NATIONAL PARCS BRASIL

GUIANA FRANCESA

3

AMAPÁ

MACAPÁ

Ilha de Marajó

BELÉM

SÃO LUÍS

17

16

FORTALEZA

Rio Amazonas

Tapajós

PARÁ

MARANHÃO

22 23

CEARÁ

RIO GRANDE DO NORTE

15

NATAL

TERESINA

JOÃO PESSOA

PARAÍBA

Rio Xingu

Rio Araguaia

Rio Tocantins

PIAUÍ

PERNAMBUCO

RECIFE

21 20

ALAGOAS

MACEIÓ

SERGIPE

MATO GROSSO

2

PALMAS

Rio São Francisco

ARACAJU

BRASIL

TOCANTINS

13

BAHIA

26

SALVADOR

GOIÁS

DF

24

32 31

GOIÂNIA

BRASÍLIA

MINAS GERAIS

14

18

19 12

27

37

ESPÍRITO SANTO

MATO GROSSO DO SUL

36

30

CAMPO GRANDE

BELO HORIZONTE

VITÓRIA

SÃO PAULO

RIO DE JANEIRO

33 38 34

42

35 39

SÃO PAULO

RIO DE JANEIRO

PARANÁ

47

41

CURITIBA

44

SANTA CATARINA

45

FLORIANÓPOLIS

RIO GRANDE DO SUL

46

PORTO ALEGRE

40

43

Oceano Atlântico

URUGUAI

HORIZONTE

GEOGRÁFICO

0   290   580 km

ESCALA

∿	River
⊚	State's Capitals
–··–··–	Country Border
–·–·–·	State Border
▬	South Region
▬	Southeast Region
▬	Centre West Region
▬	Northeast Region
▬	North Region

N O L S

NATIONAL
PARKS

BRAZIL

PROJETO
PHILIPS
BRASILIS

THIS GUIDE IS PART OF
THE PHILIPS BRASILIS PROJECT
WHOSE AIM IS TO PROMOTE
BRAZILIAN CULTURE AND
ART, AS WELL AS ITS HISTORICAL
AND NATURAL HERITAGE

NATIONAL PARKS

BRAZIL

HORIZONTE
GEOGRÁFICO

HORIZONTE
GEOGRÁFICO

General Director: Peter Milko

GUIAS PHILIPS
NATIONAL
PARKS
BRAZIL

Editor-in-chief: Peter Milko
Managing Editor: Nilton Pavin
Art Editor: Fernando Hotz Fonseca / Jorge Toth

Research Coordinator: Claudia Vieitas
Assistant Editor: Maíra Rocha
General Coordinator: Beatriz Santomauro
Reporter: Gabriela Michelotti
Copy Editor: Pier Luigi Cabra (Portuguese) and Peter Jonathan Webb (English)
Translation to English: Cláudio Blanc
Art Manager: João Carlos Botelho Ferraz
Page Layout: Ana Cristina Silveira, João Carlos Botelho Ferraz,
Jorge Fernando Gallina, Ariana Assumpção Silva
Photography Editor: Lizimar Dahlke
Associate Contributors: Adriano Gambarini, André Pessoa, Araquém Alcântara, Carolina da
Riva, Claudia Vieitas, Christian Knepper, Cristiano Burmester, Denise Greco, Enrico Marone,
Fernando Fonseca, Gabriela Michelotti, Haroldo Palo Jr., Ivan Carneiro, José Ayrton Labegalini,
Jurandir Lima, Leonardo Papini, Leonide Príncipe, Lizimar Dahlke, Marcelo Andrê, Marcelo
Venturini, Marcio Cabral, Mário Friedlander, Mauri Santos, Paulo Miranda, Paulo Robson de
Souza, Peter Milko, Renato Grimm, Rômulo Campos, Taylor Nunes, Vitor Andrade, Zig Koch
(photography); Adriana Férrer, Célio Albuquerque, Elisabeth Sloniewski, Guilherme Sierra,
Malu Campos, Sérgio Simões, Sylvia Estrella, Tarcila Ferro (content), Sérgio Dieguez (maps),
Leonardo Bussadori (page layout and cover), Levi Grau, Geraldo Moura Filho (Illustrations).
Administrative Manager: Mauro de Melo Jucá
Directory Assistant: Ana Maria Yahn
Administrative Assistants: José Augusto Pires de Abreu and Paula Bianchi
Support Services: José Antônio dos Santos
Customer Service: Marcos Fernandes
Graphic Production: Mauro de Melo
Photolithography: Retrato Falado
Impressão: R.R. Donnelley América Latina

Philips Guides - National Parks
Copyright©Horizonte Geográfico

Editora Horizonte Geográfico
Av. Arruda Botelho, 684, 5° floor
ZIP 05466-000, São Paulo, SP, Brasil
Phone: 55 (11) 3022-5599 – Fax 55 (11) 3022-3751
E-mail: horizonte@horizontegeografico.com.br
www.horizontegeografico.com.br

All information in this guide was obtained by December 2001.
We recommend users to always check schedules, prices and other useful data.
The Publisher cannot hold responsible for possible losses due to changes in information.

Horizonte Geográfico would like to thank you for sending
data to help us update the information and services
included in this publication. Please send us information by mail,
fax or e-mail: redacao@horizontegeografico.com.br.
To keep updated and get further information, visit our site:
www.horizontegeografico.com.br

Series Philips Guides of Brazilian Ecological Tourism
Published in 2002 by Horizonte Geográfico

São Joaquim National Park, in Rio Grande do Sul state ▶

Summary

DEAR READER,

It was in 1876 that engineer André Rebouças brought from abroad the idea of conceiving national parks in Brazil as a means of protecting and valuing the areas of great scenic beauty where people could enjoy nature. An admirer of natural landscapes, Rebouças put forward a proposal to the Emperor Dom Pedro II for the creation of a protected area for the forests which spread from Sete Quedas, in the Paraná River, to the Iguaçu Falls.

However, it was only in 1937 that the first national park in Brazil was founded in Itatiaia, state of Rio de Janeiro. Since then, dozens of parks have been created forming a mosaic of spectacular landscapes, areas of biological, geological and geographic relevance with such a scenery diversity that only few countries in the world are lucky to have.

And this is what you will find in this guide: hundreds of destinations and attractions to visit, as contrasting as the extensive sand dunes from Lençóis Maranhenses, which move according to the wind's wishes, and the monumental cliffs of Aparados da Serra, surrounded by waterfalls and filled with the lushness of the forest.

If there is something that all Brazilians point out as a virtue of their land, that would be the beauty of its scenery and the abundance of its natural resources. And now you have the chance to get to know these natural beauties, which used to be reserved only for scientists and a few adventurers who dared to discover those regions by themselves.

Not all parks have the ideal infra-structure to make the most of a visit, but with the information you now have in your hands, we are sure that you will be able to choose your favorite itineraries. The data were collected with the most valuable cooperation of Ibama, the bureau of the Environment Ministry responsible for the parks management, which guarantees the precision of the information.

New national parks have been planned and created in a praiseworthy effort in order to enlarge the protected areas. Most are being equipped in order to promote visitation and environmental education. Visit our site at www.horizontegeografico.com.br in order to always get up-to-date information.

It is worthwhile to remember that the national parks are a Brazilian public patrimony. Each person who visits them has an important role to play in the upkeep of those protected areas, not only as nature reservation and ecotourism destination, but also as a legacy for future generations.

Peter Milko
Editor-in-chief

View from the Boldró Fort, in Fernando de Noronha ▶

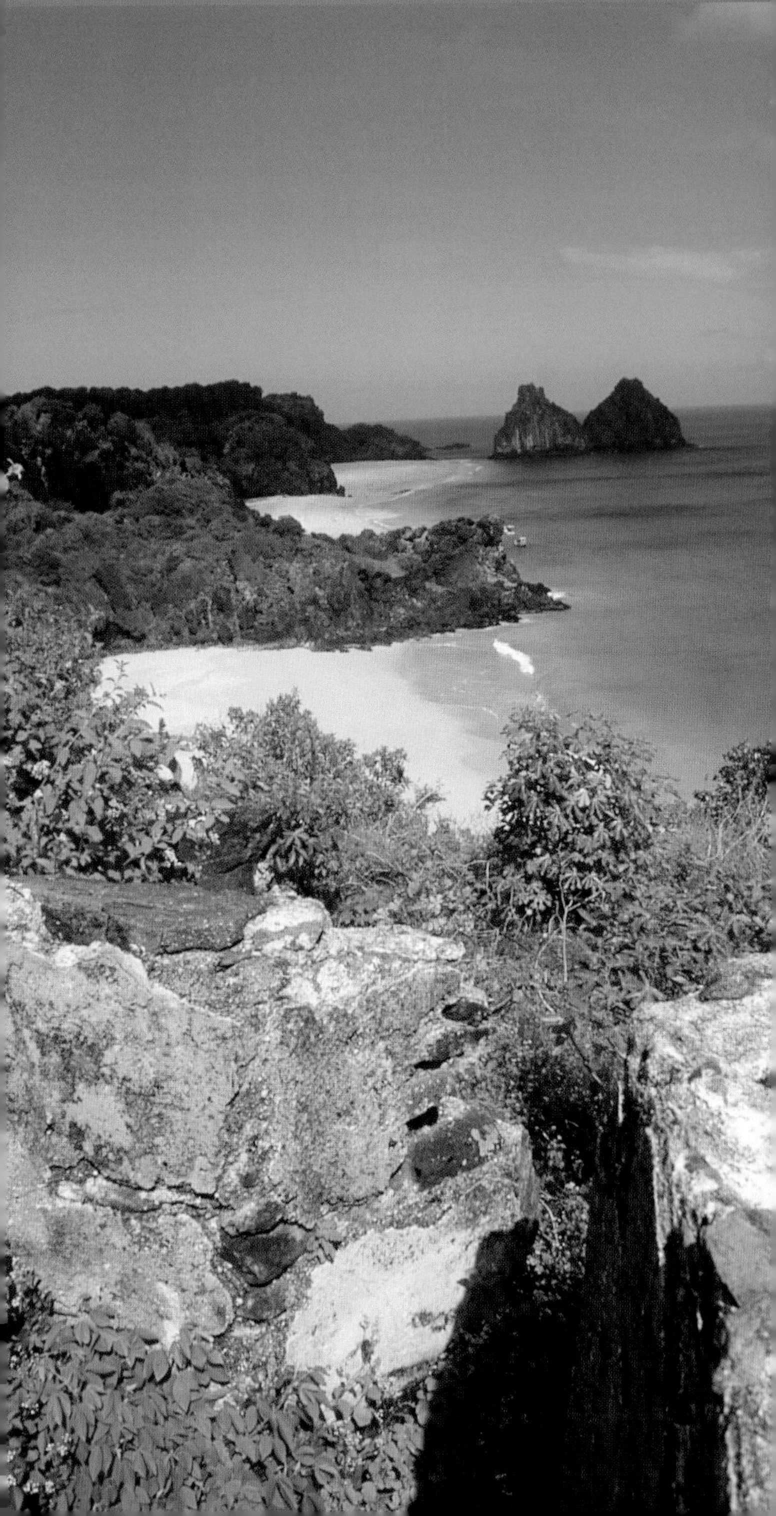

PRESENTATION

Brazil has in the conservation of its biologic diversity the greatest potential for economical development and for improving the quality of life of its people. This action includes the preservation of the wild fauna and flora, its ecosystems, forests, genetic resources and the quality of its waters.

The change of the model of development to a way which is environmentally sustainable and fair should be the greatest opportunity of economical, commercial and social growth in our history.

The National Parks must be an example, a reference and support for this new way of sustainable development; preserving, valuing nature, learning and teaching feasible economical alternatives, such as ecotourism and the sustainable use of genetic resources, and mainly achieving these goals in a participatory and socially fair way.

The ecologic tourism is a partner of the National Parks because it includes the preservation of natural resources by means of orderly visits on trails which intend to interpret nature. And also because it values and integrates manifestations of the traditional regional culture, such as folk-lore, handicraft, music, festivals, arts, cookery and the singular way that the communities around the Parks welcome visitors.
This is an opportune moment for releasing this guide, certainly a ecotourism landmark in Brazil.

Ecosystems Directory
IBAMA (Brazilian Institute of Environment and Renewable Natural Resources)

Temporary lagoons that form among the dunes of the Lençóis Maranhenses

The Tapajós is the most voluminous river in the Amazônia National Park ▶

Buriti, or Wine Palm, groves in the fields which surround the Mount Roraima National Park

HOW TO USE THIS GUIDE

This guide will lead you through the natural and cultural wonders of the National Parks and their surroundings. In order to help you to plan your trip, the guide supplies useful and detailed information, like how to get to the Park you want to go, its main attractions, best time of year to visit it and the history of the region.

Opening text:
Text with the main highlights in terms of geography, fauna and flora, topography, climate, vegetation and animals.

Box:
Some interesting subjects of the culture which deserve to be highlighted: culture, history, fauna and flora.

History:
Information on the history of the Park and its region; the early inhabitants, how the Park was created and why; which present-day facts deserve to be highlighted in the place.

Data
Foundation: month and year in which the Park was founded.
Area: total area of the Park in km².
Distance: approximate distance in kilometers from the four most important cities closest to the Park. The distance may exceptionally be calculated in terms of days spent on boat trips.
Indication about possibility of visiting the Park: The Parks which have the indication "not open for visitation" can not be visited. The icon "open for visitation" shows that it is possible to visit the Park, but this does not mean that there is infra-structure.
Telephone area code of the Park Headquarters
Telephone of the Park Headquarters

To keep uptaded and get further information, visit our site:
www.horizontegeografico.com.br

Index
In order to make the search easier, we included at the beginning of the guide a general index which envelops all chapters.

Each chapter has its own colour, identified by the upper border

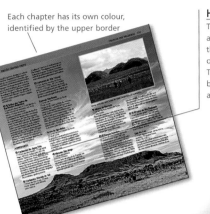

Highlights and Surroundings

The attractions of the Park are arranged alphabetically. The distance between the gate of the Park or between any other reference already mentioned. The length of time to go and to come back: average estimate which varies according to the age and fitness.

Map

Map of the Park indicating its principal attractions, rivers and forms of access.

Tips and Services

Indicates the best time to visit the Park, the appropriate ways of visiting it, whether it is necessary to hire guides, what is necessary to take and that which is not possible to miss in the visit. Indication of useful addresses, such as City Hall, hospitals and support services for the visitor; places to stay and to eat in the towns near the Park.

Glossary for the maps

Rio: river
Limites do Parque: Park limits
Trilhas: Trails
Estrada de Asfalto: Paved Road
Estrada de terra: Dirt Road
Fronteira de Estado: State Border
Fronteira de País: Country Border
Ferrovia: Railway

To visit

Access: the hours of the Park, admission fees, whether it is necessary to hire guides. It is also indicated if the Park is not open for visitation or if it demands help from Ibama to lead the visit. It is advisable to call the Park headquarters before travelling anyway.

Address: Address and telephone of the Ibama Headquarters.

How to get there: The easiest access either by car, boat, or plane. However, it is advisable to call before going; roads might get impassable during some seasons.

Infra-structure: What the Park has to offer to the visitor: facilities for handicapped people, ambulatory, quarters, camping ground, diners, rest rooms, visitor's centre etc. It also indicates when there is no structure at all.

To know more

Books and sites with more information about the Park, local culture and history.

WHAT IS A NATIONAL PARK?

The 47 National Parks of the Brazilian territory stretch from the south of the country - under the influence of the sub-tropical climate of the Serra Geral and Aparados da Serra - up to the northernmost borders, near the Equator line, like the Monte Roraima and Cabo Orange Parks. Harbouring the most varied ecologic scenarios, they preserve samples of biologic diversity and the natural landscapes of Brazil. Getting to know the National Parks - either by visiting them or by reading about them - is like immersing in the different Brazilian ecosystems: from the Caatinga to the Amazonian Rain Forest, on a trip through the Atlantic Forest, Pantanal, Cerrado, dunes, sea islands and Fields. It is to know that Brazil harbours the oldest archaeologic sites in the Americas, preserved in the Serra da Capivara, and some of the most beautiful scenarios of the planet, such as Fernando de Noronha and Foz do Iguaçu, both acknowledged by Unesco as natural heritage of human kind. From the 47 Brazilian Parks, 28 are open for visitation. Some have complete infra-structure, such as the Foz do Iguaçu National Park, with 700 thousand visitors per year, and the Itatiaia National Park,

Chapada dos Guimarães is one of the Parks with good infra-structure for visiting

Iguaçu Falls receive 700.000 people yearly ▶

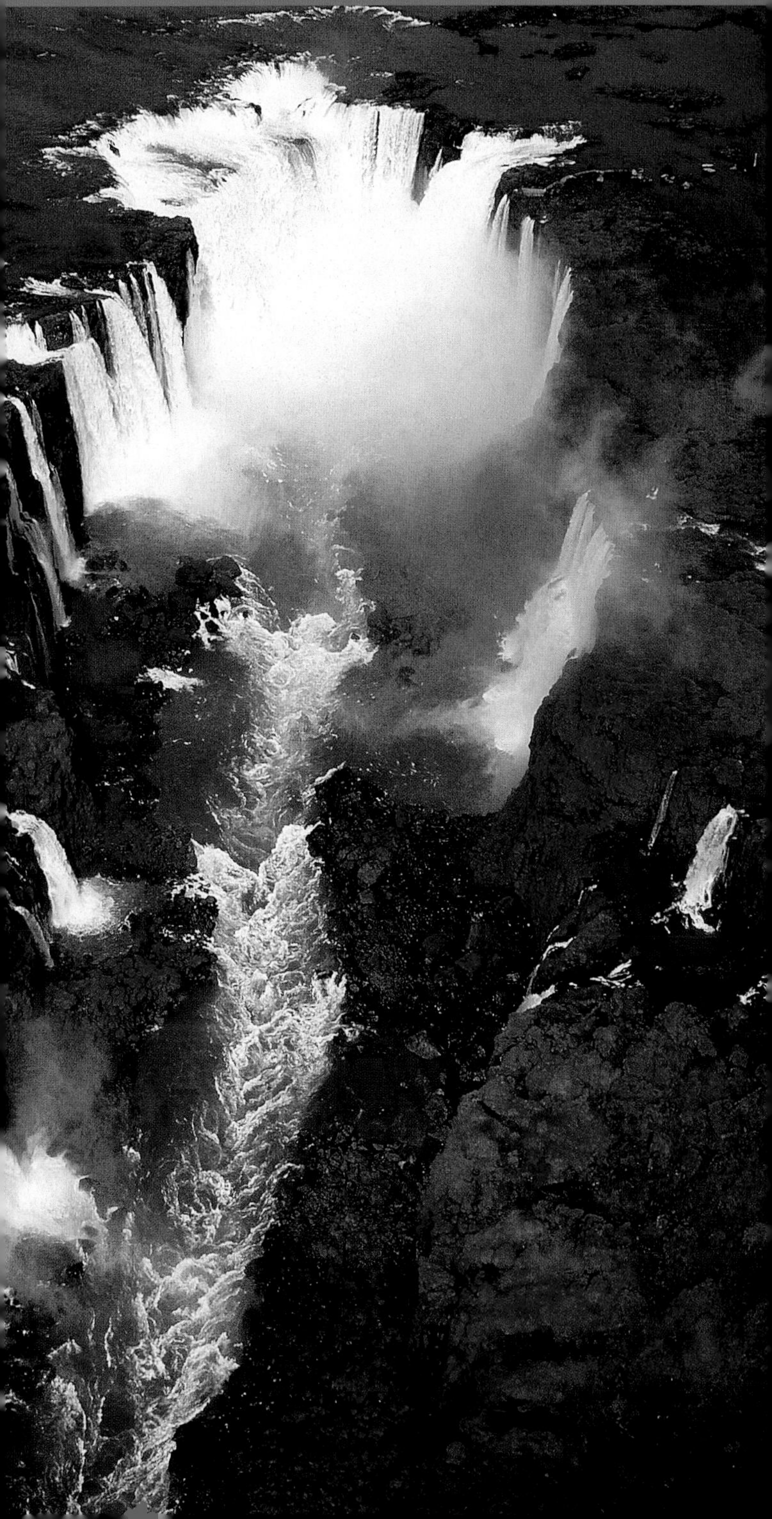

with 100 thousand; others can only be visited with a permit and help from Ibama, like Pico da Neblina and Serra das Confusões. Some National Parks were founded in 2000, like the Serra da Bodoquena and the Descobrimento National Park, but they have not had their management plan approved yet and are not open for visitation.

The guide supplies information on all Parks, including those which are not open for visitation.The exception is for the Parks which have been created recently: Serra da Cutia, Saint-Hilaire/Lange and the Jericoacoara Beach. In the Parks not open for visitation the data is limited to the information about their history and environmental characteristics, without the inclusion of the cities nearby. All the Brazilian National Parks are run by Ibama (Brazilian Institute of Environment and Renewable Natural Resources).

Some Parks, despite being protected by law, still face challenges in dealing with problems such as land expropiation, invasion of miners, predatory fishing and hunting and conflict with Indians, whose land superposes that of the Park.

In 2001, two new Parks were created: the Saint-Hilaire, in the southern coast of the state of Paraná, aiming at protecting and preserving the Atlantic Forest ecosystems that exist in the area, and the Serra da Cutia, in the city of Guajará-Mirim, in the state of Rondônia, to preserve samples of Amazonian ecosystems.

In February 2002, 84 km² of dunes, mangroves and lagoons in the Jericoacoara Beach were raised to the status of National Park.

Pedra Furada, in the Serra da Capivara National Park

The legal part

According to the Brazilian legislation "the National Parks belong to the group of conservation and protection units and are destined to the integral preservation of natural areas with very relevant characteristics in terms of ecology, scenic beauty, cultural, educative and recreational aspects, being forbidden environmental modifications and the direct human interference. The National Parks can receive visitors with recreational and educational ends, according to the management plan of the unit. Scientific research, when authorized by the bureau in charge of the management, is subject to the conditions and restrictions determined by this very bureau, as well as to that which is stated on its management plan".

HOW TO PREPARE

Each National Park has tips about what to take, the best time to go, what you must see during the visit. However, as some items are common to all Parks, we made a list of the things that you can not fail to take.

WHAT TO TAKE

Insects repellent
Sun block
Comfortable and light clothing
Tennis shoes or hiking boots, with waterproof sole
Long sleeve T-shirts
Small back-pack
Hat or cap
Bathing suit
Plastic bags or waterproof packs for documents, papers, cameras

Whistle, sunglass, canteen with water, dry fruits, cereal, lighter or matches, torch with extra batteries, mosquito net, kit with glass, fork, knife and plate, first aid kit with the usual medicines.

BEFORE THE TRIP

• If you are going to the Parks in the North and Northeast regions, take yellow fever vaccination ten days before the trip (the disease is common in many Brazilian states). You can get the vaccination at the main airports

Visitors hike in the Chapada Diamantina National Park

and vaccination offices of the country. The vaccine is valid for ten years.

• Call the Park Headquarters before going, as some roads and attractions may be impaired because of rains and other setbacks. The Park staff can also advise the best way to enjoy the visit. Do not forget to tell them the reasons of your trip - camping, climbing, rappel etc. - and make sure they are permitted in the Park. Check for the need of taking specific gear or other things, such as the hiring of guides.

REMINDER . . . .

• Malaria and other tropical diseases occur in the North region: do not fail in using insect repellent and do wear long sleeve T-shirt, specially at dawn and sunset hours.

• Try to drink only mineral water, water boiled for more than five minutes, or,

if the other options are not available, use chlorine water purifier, sold in pharmacies.

• In the North region, "summer" is when it rains more, and winter is when it rains less. As the months of the seasons change very much according to the state, each Park of this region has the summer and winter months specified.

• For information on how to prevent and treat diseases contracted while travelling, check with Disk-saúde, a service of the Health Ministry: telephone 0800 611-997. In São Paulo, Hospital das Clínicas – phones (11) 3069-6392/ 3069-6000 – and Hospital Emílio Ribas – phone (11) 3896-1200, extension 1366 – have established the Traveller's Ambulatory, where there are medical services and information for those who are going to travel.

Sites
www.mma.gov.br
www.ibama.gov.br
www.parquesdobrasil.org.br
www.redeprouc.org.br

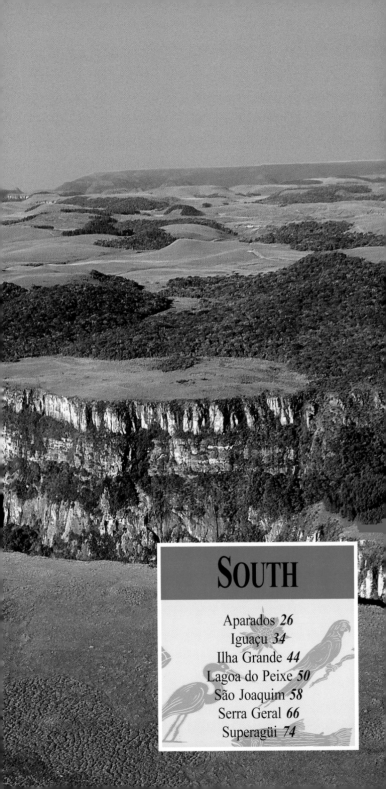

SOUTH

SOUTH REGION

Most National Parks of the South Region preserve the remains of the Atlantic Forest and its landscape variations. In the state of Paraná, the one which stands out is the Iguaçu, the most visited Park in Brazil, with 700.000 visitors per year and also the first experience in farming out tourist services. The falls, formed by 275 waterfalls, are the greatest highlight. They can be observed from trails, pathways and boats which go near by the falls. The Ilha Grande is in the same state; the Park is formed by a complex of 300 islands and islets in the Paraná River. The Superagui, formed by sea islands, harbours archaeologic vestiges of people who lived there between one and seven thousand years ago, and is also the habitat of the Cara-roxa Parrot and the Mico-leão-da-cara-preta -

a capuchin monkey -, both endangered species. The Serra Geral and Aparados da Serra are on the border of the states of Rio Grande de Sul and Santa Catarina, with one of the biggest complexes of canyons in the country. The canyons which stand out are the Fortaleza, with 7 km in extension and a difference in level of 990 m, and the Itaimbezinho, 720 m in depth. The São Joaquim is in the Geral Mountain Range and its landscape is taken over by Brazil Pines and fields-atop-the-mountains, as the altitude fields are called there. The Lagoa do Peixe, on the southern coast of Rio Grande do Sul, protects a coastal ecosystem which gives shelter to more than 180 different species of birds. The one with the best infra-structure for visitors is the Iguaçu Park.

São Be

Uruguaiana

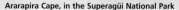

Ararapira Cape, in the Superagüi National Park

Aparados da Serra

Between 150 and 200 million years ago, massive earthquakes shook this region forming, through erosion and other factors, steep cliffs and open cracks in the rocks. The slightly ruffled topography of the *coxilhas* - pronounce *coshilha*, a rolling prairie land - is abruptly cut by extensive and deep canyons which are still being water carved. Several ecosystems and transition zones stand out in the landscape. The Coastal Rain Forest, or *Mata Atlântica*, with its many Brazilian Pines, appears at the foot of the canyons and spreads in groves on the upper lands and on the edge of the escarpments; here, it is referred to as *matinha nebular* (small cloud forest). The fields spread over the plateau and are intermingled with peat bogs in the moister parts. Seasons are very well defined, with rains from December to March, when there is much thunder and lightning, and bitter frost from June to September. There is haze all year round, shrouding and clearing from the deep valleys in several minutes. On the mountain sides, the green colour stands out from the rocks in the form of ferns, bromeliads, lilies, and larger bigger bushes. The Bigstinging Nettle, a plant with huge leaves up to 1,5 m, grows on the rocky mountainsides.

Foundation: December 1959
Area: 102 km²
Praia Grande: 20 km; Cambará do Sul: 18 km; São José dos Ausentes: 70 km; Porto Alegre: 163 km
○
⊕ (54)
☎ 251-1277

In the drier areas, the mountainsides are covered in lichen. Groves of trees, locally called *capões*, dye the grassy fields which dominate the plateau a different tone of green. Brazilian Pines are everywhere, feeding several species of the local fauna. Scotch pines also appear in the forest together with Tabebuias, California pepper trees, Canchara Cabralea, several species of Cinnamon, and Nutmegs.

The fauna is rich and includes Azure Jays, Hawk-headed Parrots - which feed on *pinhão*, the edible pine seed -, Great Grey Tinamous, Guans, several species of humming bird and Red-breasted Toucans. Among the mammals, Opossums, Agoutis and Monkeys - such as Capuchin Monkeys - can be easily seen. In the fields there are species which survive because they managed to adapt themselves to the conditions of cold, frost, and the formation of crusts of ice. In the rainy season, the water accumulates in the the peat bogs, where there are moss, lichen, Asparagus fern and bromeliads, forming quagmires in a soil rich in organic matter. Here animals such the Agouti, the Wild Dog - here called *graxaim* -, Partridges, Rufous Tinamous, Brazilian Lapwings, Ibis and Wild Ducks are common.

The Boi River flows through the 5.800-m Itaimbezinho canyon

HISTORY

The Geral Mountain Range, where the Aparados da Serra National Park is, was once inhabited by several indigenous groups of Tupi-Guarani origin. They were the Charruas, Guaranis, Arachanes, Carijós and Jaros, among other tribes. A peculiarity of these tribe was that they hunted using a weapon similar to the boleadeira - a leather thong with iron balls or stones attached to its end, which is hurled at animals to entangle their legs, thus causing them to colapse - and drunk mate tea. They would sit in groups around fires dug into the ground, which served as protection against the strong winds. Here they would drink the ground leaves of the mate herb mixed with hot water, while begging for protection to the god Tupã. This tradition was passed down to the *gaúchos* - the wranglers from the southern meadows - who preserve it up to this day. The mountain range

was one of the last regions to be occupied by the Europeans.

The term itambé, which gave origin to the name itaimbezinho, is Tupi-Guarani and means cut rock, a name which describes very well the canyon landscape of the Serra Geral. Apart from the indigenous peoples, the country was also occupied by Jesuits who brought cattle with them. In time, the Europeans and Indians became mixed and the gaúcho people and culture were formed. Cattle ranching became a common activity in the region even within the Park's area, which until recently had some small farms within its limits. In order to further protect the Park's outskirts, another Park was created in 1992 uniting with Aparados in its northeast and southwest regions: the Serra Geral. From 1996 to 1998 the Park was closed to make improvements and was re-opened with better infra-structure for visitors.

HIGHLIGHTS

⚫⚫ Itaimbezinho Canyon
The Park's most famous canyon is 5.800 m in extension and has a maximum depth of 720 m. It is cut through by the rivers Perdizes and Preá rivers which together form the river Boi.

⚫⚫ ⚫Andorinhas Cascade
Formed on the escarpment of the Itaimbezinho canyon, where the Perdizes River falls off; it is possible to see the waterfall from the Vértice Trail or from the Cotovelo Lookout. There is a crack in the

Bigsting nettle: plant with huge leaves

◄   Agouti spreads seeds (above); some cliffs are more than 700 m high rocks behind the waterfall, which allows swifts to live there, getting in and out through the water.

🔟 ⏺ ⏺ Véu da Noiva Cascade

At the Préa ravine, this waterfall is near the Cotovelo Lookout and can be seen from the Vértice Trail.

⏺ 🔟 ⏺ Cotovelo Lookout
⏱ Six hours

A natural lookout on the rim of the Itaimbezinho canyon, allowing you to see the surroundings if the weather and the haze allow. It can be reached via a 6,6-km trail on flat terrain which lies along the canyon rim. It is necessary to go with an official guide.

🔟 ⏺ ⏺ Boi River
⏱ Three days

It flows in the Park's low lands, allowing the Itaimbezinho canyon to be seen from the bottom. The trail with the same name is a hard 8,3-km hike in the Park's lowland. Most of the way is along the riverbed, upon slippery rocks. In several points it is necessary to cross the river with the water level at the knee, which can make it difficult to continue. You must go with an official guide.

🔟 ⏺ 🔟 Vértice Trail

Along the Itaimbezinho canyon. It is a mild 1,4-km trail with information along the way, explaining things with which you come across. It has nice views of the Andorinhas and the Véu da Noiva Cascades.

SURROUNDINGS . . . .

⏺ 🔟 ⏺ Ferradurinha - Passo do Inferno Waterfall
⏺ 12 km from the Park ⏱ Two hours

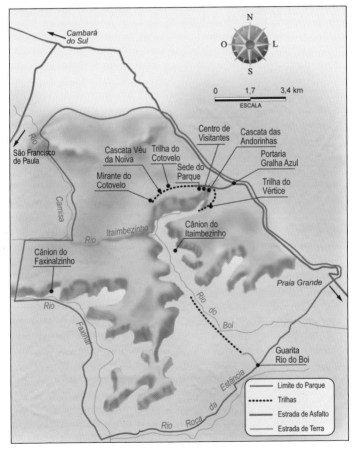

Araucária: source of food for the local fauna

The 10-km dirt road is along the Santa Cruz and the Ferradurinha rivers and takes half an hour to be travelled. From the metal bridge above the Santa Cruz, it is possible to see the Passo do Inferno Waterfall. The waterfall forms a large pool where it is possible to slide into the water on a buoy.

🐾 🌑 🌕 Ferradura Park - Rio Santa Cruz Valley
⊖ 15 km from the Park ⏲ Three hours
The hike is a 1-hour descent which goes past three lookouts from which it is possible to see the Caçador Ravine waterfall, where you can have a dip. The way back is a milder trail.

🐾 🌑 Rafting on Paranhãna River - Laranjeiras Park
⊖ 30 km from the Park ⏲ Five hours
The rafting tour starts at the Canela - Três Coroas road. It takes half an hour to go down the Paranhãna River, surrounded by well preserved native vegetation. Most of the way is formed by rapids. At the end you reach the La-ranjeiras Park, where canoeing tournaments are held.

São José dos Ausentes
⊖ 70 km from the Park ⏲ Twelve hours
On the "fields atop the mountains", by São José, lies the highest peak in the state of Rio Grande do Sul, the Mount Negro, with 1.403 m. There is a hanglider ramp here. Some of the other local attractions include wooden houses without heating (in one of the country's coldest weathers - the record is -7.9°C), and snow.

Thick haze and cold wind are always present during the winter in the Serra Geral

Hawk-headed Parrot

A native of South America forests, the Hawk-headed Parrot *(Amazona vinacea)* is found from Bahia to Rio Grande do Sul, as well as in eastern Paraguay and Argentina. Today, it is a rare species which lives in small and isolated populations in fragments of the forests. It is an endangered species mainly due to the loss of its environment, but also because of hunting and illegal trading. They live in the dry forests of the heartland, in pine forests and moist woods where bamboo grows. They gather in noisy flocks which can be heard from far away. In Brazil, they live on the mountainsides at higher altitudes, above 1.000 m, and are found mainly in natural preserved areas, such as

Bird runs risk of extinction

Aparados da Serra. They feed on leaf sprouts and flowers, including those of Eucalyptus and Pines as well as the seeds, or *pinhão,* of the Brazilian pine.

TO VISIT

Access – Open from Wednesday to Sunday from 9 am to 5 pm. Admission fee: R$ 6,00.

Address – Estrada RS-429, Caixa Postal 10, Cambará do Sul, RS, 95480-000. Phones: (54) 251-1277 and 251-1262. Fax: (54) 251-1305.

How to get there – By car from Porto Alegre: take BR-101 up to Novo Hamburgo, then the road to Taquara. Afterwards, take RS-020 towards São Francisco de Paula, Tainhas and Cambará do Sul – only the last 10 km are dirt road. Access to the Park and Itaimbezinho from Cambará do Sul is well signalized. The Gralha Azul gate is by the Cambará - Praia Grande (CS-360). By coach: there are departures from Cambará do Sul to the Park from Monday to Saturday.

Infra-structure – Visitors' Centre, cultural area with a photographic exhibition, and auditorium for 50 people, snack bar, rest-rooms, handicraft shop, and parking lot.

TIPS

➋ The dry season, from June to September, when it is coldest, is the best time to visit the Park.

➋ Open areas and constant wind make a raincoat and warm clothes necessary items.

➋ During the rainy season, between April and May, the rivers tend to rise many meters quickly. It is important to heed and to follow the Parks rules.

➋ In case of *viração* - the thick fog which appears all of a sudden - make sure you do not lose the trail and do not move if you do not know where you are. The fog prevents you from seeing and the canyon might be just ahead of you.

To know more
www.bdh.com.br/itaimbezinho
www.praiagrande-sc.com.br

SERVICES

Cambará do Sul, RS
⊕ 65
◎ 95480-000

Useful Addresses
City Hall. Av. Dona Ursula, 475. Phone: 251-1174.
Bus station. Rua Dona Ursula, 700. Phone: 251-1343.
Hospital. Rua Padre João Pazza, 197. Phone: 251-1167.
Telephone station. Rua 28 de dezembro. Phone: 251-1203.
Post Office. Av. Getúlio Vargas, 663. Phone: 251-1250.
Bank. Banrisul.

Support for the Visitor
City bureau for Tourism and Development. Rua Dona Ursula, 475. Phone: 251-1320.

Lodging
Pousada Alvorada. Av. Getúlio Vargas, 1184. Phone: 251-1284. 15 rooms, tv, minibar, tel. Restaurant. $
Pousada Cambará do Sul. Rua Adail Lima Valim, 23. Phone: 251-1131. 5 rooms, tv. Parking lot. $
Pousada das Corucadas (rural lodging). Road to Ouro Verde, km 1 (Baio Ruano Farm). Phone: 251-1128. 7 rooms. Lake, waterfall, corral, horses, fishing. $$
Pousada Fortaleza. Av. Getúlio Vargas, 296. Phone: 251-1224. 8 rooms, tv, tel. $
Pousada dos Lobos. Rua da Úrsula, 148. Phone: 251-1263. 3 rooms. (family home). Parking lot. $
Pousada Paraíso. Rua Antônio Raupp, 678. Phone: 251-1352. 15 rooms, tv, tel. Restaurant. $
Pousada Recanto dos Amigos. Lajeada da Margarida Road, 4 km on dirt road. Phone: (51) 9832-1615. 6 rooms. Lake, waterfall, horses, fishing. $ $
Pousada Simoni. Rua 20 de Setembro, 570. Phone: 251-1116. 6 rooms, tel., restaurant. $

Dining
Altos da Serra. Av. Getúlio Vargas, 696. Phone: 251-1259. Pasta/Meat. $
Garfo & Bombacha. Caracol Road, 7 km. Phone: 282-2677. Meat/Typical local food. $ $
Sabrina. Av. Getúlio Vargas, 586. Phone: 251-1147. Meat. $

São José dos Ausentes
⊕ 54
◎ 95280-000

Useful Addresses
City Hall. Rua Professor Eduardo Pereira, 442. Phone: 234-1100.
Bus station. Av. Ismênia Batista Velho s/n.
Post Office. Rua Professor Eduardo Pereira, 442.
Ambulatory. Rua do Hospital. Phone: 234-1061.

Support for the Visitor
Tourist Bureau. Rua Professor Eduardo I. Pereira s/n. Phone: 324-1100.
Ecotourism local guides. Phone: 234-1072.

Dining
Pousada Fazenda Cachoeirão dos Rodrigues. Access via Potreirinhos Farm, 34 km on dirt road. Phone: 237-2337. Internet: www.guiatelnet.com.br/cachoeiraodorodrigues. 6 rooms. Waterfall, horses, fire place, dining hall. $ $
Pousada Fazenda Monte Alegre. Brasília Road, 6 km on dirt road. Phone: 9996-1697. 4 rooms. Cascade, horses. $$$
Pousada Fazenda Monte Negro. Access via the road to Bom Jardim da Serra, 39 km on dirt road. Phone: 9978-2299. 3 rooms, 12 bedrooms. Horses. $$$ rooms and $$ bedrooms.
Pousada Fazenda Paraíso. Access via km 35 of BR-285 to Bom Jesus, 10 km. Phone: 504-5002. Fax: 237-1500, reservation: 237-1073. 2 rooms, 2 huts, fire place. Target practice, corral, waterfall, horses. $$$
Pousada Fazenda Potreirinhos. Access via road to Bom Jardim da Serra, 34 km on dirt road. Phone: 9977-3482. 8 rooms, horses, fishing. $$$
Pousada Fazenda São José do Silveira. Access via Silveira district, 21 km on dirt road. Phone: 9972-4035. 8 rooms, 3 bedrooms, heating. Corral, horses. rooms.bedrooms. $$$
Sítio Vale das Trutas. Phone: 504-5693. Internet: www.valedastrutas.com.br. 2 chalets, tv, fire place, kitchen. Restaurant, lake, waterfall, fish-and-pay. $$$

Dining
Café Serrano. Av. Ismênia, 508. Phone: 234-1072. Typical local food. $
Família Cesa. Rua Ismênia, 368. Phone: 234-1202. Varied menu. $

Iguaçu

Iguaçu means "big water" in the language of the Tupi Indians. The huge waterfall began to be formed around 200 million years ago, when South America and Africa split apart. This rupture provoked huge geologic changes in the continent and one of the main consequences was a basaltic overflow, which began to occur around 110 million years ago. The many layers of lava, set upon one another, can still be seen today in the waterfalls. Land was exposed to erosion by the rivers and in time the Iguaçu Falls were formed. The Park lies in the heart of the Prata basin, which envelops many rivers, the most important being the Paraná, the Paraguay and the Uruguay. It is one of the most important protected areas within the region, together with the Iguazú Park, in Argentina. Rain is more intense from October to March, when the water volume of the falls increases, reaching 6,5 thousand m³ per second. The region of Iguaçu is the realm of the Coastal Rain Forest, with three major vegetation formations: the Brazilian pine forest, at altitudes above 600 m, where the climate is colder; the semideciduous forest, whose trees lose their leaves in winter, at altitudes between 400 m and 500 m; and the riverine forests, along the banks of the seasonally flooded rivers. Besides the Brazilian Pine, other common trees in the Park are

Foundation: January 1939
Area: 1.853 km²
Curitiba: 668 km; Cascavel: 167 km; Guaíra: 225 km; Assuncion: 356 km

○
⊕ (45)
☎ 529-8383

Guaicá, *Vassourão-branco*, *Guabirova* (tree of the genus Campomanesia, family Myrtaceae), *Mamica-de-cadela*, the Chaste tree, *Laranjeira-do-mato*, *Angico-vermelho* (a tree of the mimosa family), *Miguel-pintado,* and *Baga-de-morcego*. In the riverine forests, it is possible to find Whiptrees, Apes ear-rings, Queen palms, *Guabirovas*, *Cuvatã*, *Ingá* (another tree of the mimosa family), Tree ferns, and the Parana Peltophorum. All environments are adorned by many species of orchids and bromeliads and, of course, the plant diversity fosters a very rich fauna. Among the species found in the Park are the Coati (a tropical carnivore allied to the Raccoon), Peccary, Otter, Paca, and the *Tapiti* (a small hare-like rodent). Jaguars, Pumas and Ocelots are also found in the area and are monitored by a team from the National Predator Centre, who research these animals. The Park is also home to many bird species, such the Yellow-headed Paroquet, *Guaxos* with their hanging nests, the Green-backed Trogon, the Red-breasted Toucan, the *Flautim*, the Green-

headed Tanager, the great *Gavião-pomba* (a species of hawk), the endangered Tyrant hawk, the *Falcão-de-peito-vermelho* (another species of hawk), and the Black-fronted Piping Guan. By the rivers, many species of herons and bitterns can be seen. Among the reptiles that are prominent, there are several species of snakes. Do not miss watching the countless butterflies searching for mineral salts on the river banks.

The violence of the waters falling from the heights impresses visitors

HISTORY

The early inhabitants of the region were the Guarani Indians. The first European to arrive at the waterfalls, in 1542, was the Spanish Captain Nuñez Cabeza de Vaca, who named them the Santa Maria Falls. His expedition opened the pathway for European civilization and the Jesuits' missions. However, with the arrival of the *Bandeirantes* from São Paulo, the missions were harassed and the Indians nearly exterminated. These *bandeirantes* were members of the *bandeiras*: armed bands which entered the backwoods hunting for Indians to enslave and prospecting for precious minerals. In 1888, the western region of the state of Paraná received a new and more intense wave of migration, which brought the felling of the forests and the cultivation of mate tea to the region. At

Morning mist invades the Atlantic Forest in the lower Iguaçu region

◀ Jaguar (above); 257 waterfalls form the famous Iguaçu Falls that time, the waterfalls were already famous for their beauty. They attracted notorious visitors such as Santos Dumont, the Brazilian who invented the aeroplane. He visited the waterfalls back in 1916, when the first proposition to create a conservation unit arose. But the Iguaçu National Park was only created in 1939, somewhat late in following the international trend of creating protected wild areas.

Until the 1940's, the region had few inhabitants, which helped to preserve its ecosystem. With the arrival of the *gauchos* - a term which refers both to the people from the state of Rio Grande do Sul and to their culture - the scenery started to change. In the 1950's, they were looking to increase their agricultural land and in the 1970's, already populous, the region suffered changes due to the introduction of soya plantations. To complicate further still, the Argentinean side was rapidly deforested during the 1980's.

Toucan: a common bird in the trails

The legend of the waterfalls

The Guarani Indians, who live on the banks of the Iguaçu River, believe that the world is ruled by Tupã and his serpent son M'boi. Igobi, the village's medicineman, had a beautiful daughter called Naipi; so beautiful that the waters of the river became still when the young Kaingangue woman looked at herself on the water-mirror. But her beauty was also her curse: because she was so gorgeous, Naipi was to be consecrated to the god M'boi. However, on the the day of the consecration festival, Tarobá, a brave warrior himself, fell in love with Naipi and ran away down river with her, by canoe. When M'boi learned

that they had gone, he became very angry. He got into the entrails of the earth, winding his huge body, and dug out a gigantic cleft which formed the waterfalls. Enveloped by the waters of the enormous waterfall, the pirogue and the runaway lovers fell from a lofty height and disappeared forever. Naipi was transformed into one of the central rocks of the waterfalls, forever whipped by the waters, and Tarobá into a palm which stands by the abyss, leaning over the gorge of the river. Beneath the palm tree there is a cave, from which the revengeful monster keeps an everlasting watch upon its two victims.

The Guarani story links the appearing of the waterfalls to a love tragedy

HIGHLIGHTS

The first National Park in the country to farm-out its services promises to create new tours and to enlarge its visiting infra-structure. The plans include building panoramic lifts, suspended pathways in the canopies for looking at the flora and fauna and special trails for handicapped people, some new trails and even a tour to go on on full moon nights.

Iguaçu Falls
⊕ One hour

Between Brazil and Argentina, the falls are formed by 275 waterfalls, which can be seen from both countries although the view is better from the Brazilian side. The bus to the falls departs from the Visitors Centre and stops at the beginning of the Cataratas trail: a 1,2-km paved pathway with stairways. Look out for the Coatis (a tropical cousin of the Raccoon), which are accustomed to human presence (remember not to feed the animals) and the great number of butterflies. The trail ends at the Garganta do Diabo lookout-pathway. Groups of more than 15 people must be accompanied by a guide (R$ 50,00). To go to Porto Canoas from here, it is necessary to take the lift or the stairways.

Macuco Safari

Monday, from 1 to 5:30 pm; Tuesday to Sunday from 8 am to 5:30 pm. Admission fee: US$ 33,00 for adults and US$ 16,50 for children from 8 to 12 From the Visitors' Centre, this is the first stop. The first part of the tour is by jeep, accompanied by a guide who describes the local fauna and flora. Afterwards, you can conti-nue to the river by jeep or on foot, along a trail for half an hour through the forest. It takes you past the 25-m-high Macuco waterfall, where you can go for a dip. The trail ends at the Iguaçu River which is also the starting point for the third part of the Macuco

trail: a boat ride to the waterfalls. The tour is very thrilling, as the boat navigates fast rapids and gets very close to the falls, soaking the passengers.

Canoas Port

From Tuesday to Sunday, from noon to 6 pm
The Community Centre, at the end of the Cataratas Trail and asphalt road, has a souvenir shop, food plaza, snack bar and restaurant.

SURROUNDINGS . . . .

Itaipu

⊖ 12 km from Foz city centre
⊙ Three hours. Access via
Av. Tancredo Neves, km 6.
From Monday to Saturday, 8 to 10 am
and from 2 to 4 pm (power station).
From Monday to Saturday,
9 to 11:30 am and from 2 to 5 pm
(Ecomuseum) Free admission
The biggest electric power station in
the world - (while one in China is still
being built) - can be visited. At the
power station you can watch a film
about its history and go to the
Ecomuseum, which has archaeologic
and ethnographic collections.

⑪ Bertoni Museum (Paraguay)
⊙ Five hours
The tour to the house of the Swiss scientist
Moisés Bertoni departs from Meira and
goes past the meeting of the waters of the
Paraná and Iguaçu Rivers, and the borders
of Argentina, Brazil and Paraguay.
The incredible museum in the forest
precariously preserves the fantastic
research collections of Bertoni and his sons
(1890 to 1929). It is a 1:30-hour walk and
you may also take advantage of being
there and visit the indigenous village of the
Guarani M'bya.

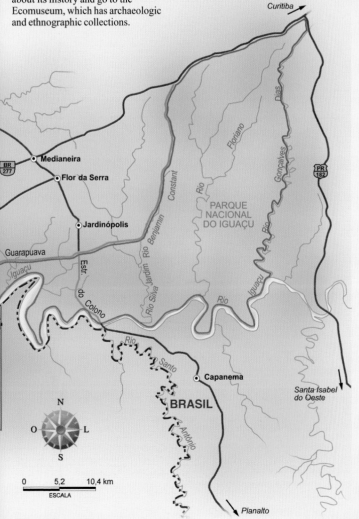

The Bird Park

⊖ 500 m from the Park
⊕ One hour. Open daily from 8:30 am to 5:30 pm. Admission fee: R$ 16,00

Across from the Park's gate. The 17 ha of native forest shelters 900 tropical birds of 150 species from all continents. Visitors can watch the fauna along the 1-km trail by getting into gigantic cages and by visiting the butterfly house with at least 30 different butterfly species.

Iguazú National Park (Argentina)

⊕ One day. From 9 am to 6 pm
Admission fee: from US$ 10 to 30,00

In Argentina, the Iguazú National Park borders the Brazilian Park. On the southern bank of the Iguaçu River, it harbours the *Mata Missionera*, or Coastal Rain Forest, with a rich native flora and fauna. You can get to the Park by crossing the border to Argentina overland; there you can watch the waterfalls along a 3-km network of trails and pathways.

The coatis are used to the human presence. However, one should not feed them

To Visit

Access – Open from Tuesday to Sunday, from 8 am to 6 pm; on Monday from 1 to 6 pm: Admission fee R$ 8,00 (adults), R$ 2,00 (children under 7 and people older than 70) and R$ 4,00 (local residents with an address proof).

Address – BR-469, km 18, Caixa Postal 05, Foz do Iguaçu, PR, 85851-970. Phone/fax (45) 529-8383. E-mail: parnaiguassu@foznet.com.br.

How to get there – There are regular flights to the Foz do Iguaçu International Airport, 2 km from the Park. By car from Curitiba: take BR-277 up to Foz do Iguaçu. Then, take BR-469 and it is 23 km more to the Park. By coach: there are several daily coach departures to the Park from the main cities in the southern states.

Infra-structure: parking lot (R$ 6,50 cars and R$ 10,50 coaches), visitors' centre, the *Cataratas* community centre, souvenir shop, rest-rooms (also for handicapped people), ambulatory, facilities for toddlers, bank, telephone, police station, snack bar and restaurant. There are eight buses with capacity for 72 people which make the trip to the waterfalls and to the Macuco Safari.

Tips

❏ It is possible to visit the Park all year round. It rains less from June to August. Between October and March, because of the rains, there is a greater volume of water which makes the waterfalls very full and the boat tours more thrilling. In spring, the trails have more flowers.

❏ Wear a raincoat if you don't want to get soaked on the lookout paths over the waterfalls or on boat rides on the rivers.

To know more

ZOTZ, W. **Iguaçu**. Florianópolis: Mares do Sul, 2000.
AZEVEDO, O. **Nossa Terra: Foz do Iguaçu.** Curitiba: Bancos Bamerindus do Brasil, 1989.
www.pr.gov.br/turismo/
www.iphan.gov.br/bens/mundial/p7.htm

◀ Two arms of the Iguaçu River converge into the waterfalls with height superior to 75 m

SERVICES

Foz do Iguaçu

🌐 45
✉ 85866-000

Useful Addresses
City Hall. Rua Xavier da Silva, 660. Phone: 521-1000.
Bus station. Av. Costa e Silva, 5 km. Phone: 522-3633
Airport. Cataratas Road, 13 km. Phone: 523-4244.
Hospital. Av. Brasil, 1637. Phone: 523-1404.
Post office. Praça Getúlio Vargas, 72.
Banks. ABN/Real, América do Sul, Bandeirantes, Banespa, Banestado, do Brasil, Bemge, Bradesco, CEF, HSBC, Itaú, Mercantil/SP, Unibanco.

Support for the Visitor
Tourist Information. Kiosk at the airport. Bus station. Phone: 522-2590, extension: 224.
Tourist Bureau. Rua Almirante Barroso, 1300. Phone: 523-0222. Teletur. Phone: 0800 451-516.
Tour agency. Da mata ecoaventuras. (45) 9963 1701/529 6279. Email: da_mata@fnn.net.

Lodging
Albergue Paudimar. Rua Rui Barbosa, 634, Centro. Phone/fax: 574-5503. Internet: www.paudimar.com.br. 60 rooms, tv room, laundry, common kitchen and bathroom. $
Bourbon & Tower. Cataratas Road, km 2,5. Phone: 523-1313. Fax: 574-1110. Reservation: 0800 451-010. Internet: www.bourbon.com.br. 308 rooms, tv, air conditioning, minibar, tel., safe. Heated swimming pool, sauna, massage, billiard room, sports court, jogging trail, playground, bar, parking lot, valet service. $$$$
Cassino Palace. Rua Rio Branco, 381. Phone/fax: 523-2300. Internet: www.cassino.com.br. 47 rooms, tv, air conditioning, minibar, safe, tel. Swimming pool, parking lot. $$$
Florença. Cataratas Road, km 13. Phone: 523-4555. Fax: 572-2524. Internet: www.hotelflorenca.com. 63 rooms, tv, air conditioning, minibar, central heating, tel. Swimming pool, billiard room, sports court, playground, bar, parking lot. $$
Líder Palace. Av. Juscelino Kubitschek, 3146. Phone/fax: 522-2121. Internet: www.liderpalace.com.br. 111 rooms, tv, air conditioning, minibar, tel. Swimming pool, bar, parking lot. $$$$
Mabu Thermas & Resort. Av. das Cataratas, 3175. Phone: 523-4000. Fax: 523-3432. Reservation: 0800 417-040. Internet: www.hoteismabu.com.br. 208 rooms, tv, air conditioning, minibar, tel. Swimming pool, bar, safe, central heating, lake, sauna, massage, sports court, playground, fishing, parking lot, valet service. $$$$
Rafain Centro. Rua Marechal Deodoro, 984. Phone/fax: 523-1213, reservation: 0800 451-213. Internet: www.rafaincentro.com.br. 120 rooms, tv, air conditioning, minibar, safe, central heating, tel. Swimming pool, billiard room, parking lot. $$$$
Royal Park. Cataratas Road, km 11. Phone/fax: 572-2424. Internet: www.brasil.com/royal. 80 rooms, tv, air conditioning, minibar, central heating, tel. Swimming pool, sauna, football, bar, parking lot. $$$
Santa Ana Park. Av. Costa e Silva, 1850. Phone/fax: 522-1012. Internet: www.santaanapark.com.br. 67 rooms, tv, air conditioning, minibar, central heating, tel. Swimming pool, bar, football, parking lot. $$$
Suíça. Av. Felipe Wandsheer, 3580. Phone: 525-3232. Fax: 525-3044. 30 rooms, tv, air conditioning, minibar, central heating, safe, tel. Swimming pool, playground, bar, parking lot. $$$$
Sun. Av. Juscelino Kubitschek, 3485. Phone/fax: 522-2926. 75 rooms, tv, air conditioning, minibar, tel. Swimming pool, parking lot. $$$
Tropical das Cataratas. BR-469, km 28. Phone: 521-7000. Fax: 574-1688. Internet: www.tropicalhotel.com.br. 200 rooms, tv, air conditioning, minibar, safe, tel. Swimming pool, bar, restaurant, sports court, playground, parking lot. $$$$

Dining
Antônio Maria. Rua Almirante Barroso, 1466 (Galeria Viela). Phone: 574-3388. Varied menu. $$
Búfalo Branco. Rua Rebouças, 530. Phone: 523-9744. Meat. $$$
Don Bruno Ristorante. Rua Almirante Barroso, 1713. Phone: 574-5969. Italian. $
Galeteria la Mamma. Rua das Cataratas, 1327. Phone: 574-3272. Italian. $

Grande
Ilha Grande

Deposition of sediments formed the Paraná flood plain between 7.500 to 8.000 years ago. The present day aspect was reached 1.500 years ago during a time of much rain, when lakes, marshes and a system of channels connecting them were formed. The Park is a complex of 300 islands and isles which form one of the biggest river archipelagos in the country. It is only smaller than Anavilhanas and Mariuá, in the Amazon, and is the only part of the Paraná River where there is no dam or artificial lake. The islands are subject to seasonal flooding and its vegetation is composed mainly of Coastal Rain Forest. These moist zones, together with the transition zones, contribute to the great local biologic diversity. Ingas and the Brazilian Beauty leaf are found in the regions where soils are usually flooded. Drier lands foster Mastic-resin trees and Bastard Cedars. Dikes have a thicker vegetation, with trees such as the *Pateiro*, *Pau-d'alho*, and White fig tree reaching up to 25 m in height. On the seasonally flooded plains, and around lagoons, small bushes, herbs and water plants such as Waterlilies and

Water-lettuce abound. Other species that are found are trees with prop roots, such as *Jequitibás*, Chaste trees, Piptadenias, *Angico-vermelho*, *Peroba-rosa* and *Fávia*.

Research has found 60 species of mammals, 298 of birds, 37 of reptiles and 22 amphibians. There are many Marsh Deer, Agouti Pacas, Jaguars, Pumas, Capybaras, Howling Monkeys, Wild Dogs, Peccary, Otters, Giant Otters and Tayras - a weasel closely allied to the grison. Water fowl such as Jacanas, Egrets, Roseate Spoonbills, and Herons are also very common. Among reptiles, the Broad-nosed Cayman stands out and among the fish, *Doura-dos*, *Piaparas* and *Pintados*.

HISTORY

The first Europeans who arrived in this region, inhabited by the Guarani and Xetá Indians, were Spaniards who sailed up the rivers from the Prata basin. In the 16th century, Spanish Jesuits settled many missions in the continent's heartlands, becoming known as Las Missiones del Guayra. The ruins of

Foundation: September 1997
Area: 788,7 km²
Curitiba: 637 km; Umuarama: 118 km; Cascavel: 156 km; Foz do Iguaçu: 202 km

⊘
⊕ (44)
☎ 642-2317

these old settlements can still be found on the outskirts of the Park. The *bandeiras* caused many Indians to escape from the region, as these bands of armed men - the so called *bandeirantes* from São Paulo -, who hunted for Indians to enslave, had gone to Sete Povos das Missões, in the state of Rio Grande do Sul. The second wave of Brazilian occupation came

with the boom of coffee plantations. The region which lies between the Paraná, Paranapanema and Piquiri Rivers, where Ilha Grande is, was the last area to be occupied. In the 1960's, the coffee plantations declined and were substituted by cattle ranching and agriculture. Many dams and power stations were built along the whole extension of the Paraná River.

Only a small part of the river with more than 200 islands and isles was not affected by the dams and power stations and is now a refuge for many plant and animal species. In 1993, there was a huge flood which overflowed onto the

cattle ranches. This made it easier to obtain land for the creation of the National Park, which was founded some years later, in 1997.

The Park is part of the Paraná River Corridor of Biologic Diversity, a set of natural protected areas in Brazil, Argentina, and Paraguay with more than 1,5 million hectares. It stretches from the Porto Primavera power station, along the border of the states of Paraná, Mato Grosso do Sul and São Paulo, up to the Itaipu dam on the border of Brazil, Argentina and Paraguay. It is a corridor of water ecosystems and of forested areas for terrestrial fauna.

Sete Quedas: submerged by Itaipu

The fight for preserving Sete Quedas, formed by a set of 19 waterfalls where the Paraná River narrows, was one of the first big movements to defend nature in Brazil. They were submerged by the building of the Itaipu dam in 1982 and, together with them, the National Park of the same name. In the middle of 2001, the Itaipu dam reached such a low level that a small part of Sete Quedas rose above the water level.

At the same time, Brazil also experienced the biggest energy crisis in its history.

HIGHLIGHTS

The best way to know the Park is by boat. It is possible to schedule tours in canoes or on launches, which may take one day, with stops on beaches and islands.

🐾 🦜 Cartão de Visita Island

On the outskirts of the city of Vila Alta with access via Porto Figueira. It has a nice white sand beach, huge fig trees and a trail in the forest. Watch the Pink and White Egrets, Parrots, Trivium and other fowl flying overhead. You may also go on a boat tour from Porto Figueira, with views of archeologic sites.

Parrot: common in the region

🦜 Gaivotas Island

With extensive beaches, many Seagulls and Capybaras spend the night here. This is one of the most visited beaches in the Park. Boats depart from Guaíra.

🦜 Grande Island

The island is around 110 km in length and up to 30 km in width. There are parts of preserved forest, where Brazilian Beauty leaves, *Vacuns*, Tabernaemontana and *Tarumãs* grow. You can reach the island from the south via Guaíra or from the north via Porto Figueira, a small balneary city where there is an ecologic lodge.
Phone: (44) 624-2157.

🐾 Saraiva Lake

The archipelago's most important natural lake is on Grande Island; it is around 20 km in width and has floating masses of waterlilies on it. The water is dark and clean and reaches up to 12 m in depth. Here, apart from the waterlilies in flower, it is possible to watch fowl, Howling Monkeys, Capybaras and other animals on its banks. There are boat tours of 11 km on the lake, departing from Guaíra.

Xambrê Lake

A good place for a picnic and watersports. Access is via Altônia. Get in touch with the city hall to get permits and information.

Paracaí Beach

In the city of São Jorge do Patrocínio, there are rustic facilities for picnics and a white sand beach with good condition for bathing and nature watching. The sunset is

◄ Roseate spoonbill and egrets (above); islands in the Paraná River compose the archipelago

a spectacle. Get in touch with the city hall to get permits.

Luiz Eduardo Magalhães Bridge

The biggest river construction in Latin America is now in the final phase of its building. It allows you to see the beautiful scenery of the Bandeirantes Island and the Amambai River lowlands. Access is via Porto Figueira and Porto Camargo. Take advantage of being there and visit the Bugio and Angico Forests and keep walking along the Paraná River up to the Araras cliff with its rich vegetation and bands of Howler Monkeys and flocks of birds flying overhead. It is also possible to watch families of Otters from the foot of the cliff.

Porto Camargo: bases for visiting the Park

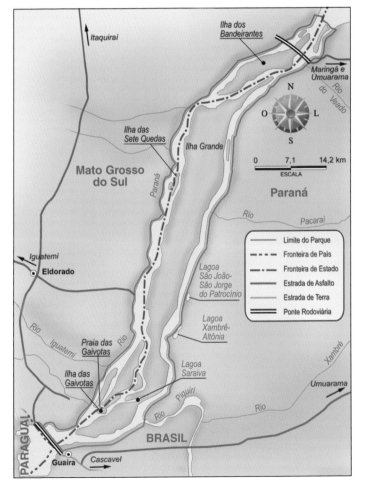

To Visit

Access – The Park is not
open for visitors yet.
Address – Rua Barão do
Rio Branco, 787, Vila Velha,
Guaíra, PR, 85980-000.
Phone: (44) 642-2317.
Fax: (44) 642-2196.
How to get there – By plane:
Guaíra and Umuarama have
small airports. By car: take the
PR-498 road, continuation
of PR-485 or the BR-487
on the Londrina–Maringá axis
up to Umuarama, then towards
Vila Alta and Icaraíma. From
the south, come via the BR-272
or BR-467 or BR-163, via
the Cascavel/Toledo axis up to
Guaíra. All of them are paved.
You may also have access
from Mato Grosso do Sul
and via the Paraná River.
Infra-structure – None.

Tips

◑ One of the typical local dishes
is *Pintado na telha* - a delicious
fish cooked in a roof-tile.
◑ The river beaches can
be seen from April to
November. The other months
are the flood season.

To know more
CABRAL, S. **Las missiones
jesuiticas del Guayrá**.
Buenos Aires: Manrique
Zago, 1993.
CAMPOS, J.B. (org.). **Parque
Nacional de Ilha Grande:
Reconquista e desafios.**
Maringá: IAP, 1999.
www.iap.gov.br
www.celepar.br/celepar/sema/
parques/ilhagrande

SERVICES

Guaíra, PR

🌐 44

✉ 85980-000

Useful addresses

City Hall. Rua Coronel Otávio Tosta, 126. Phone: 642-1311.
Bus station. Av. Dr. Oliveira de Castro. Phone: 642-1224.
Hospital. Rua Bandeirantes, 1820. Phone: 642-1400.
Port. Rua Monjoli s/n. Ferry to Salto Del Guayra (Paraguay).
Telephone station. At the bus station. Phone: 642-1538.
Banks. Banestado, Bradesco, CEF, do Brasil.

Lodging

Deville. Rua Paraguai, 1205. Phone/fax: 642-1671. Reservation: 0800 411-866. 67 rooms, tv, air conditioning, minibar, tel. Mini tennis court, billiard room, bar, playground. $$$

Dining

Jangada. Rua Monjoli, 685. Phone: 642-1649. Fish. $

Umuarama, PR

🌐 44

✉ 87501-130

Useful Addresses

City Hall. Av. Rio Branco, 3730. Phone: 623-4141.
Bus station. Praça do Bíblia. Phone: 622-2175.
Airoport. Km 155, PR-323. Phone: 622-3223.
Hospital. Av Ângelo Moreira da Fonseca, 3415. Phone: 623-2007.
Telephone station. Rua Ministro Oliveira Salazar, 5004. Phone: 622-1404.
Post Office. Av. Rio Branco, 3886.
Banks. ABN/Real, América do Sul, Banestado, do Brasil, CEF, HSBC, Itaú, Mercantil/SP, Unibanco.

Lodging

Caiuá. Av. Presidente Castelo Branco, 3745. Phone/fax: 622-5457. 62 rooms, tv, air conditioning, minibar, tel. Swimming pool, bar, parking lot, parking lot service. $$$
Olinda Palace. Av. Flórida, 4069. Phone/fax: 623-3444. 35 rooms, air conditioning, minibar, tel. Bar. $$
Presidente. Av. Rio Branco, 3845. Phone/fax: 622-2366. 62 rooms, tv, air conditioning, minibar, tel. Bar, parking lot. $$
Saving. Rua Aricanduva, 4061. Phone: 623-3888. Fax: 622-8651. 60 rooms, tv, air conditioning, minibar, tel. Parking lot. $$
Spazio. Pça. Mascarenhas de Moraes, 5039. Phone/fax: 623-2010. E-mail: spazio@spaziohotel.com.br. 66 rooms, tv, air conditioning, minibar, tel. Parking lot. $$

Dining

Chapelão. Av. Pres. Castelo Branco, 3858. Phone: 622-2476. Varied menu. $
Costela & Companhia. Av. Presidente Castelo Branco, 4293. Phone: 622-4654. Meat. $

The flight of Egrets is a common spectacle on many of the 300 islands in the Park

Lagoa do Peixe

The constant action of the wind as well as retreating and advancing levels of the sea due to glacial and interglacial periods helped to form the coastal plain where the Lagoa do Peixe National Park is. The yearly average temperature is 17,5°C with June and July the coldest and most humid months.

The complex of coastal ecosystems includes fresh and salty water lagoons, beaches, dunes, bogs, riverine vegetation and even a marine area. The Lagoa do Peixe is actually a lagoon as it is also linked to the sea. It is the biggest in the Park, with 35 km in length and from 10 to 60 cm in depth. On the cape, it is 2 m deep and from June to December it is linked to the sea. Strong winds and the entrance of nutrients from the sea attract a diversified fauna and flora: crabs, periwinkles, shrimp and fish inhabit its waters, attracting countless bird and mammal species in search of food. There are also *marismas*. These are banks of the lagoons, seasonally flooded by salty water, whose vegetation is dominated by herbaceous species.

The forests are low and cover the parts away from the sea, where trees such the *Canela-amarela* - a tree of the laurel family -, Fig trees, Myrtles,

Foundation: November 1986
Area: 344 km²
Mostardas: 4 km; Tavares: 12 km;
Capivari: 129 km;
Porto Alegre: 212 km

○
⊕ (51)
☎ 673-1464

and Christmas bushes are found. In the riverine forest, besides fig and smaller trees, thorny bushes, cacti and bromeliads are prominent. In the areas with peat bogs that are seasonally flooded, a type of forest develops with Brazilian Guavas, a species of Rapanea called *Capororocão,* the Queen palm and the Shadow palm. In the bogs, besides grasses and sedges, there are groves of Queen palm and many Trumpet trees. On the dunes, Clubmoss, the insectivorous Sundew, a species of Rapanea called *Capororoquinha* and *Vassourão* stand out. The Park has areas influenced by human presence: natural grazing land, farms producing onions and areas of reafforestation with Pinus. These areas are in the recreation zones of the Park where the original vegetation will be recovered.

There is no doubt that it is the birds and animals which most draw our attention. One hundred and eighty species have been identified of both dwelling and migratory species. The Lagoa do Peixe National Park is the only place in Brazil where you can go Flamingo watching all year round. Both species which visit the Park come from Chile and Argentina and are more easily seen between April and September. Ruddy Turnstones and American Oyster Catchers come here from North America to mate.

The flocks of Long-billed Terns, for instance, are likely to have 12.000 individuals. On the beaches, *Piru-pirus* run about, sometimes leaping on one leg, side by side with *Garças-mouras*, South American Stilts and Ruddy Turnstones. They come to this environment in order to hunt for invertebrates buried in the sand, such as *Tatuíras* and *Linguarudos* - small beach snails. In winter, a species of penguin called *Magalhães*, Sea Lions and Wolves are common on the beaches. Between June and September, watch the sea for Right Whales, which travel past these waters going to or returning from their mating and feeding grounds.

In the bogs, Capybaras, Otters, Crab-eating Raccoons, Coypus and Broad-nosed Caymans represent the mammals and reptiles. Egrets, Brazilian Lapwings, Jacanas and many species of hawk are also common in the Park. At the lagoons, watch for Black Skimmers with their long bills, for *Coscorobas* - a large bird of the swan family -, and for the endangered Black Necked Swan, in December.

In the riverine vegetation animals such as the Crab-eating Raccoon, Armadillos, Red-throated Oven-birds, Wood Rails, Guira Cuckoo, and Brazilian Burrowing Owls are common. On the sand dunes, the *Tuco-tuco*, a small burrowing, gopherlike rodent, draws the visitor's attention when burrowing themselves in the sand.

White-faced tree-duck: one of the 180 bird spec

HISTORY

The early people who inhabited the Peixe Lagoon lived from hunting and gathering shellfish, whose leftovers were dumped in shell mounds or *sambaquis*. There are 21 archaeologic sites in the Park and on the outskirts, where arrow heads, polished stone artifacts and beads have been found. The men and women who left these vestiges lived around seven thousand years ago and it is believed that they belonged to the Umbu and Humaitá traditions. Two thousand years ago, the people of the Vieira tradition, who made ceramics, assumed the region. In the 16th and 17th centuries, the region was occupied by the Minuano, Arachane and Carijó Indians, who nearly vanished with the arrival of the *bandeiras* - armed expeditions from São Paulo which entered the forests hunting for Indians to enslave and to prospect for precious minerals. In 1763, the village of São Luiz de Mostardas was founded by settlers from the Azores and, to this day, it keeps the architectonic and cultural features of its founders. Difficult access to the sandy plain, the inhospitable environment and the climate kept the region isolated and, until today, the occupation rate is low. For this reason, the coastal ecosystems have remained relatively well preserved. Today, the main economic activities are cattle ranching and fishing.

Research done back in the 1980's by the

The queenpalm and the guaricanga palm are typical of the areas that flood

◀   Long-dilled tern (above); Lagoa do Peixe is 35 km long

Research Centre for the Preservation of Wild Birds (Cemave) drew attention to the presence of a great number of bird species at the Lagoa do Peixe and, in 1986, this resulted in the transformation of the area into a National Park. The importance of the area was also internationally acknowledged. In 1991 it was included in the Hemisphere Network of Limicolous Birds; in 1992 in the Coastal Rain Forest Biosphere Reserve; and in 1993 in the Ramsar Convention which is concerned about moist zones of international relevancy.

HIGHLIGHTS

It is possible to get into the Park via three distinct accesses. Bicycle riding is permitted in the conservation unit. Before you go for adventure, visit the headquarters, at the centre in Mostardas. There are videos, books, a permanent photographic exhibition and a model of the Park.

Lagoa do Peixe Cape

Here the greatest migratory bird flocking occurs in the Park. The small, local community live on fishing prawns, crabs, mullet, *peixe-rei* - a fish of the wrasse family -, and sole fish. When it begins to rain, an amazing amount of mosquitoes appear - do not forget your insect repellent!

Beaches

The 36 km of beaches in the Park are called Flamingos' Trail. It is 18 km from Mostardas lighthouse - which actually belongs to the city of Tavares and not to Mostardas, as the name may suggest - to Lagoa do Peixe Cape, and then 18 km more to the Park's south border. The lighthouse was built in 1940, and is totally covered in tiles. On these beaches, you can watch birds such as Ruddy Turnstones, *Garças-mouras*, *Pirus-pirus* and Flamingos. From June to December the cape is flooded and thus impassable.

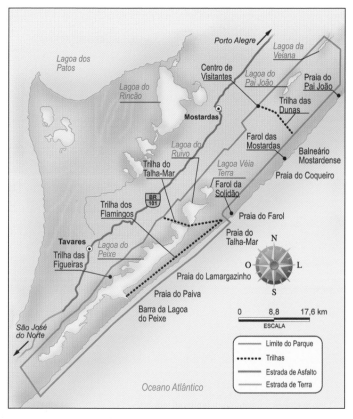

Bird research and preservation

Piru-piru: a migratory species

The Research Centre for Wild Bird Preservation (Cemave) is an institution bound to the government bureau for environmental affairs, Ibama, who does research with birds all over Brazil. In the state of Rio Grande do Sul, because of the plenty of bird species in the Peixes Lagoon, there is a particularly special research involving the migratory species. Researchers make two yearly expeditions in order to watch the animals, to catch and ring-mark birds, as well as to train the Centre's staff in ring-marking. They do research on the preservation of these animals and their environment. Phone: (51) 3226-4871.

🐦 Dunas Trail
Or Balneário Mostardense road, around 12 km long, cuts through the Park past bogs, riverine vegetation and dunes all the way to the shore. It is outside the border of the conservation unit.

🐦 Figueiras Trails
From Tavares to the trail it is 6 km on sand. You can not drive this 1-km way during the flood season.

🐦 Talha-Mar Trail
Better known as Véia Terra road, it is 10 km long and links the main road to the shore. Watch for the big moving dunes along the way. From June to August, the passage may be flooded by water.

SURROUNDINGS

Solidão Lighthouse
⊖ 60 km from the Park ⌚ Four hours
The 21-m-high lighthouse, which was built back in 1929, is on Farol beach. Despite the bad condition of the access, the sand dunes and flooded areas along the way re-pay the effort.

Patos Lake
⊖ 12 km from Mostardas, 10 km from Tavares ⌚ Six hours
The biggest lake in the country occupies an area greater than 100 km². It is rich in prawn and other invertebrates and for this reason attracts a huge quantity of birds which feed on these animals. Barquinho Port, by the lake, is 25 km from Mostardas and can be reached by walking 6 km in the forest. Also visit the Capão da Marca Lighthouse, one of the oldest, on the banks of lake Patos. Here you can see archaeologic vestiges of the indigenous peoples occupation.

Mostardas
⊖ 4 km from the Park ⌚ Six hours
The small town still has traces of its Azorean colonization and its customs, with low houses and narrow streets. The Casa da Cultura has a good collection with antiques, photographs and library. Pure wool clothes, woven on manual looms, and miniatures of sea birds are the main handicrafts in the town.

São José do Norte
⊖ 127 km from Tavares ⌚ Six hours
The small village is at the end of the narrow stretch of sand between the sea and the Patos Lake. Do not miss the *molhe*; a kind of sand bank, 4 km long, over the cape of Patos Lake. Walk here on days when the sea is calm watching for Sea Lions. On the way, do not miss a visit to Bojuru, a small colonial village also in Azorian style.

Tavares
⊖ 12 km from the Park
⌚ Six hours
The city's highlights are the festivals and cultural manifestations. The Ternos Juninos and Cavalhadas, both of Azorian heritage, occur in June. The Prawn and Onion festival occurs in March.

The dunes in the Park stretch out for more than 10 km ▶

TO VISIT

Access – Get information about hours and visiting rules at the Park's headquarters.

Address – Pça. Prefeito Luiz Martins, 30, Mostardas, RS, 96270-000.

Phone: (51) 673-1464. E-mail: lagoadopeixe@terra.com.br.

How to get there – By car from Porto Alegre, take the RS-040 up to Capivari and then take the BR-101 up to Mostardas. The roads are flat and the pavement has just been re-made. By coach: there are regular coaches from the Porto Alegre bus station to Mostardas. From this city, there are city buses to the coast through the Park.

Infra-structure – The office at Mostardas is open from 8 to 12 am and from 2 to 5 pm. It is also a temporary visitors' centre with information and a video show about the Park.

TIPS

❍ The Park is more visited in summer, which is from December to March, and in winter, from June to September, when migratory birds flock to the Park. In winter, Sea Lions can also be spotted along the beach. The temperature is more pleasant in summer, when the *minuano* - a cool and dry wind - does not blow.

❍ Before arriving in Mostardas, take a look at the Crab-eating Racoons, King Fishers, Southern Limpkin, Egrets and water plants of the region.

❍ If you are visiting the Park in the winter and want to take a walk on the dunes, make sure you are wearing coat, bobble hat and scarf.

To know more

NASCIMENTO, I. de L.S. **Aves do Parque Nacional da Lagoa do Peixe**. Brasília: Ibama, 1995.

PEDRAZZI, I. e GRIMM, R. **Lagoa do Peixe**: Paraíso das Aves. Florianópolis: Mares do Sul, 1999.www.proaves.org.br

The sand banks by the Lagoa do Peixe reflect the sun light

SERVICES

Mostardas
🌐 51
✉ 96270-000

Useful Addresses
City Hall. Rua Bento Gonçalves, 1020. Phone: 673-1157/ 673-1307.
Bus station. Rua 15 de Novembro, Phone: 673-1255.
Hospital. Rua Almirante Tamandaré, 864. Phone: 673-1411.
Telephone station. Rua Bento Gonçalves, 960.
Post Office. Rua Independência, 839. Phone: 673-1221.
Banks. Do Brasil, Banrisul.

Support for the Visitor
Tourist Services. Av. Padre Simão, 141. Phone: 673-1177/1433.
Tourist Bureau. Rua Bento Gonçalves, 1020. Phone: 673-1166.
Tour agencies. Garça. Rua Almirante Tamandaré, 847 . Phone/fax: 673-1463.

Lodging
Estrela do Mar. Balneário Mostardense. Phone: 673-1500. 11 rooms, tv, tel. Bar, restaurant. $
Mostardense. Rua Bento Gonçalves, 203. Phone: 673-1368. 11 rooms, tv. $.
Municipal. Rua Independente, 761. Phone: 673-1500. 8 rooms, tv, tel, fan. Restaurant. $
Scheffer. Rua Almirante Tamandaré, 1191. Phone: 673-1277. 8 rooms, tv, tel. $
Camping Fazenda Capororoca. RST-101, km 86. Phone: 9959-1630. Electricity, tap water, bathrooms, kiosks, fishing, football field.
Camping Lagoa da Reserva. RST-101, km 98. Phone: 9973-7146/ 9136-3262/9912-0733. Rural property, electricity, tap water, bathrooms, vacancies for tents, trailers, motor-homes.

Dining
Alternativa. Av. Pe. Simão s/nº. Varied menu. $
Edmundo's. Rua Bento Gonçalves, 908. Phone: 673-1553. Fish/Meat. $
Ponto de Encontro. Rua Emílio Ferreira de Lemos, 867. Phone: 673-1314. Varied menu. $
Recanto. Rua Luiz Araújo, 935. Phone: 673-1527. Pizza. $
São Francisco. Rua 11 de Abril, s/nº. Phone: 673-1460. Varied menu.$

Tavares
🌐 51
✉ 96000-290

Useful Addresses
City Hall. Rua Abílio Vieira Paiva, 228.
Bus station. Rua Edgardo Pereira Velho, s/nº. Phone: 674-1175.
Ambulatory. Rua Alfredo Lisboa, s/nº. Phone: 674-1221.
Telephone station. Av. 11 de Abril, 261.
Post Office. Rua Abílio Vieira Paiva, s/nº.
Bank. Banrisul.

Support for the Visitor
Support Centre for the Ecotourist. Av. 11 de Abril, s/nº.

Lodging
Paiva. Av. 11 de Abril, 218. Phone: 674-1329. 8 rooms, tv. $

Dining
Arco Íris. Rua Edgar Pereira Velho, s/nº. Phone: 674-1305. Varied menu. $
Colares. Av. 11 de Abril, 232. Phone: 674-1132. Varied menu. $

São Joaquim

São Joaquim

The topography of the Geral Mountain Range started to be shaped 120 million years ago, when lava overflows set on a sandstone base formed the plateau which today spreads over the greater part of the country's southern region. The Catarinense or Serrano plateau, where the São Joaquim Park is, lies on the eastern rim of the mountain range where earthquakes and river erosion formed valleys and canyons. The highest summit, Igreja Hill with 1.822m, is normally enshrouded in a thick mist. This is where the rivers Pelotas, Urubici, Cachimbo and Bispo have their sources. The Park englobes the high plains, which is the coldest region in the country, where snow falls are not rare, and the "mountain below", with an average temperature of 20°C.

In the area of the Coastal Rain Forest, the principal landscape is formed by forests of Brazilian Pine, which occur between 500 and 1.200 m above sea level. Apart from this pine, the forest also harbours the Imbuya Phoebe, two species of cinnamon called *Fogo* and *Lajeana*, and the Scotch Pine. At higher altitudes, a type of dwarf forest develops,

Foundation: July 1961
Area: 493 km²
Florianópolis: 160 km; Lages: 116 km; Urubici: 12 km; São Joaquim: 53 km

⊘

🌐 (49)
☎ 278-4002

with many bushes, among which there are
Rapaneas, types of Holly such as the
Congonha and the *Caúna*, a species of
bamboo called *Taquara* and the
Vassourão-branco. On the rim of the
mountains above 1.200 m, the vegetation is
called *Nebular* Forest. *Gramimunha,
Goiabinha-do-campo, Cinzeiro* and *São-
joão-miúdo* are twisted trees, endemic to
this ecosystem. The fields on the plateau
are dominated by grasses such as the *Ca-
pim-caninha*, with *Vassoura-lajeana,
Caraguatá* and Bracken Fern. The Park's
fauna still falls prey to poachers; it is
represented by squirrels, the Cavy, Peccary,
a species of brocket called *Catingueiro*,
Wild Dogs and Little Anteaters. Puma,
already rare in the region, is locally called
Bay Lion. There are many bird species, due

mainly to the variation in altitudes.
Common birds are Azure Jays, Southern
Swallow-tailed Kites, a species of Wood
Rail, Partridges, as well as Cayenne Swifts,
Hummingbirds and King Fishers. The Park
also has two endemic bird species: the
Grimpeirinho and the *Grimpeiro*.

The azure jay feeds on pine seeds

HISTORY

Rock paintings found in the region show that the area was inhabited at least 3.000 years ago. However, very little is known about the people who left their mark in the grottos and caves. When the Jesuits travelled through the region on their way to the heart of Rio Grande do Sul to found their missions, the Xokleng Indians inhabited a territory which spread from the top of the mountains to the coastal plain. With the penetration of armed bands from São Paulo, who hunted for Indians to enslave in the backwoods of the country, and immigrants from the Azores and other European countries in their wake, the Indians ended up being annihilated. These bands were the so called *bandeiras,* and their cruel, bloodthirsty members, the *bandeirantes.* The occupation by Europeans introduced cattle ranching in the heart of the state. At this time they used typical wattle and daub walls in the grazing fields so as to form passage ways for their herds of cattle. Vestiges of these trails can still be found within the Park and in the neighbouring areas.

Until the first half of the 20th century, the "high plains" were cut through by the paths of wranglers, used by the traders of pack animals and other goods. The *tropeiro* was another adventurous, historic character, who travelled the trails transporting jerked beef, wool and cheese to the coast and bringing back *cachaça* - a rumlike spirits made out of sugar cane - and other products. In the 1950's, woodcutting exhausted the native forests, mainly of the Brazil Pine. As a result, the first ecologic movements were formed, demanding the preservation of this ecosystem and, in 1957, an agricultural engineer from São Joaquim suggested the

Legends and Brazil Pines

Up to the middle of the 20th century, Brazilian Pine forests used to cover a great part of the country's southern region, extending to part of the states of São Paulo and Minas Gerais. The pinhão - the edible pine seed - was the base of the indigenous peoples feeding; they used special arrows in order to fell the pine-cones. The tree was thus included in the regional folk-lore. The caboclos - a race and a culture resulting from the mixture of the European and the Indian - use the leaves and fruit to perform magic and to forecast the future. Among the beliefs, one states that when the pine's branches creak, it is a bad omen: someone is about to die and the tree is offering wood for the coffin. Another says that when the pine falls, it is because someone has been pierced by a bullet.

Brazilian pine: inspiration for the folk-lore

◀   Little Anteater (above); rocky formations in the Catarinense Plateau and bushy vegetation

creation of a National Park in the region. One year later, a geo-economic survey was made and the area to be the base of the conservation unit was chosen. The Park was founded in 1961.

HIGHLIGHTS

Santa Bárbara Fields
In the higher sections of the Park, the landscape is dominated by high altitude fields. Access is via a 30-km dirt road, from Vacas Gordas, by SC-438.

🔟 🌑 Laranjeiras Canyon
Despite difficult access, the canyon, to where the sources of the Laranjeiras

River flow, is a nice point for a stop. To get there, take the 25-km dirt road which starts at Bom Jardim da Serra.

🔟 Véu de Noiva Waterfall
The cold water 25-m waterfall is near by the Park's limits, 5 km from Igreja Hill.

Igreja Hill
Here the high altitude fields finish abruptly and fall in cliffs of more than 1.500 m in height. An excellent view on clear days, overlooking the Serra Geral escarpments and the coast, 60 km away. Here, at 1.822 m in height, where it is very windy, the lowest temperature in the country has been recorded: - 17,8°C.

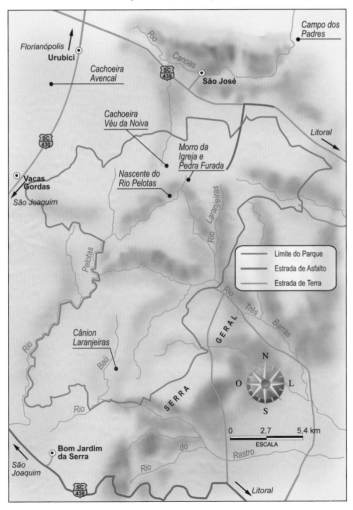

Furada rock overlooked from the 1800-m high Igreja hill

⬤ Pelotas River Source

The source is in a flooded field which is difficult to get to. The Pelotas River cuts through the Park and unites with the Canoas to form the Uruguay River.

Pedra Furada

A rock formation which can be seen from the Igreja Hill.

SURROUNDINGS · · · · · · · · ·

⓫ Avencal Waterfall

⊖ 8 km from São Joaquim ⊕ Two hours
The access by car via BR-430 is easy;
then a 1-km walk through Maidenhair and Dicksonia Tree Fern take you to the 88-m waterfall, which falls into the canyon. It is possible to go by car to the summit of the waterfall to enjoy the view.

Rock Paintings

⊖ 10 km from Urubici ⊕ Two hours
Rock inscriptions in high and low relief, which date back to 3.000 years ago, can be visited on the way between the high and low parts of the Maidenhair field. It is easily reached via a paved road.

São Joaquim
⊖ 53 km from the Park ⊕ Six hours
The cold weather is the city's biggest attraction, as it usually snows here in the winter. The city is renowned as the best apple producer in the country.

Corvo Branco Mountain Range
⊖ 30 km from Urubici ⊕ Four hours
The road which links Urubici to Grão-Pará leads to the peak of Corvo Branco, with 1.470 m in height. The Pelotas and Canoas rivers can be seen from the steep and winding road, which leads past precipices, canyons and many lookouts. In winter, it is likely to snow in the region.

Rio do Rastro Mountain Range
⊖ 60 km from São Joaquim
In the city of Bom Jardim da Serra, the winding SC-438 follows the 1.450-m-high canyon. There are lookouts from where you can stop to enjoy the view.

The treasure of the Jesuits

The Jesuits' missions in the south had a very strong importance in the region and fostered some of the most traditional legends in local folk-lore. One of them dates back to the time when the Jesuits were being expelled from the country by order of the Marquis of Pombal; he who fought against the political power of the Catholic Church in order to strengthen the Portuguese state. It is said that the priests fled up the Uruguay and Pelotas Rivers, taking with them precious metals and jewels. The treasure is said to have been hidden near Igreja Hill. To this day, there are stories of wandering ghosts roaming about looking for the treasure.

Landscape overlooked from the Igreja hill

TO VISIT

Access – The Park is not
open for visitors yet.
Mail Address – Rua Felicíssimo
Rodrigues Sobrinho, 1542,
Urubici, SC, 88650-000.
Phone/fax: (49) 278-4002.
E-mail: pnsj@iscc.com.br.
How to get there – By car from
Florianópolis: take the BR-282 up to
km 146 (Santa Clara), then take
SC-430 - 24 km further until Urubici.
From here, it is 12 km on dirt road via
SC-439 up to the slopes of Igreja Hill.
From Lages: take SC-438 towards
Bom Jardim da Serra. In Cruzeiro,
take SC-430 for 44 km up to Urubici
(28 km on a dirt road).
Infra-structure – The Park has
an asphalt road which leads to Igreja
Hill. There are also dirt roads to
the main attractions.

TIPS

❍ The best time to visit the Park is
from June to August, when it is likely
to snow. It is also the time clear skies,
with excellent visibility and better
chances for bird watching.
❍ The weather on the top of the
mountains is very moist, with constant
rain. It is advisable to wear water-proof
clothing and shoes.

To know more
DALL'ARA, J. **O Tesouro do Morro
da Igreja**. Florianópolis: FCC, 1994.
KELLER, L. **Arte rupestre em Santa
Catarina.** Florianópolis: Rupestre, 1996.
PIAZZA, W. **As grutas de São Joa-
quim e Urubici.** Florianópolis: Editora
UFSC, 1966.
www.turismocatarinense.tur.br
www.iscc.com.br/pnsj

◀ Typical farm in the mountain region with Brazilian Pine forest in the background

SERVICES

Urubici
⊕ 49
✉ 88650-000

Useful Addresses
City Hall. Pça. Francisco Pereira de Souza, 53. Phone: 278-4211.
Bus station. Av. Adolfo Konder, 81. Phone: 278-4371.
Hospital. Rua Boanerges Pereira de Medeiros, 1196. Phone: 278-4099.
Post Office. Rua Irmã Policarpa, 48. Phone: 278-4135.
Banks. Do Brasil, BESC, Bradesco.

Support for the Visitor
Tourist Information. Av. Adolfo Konder. Phone: 278-4360.

Lodging
Amorim. Av. Prefeito Natal Zilli, 2833. Phone: 278-4491. 10 rooms, tv. $
Anderman. Av. Prefeito Natal Zilli, 2792. Phone: 278-4327. 15 rooms $
Fazenda Serra do Panelão. SC-430 Road, km 11, 14 km.
Phone: 292-1800. Internet: www.panelao.cjb.nh.net.
8 rooms, 2 chalets, tv, fireplace, heating. Swimming pool, bar, restaurant, lake, multi-sport court, fishing, horses, car park. $ $ $ $
Pousada Águas Brancas. SC-430 Road, km 3. Phone: 278-4178. 7 rooms, tv, fireplace. $
Pousada das Araucárias. SC-439 Road, km 8. Phone: 278-4532. 2 rooms, fireplace. $
Pousada Fazenda da Invernada. Access via SC-439 (B. Fetti), 2 km. Phone: 278-4131. 4 rooms Bar, horses, carpark. $ $
Pousadas das Flores. Guest House. Av. Adolfo Konder, 2273. Phone: 278-4107. 3 rooms, air conditioning tv. $
Pousada Vó Natália.
Rua Felicíssimo Rodrigues Sobrinho, 1614. Phone: 278-4194. 4 rooms, tv, fireplace. $
Serra Bela Hospedeira Rural. Geral de Santo Antônio Road, km 4. Phone: 278-4016. 6 rooms, fireplace, carpark, lake, horses, fishing. $ $
Serra Bela Hospedaria Rural. SC-439 Road, km 4. Phone: 278-4016. 6 rooms tv, fireplace. $ $
Urubici Palace. Av. Adolfo Konder, s/n°. Phone: 278-4258. 23 rooms, tv, minibar. $

Dining
Churrascaria Tio Loro. Av. Afonso Konder, s/n°. Phone: 278-4675. Meat. $
Zeca's Bar. Av. Afonso Konder, 522. Phone: 278-4490. Varied menu. $

São Joaquim
⊕ 49
✉ 88600-000

Useful Addresses
City Hall. Pça. João Ribeiro, 1. Phone: 233-0411.
Bus station. Rua Domingos Marturano, s/n°. Phone: 233-0358/ 233-0296.
Hospital. Rua Murilo Bortoluzzi. Phone: 233-0011.
Telephone station. Pça. Cesário Amaranti, s/n°.
Post office. Rua Marcos Batista, 520. Phone: 233-0125.
Banks. Do Brasil, Bradesco, BESC, CEF.

Support for the Visitor
Tourist Information. Pça. Cesário Amarante, 38. Phone: 233-0411.

Lodging
Pousada Água Santa (farm). SC-438, km 79, 3 km. Phone: 233-1140. 8 rooms, tv. Bar, restaurant, billiard room, orchard, heated swimming pool, horses, fishing, carpark. $
Pousada Caminhos de Neve. Av. Irineu Bornhausen (Morro da Bandeira farm). Phone/fax: 233-0385. 15 rooms, minibar, tel., tv, heating. Carpark, bicycles, horses. $ $
Pousada Fazenda Passo Velho (rural lodging). SC-438 towards Bom Jardim da Serra, km 34, 36 km. Phone/fax: 232-0114. 8 rooms, tv. Carpark, bar, restaurant, fishing, horses, cascade, playground. $ $ $
Pousada Santa Rita. SC-438, towards Bom Jardim da Serra, km 31, 34 km. Phone: 232-0255. 1 rooms, 7 apartments. Bar, restaurant, carpark, waterfall, horses, fishing. $ $ $
São Joaquim Park. Pça. João Ribeiro, 58. Phone: 233-1444. 13 rooms, tv, tel., heating, minibar. $ $ $ $

Dining
Bara Ramos. Rua Urubici, 580. Phone: 233-0119. Varied menu. $
Casa de Pedra. Rua Manuel Joaquim Pinto, 360. Phone: 233-0437. Varied menu. $

Serra Geral

The Geral Mountain Range dates back to 200 million years, when a large basaltic plateau appeared in the southern region of the country due to lava overflowing into the area. Later on, the terrain which had been moulded by lava suffered cracking and ruptures because of the movement of the tectonic plates. On the borders of the states of Santa Catarina and Rio Grande do Sul, the many fractures in the rocks, sculpted by erosion and harsh weather, form the biggest chain of canyons in the country. The height of the vertical cliffs reach up to 990 m. The biggest,

the Fortaleza canyon, is 7-km long. The climate is sub-tropical without a dry season; the hottest month is January and the coldest is July. But all year round temperatures raise and fall quickly during the day. Fog is formed by the temperature difference between the cold rim of the plateau and the plains below the canyons. They appear suddenly and in several minutes can spread over vast areas. Frost and the formation of ice crystals, which enshroud the fields early in the morning, are common in winter. Cachoeira, Bonito and Porteira Velha are some of the

Foundation: May 1992
Area: 173 km²
Cambará do Sul: 22 km; Praia Grande: 19 km; Tainhas: 55 km; Porto Alegre: 220 km

○
⊕ (54)
☎ 3225-2144

rivers that flow through the plateau. Apart from these, countless creeks form small swamps hidden under the water vegetation, causing the trails to become muddy. The Park's vegetation is composed of stretches of the almost extinct Brazilian pine forests. These also include California Pepper trees, Oaks, Red Quebrachos and Scotch pines. In the lower part, the Coastal Rain Forest develops and Christmas bush and the Canchara Cabralea, which may reach up to 25 m in height, appear. On the plateau, fields with grasses, herbs and small bushes predominate.

Among mammals, there are Wild Dogs - locally called *Graxaim* -, Pampas Deer, Brocket, Armadillos, Peccary, Capuchin Monkeys, Red Howlers, Squirrels, Otter and even bigger species such as the Maned Wolf and the Puma, locally called Bay Lion.

Among birds, there are some endangered species such as the Grey Eagle and the Hawk-headed Parrot. However, if you spend some time in the region you will probably be able to see Ibis, Azure Jays, and Brazilian Lapwings, which are very common in the Park.

Fields-atop-the-mountains: landscape mingles with the canyons of the Serra Geral

HISTORY

Serra Geral and Aparados da Serra, the two coupled Parks of Brazil, share the same history. The early inhabitants were the Çaágua Indians and, due to difficult access, the Geral Mountain Range was one of the last territories to be occupied by Europeans. However, in the 17th and 18th century, the region's tracks were travelled by *tropeiros* - traders of pack animals who transported the production of dried meat from the heartland to the coast. Later, wood cutting companies and cattle ranches entered the "fields atop the mountains", gaining the space lost by the Brazilian pines.

With the creation of the Aparados da Serra National Park, in 1959, part of the region's ecosystem was protected. However, as wood cutting increased, it was considered necessary to enlarge the protection area. As the process to change the area of a National Park takes a long time and must be approved by the National Congress, it was decided to create a new conservation unit. So, in 1992 the Serra Geral National Park was founded.

In the moist areas it is possible to find the bigsting nettle with its typical gigantic leaves

◀   Otter (above); Fortaleza: the largest canyon in the Park, 7 km long

SURROUNDINGS

Churriado Canyon

It is 12 km from the place where you leave your car. The hike takes three hours and must be started very early in the morning in order to avoid the evening fog.

Índios Canyon

It is a gorge smaller than the other canyons. It can be reached via a short and easy trail which starts near the inspection station at the foot of the mountains, on the border of the states of Santa Catarina and Rio Grande do Sul. It takes 15 minutes to walk.

Fortaleza Canyon

The biggest canyon in the region with a 30-km rim and 7,5 km in extension if all the bends and curves are considered.

Its name - Fortress - is due to the shape of the rocks which are reminiscent of the battlements of a fortress. On fine weather days it is possible to see the sea from the summit. There is a trail to the canyon lookout, which takes 25 minutes to walk and goes past a nice waterfall.

Malacara Canyon

With height above 900 m, this canyon can be reached via the upper part on a 8-km walk, or via the lower part into the canyon on a 3-hour trail along the riverbed. As it is very high, there is a great contrast between the upper region with forests of Brazilian Pine and the lower region of Coastal Rain Forest.

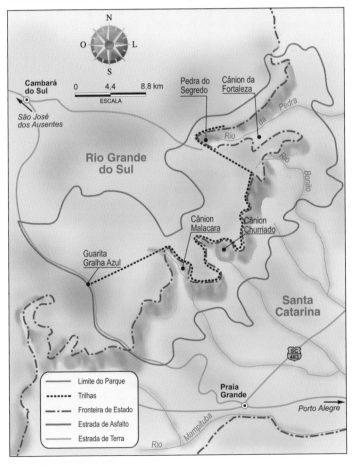

♦ ❂ Molha-Coco Canyon

This gorge, which also lies on the "fields below the mountains", saves a surprise in it: one of the nicest local waterfalls, surrounded by well preserved *Mata Atlântica*, as the Coastal Rain Forest is called in Brazil. Many mountaineers come here in order to cross through the canyon.

♦ ❂ Segredo Rock and Tigre Preto Waterfall

The level of difficulty of the trail is medium. It leads through the Segredo Gully, a shallow creek whose bottom is very slippery. The Tigre Preto Waterfall, in which you can bathe, is after the gully. Above it is the Segredo Rock lookout, a 5-m high rock formation supported on a very small and thin base, 50 cm in diameter.

SURROUNDINGS · · · · · · · · ·

❂ ❂ Buoy-cross on Mambituba River

⊖ 5 km from the Park ⊕ Two hours

The place is privileged with its transparent water which flows from a canyon. In Praia Grande, it is possible to book the tour and rent a buoy, wetsuit, and life-jacket.
Information: (48) 532-0132.

● ❂ Passo do S Waterfall

⊖ 58 km from the Park ⊕ Four hours
Access by Bom Jesus road, via Várzea do Cedro

Armadillo: an endangered mammal

Two very shallow and wide rivers which make an S and can be forded on the slippery bottom. After crossing, you reach the waterfalls which are around 30 m in height.

● ❂ Venâncio Waterfall

⊖ 40 km from São Francisco de Paula
⊕ Four hours

The Lageado River is very wide and suddenly narrows making a sequence of waterfalls. It is locally known as "mini Iguaçu Falls", as the sequence of waterfalls are reminiscent of the true ones in the state of Paraná, but much smaller.

❂ ❂ Rappelling on Costãozinho, CTG and Borges Waterfalls

⊖ 6 km from Praia Grande
⊕ Three hours

Rappelling is permitted on these waterfalls.
Information: (48) 532-0132.

Serra Geral has the biggest set of canyons in the country

◀ Waterfall on the Fortaleza canyon whose cliffs reach up to 900 m in height

To Visit

Access – Ask Ibama about the best way to visit the Park and, if you are walking long trails, the best places to go camping.
Mail Address – Estrada RS-429, Caixa Postal 10, Cambará do Sul, RS, 95480-000. Phones: (51) 3255-2144. Fax: 3226-1362, extension 507 and 508.
How to get there – By car from Porto Alegre: take RS-020 towards São Francisco de Paula and Cambará do Sul. From Cambará to the Park, it is 22 km on a dirt road. From Santa Catarina: take BR-101 up to the border with Rio Grande do Sul and take the road to Praia Grande. From Praia Grande, take the SC-360 towards Cambará do Sul. By coach: there are departures from Mondays to Saturdays from Cambará to the Park.
Infra-structure – There is none. It is possible to visit the canyons and camp in them. Guides can be hired in the nearby cities.

Tips

❍ The best time to visit the Park is in the winter, from June to August, when visibility is better and there is not so much fog. Summer, from December to March, is the best time to go bathing in the waterfalls.
❍ Woolen sweaters, which are typical products, are recommended for hikes or horse rides.

To know more
www.bdh.com.br/itaimbezinho
www.praiagrande-sc.com.br

SERVICES

Cambará do Sul, RS
⊕ 54
◔ 95480-000

Useful Addresses
City Hall. Av. Dona Ursula, 475.
Phone: 251-1174.
Bus station. Rua Dona Ursula, 700.
Phone: 251-1343.
Hospital. Rua Padre João Pazza, 197.
Phone: 251-1167.
Telephone station. Rua 28 de
Dezembro. Phone: 251-1203.
Post Office. Av. Getúlio Vargas, 663.
Phone: 251-1250.
Bank. Banrisul.

Support for the Visitor
**City Bureau for Tourism and
Development.** Rua Dona Ursula, 475.
Phone: 251-1320.
Tour Agencies. Caa-etê.
Phone: (51). 3338-3323.
Maracajá. (51) 3395-5678.

Lodging
Pousada Alvorada. Av. Getúlio Vargas,
1184. Phone: 251-1284. 15 rooms tv,
minibar, tel. Restaurant. $
Pousada Cambará do Sul. Rua Adail
Lima Valim, 23. Phone: 251-1131.
5 rooms, tv. Parking lot. $
Pousada das Corucadas. (rural
lodging). Road to Ouro Verde, km 1.
Phone: 251-1128.
7 rooms. Lake, waterfall, corral, horses,
fishing. $$
Pousada Fortaleza. Av. Getúlio Vargas,
296. Phone: 251-1224. 8 rooms, tv, tel. $
Pousada dos Lobos. Rua da Úrsula,
148. Phone: 251-1263. 3 rooms (family
home). Parking lot. $
Pousada Paraíso. Rua Antônio
Raupp, 678. Phone: 251-1352.
15 rooms, tv, tel. Restaurant. $
Pousada Recanto dos Amigos. Lajeada
da Margarida Road. Phone:
(51) 9832-1615. 6 rooms. Lake,
waterfall, horses, fishing. $$
Pousada Simoni. Rua 20 de Setembro,
570. Phone: 251-1116. 6 rooms,
tel, restaurant. $

Dining
Altos da Serra. Av. Getúlio Vargas, 696.
Phone: 251-1259. Pasta/Meat. $
Garfo & Bombacha. Caracol Road,
7 km. Phone: 282-2677. Meat/Typical
local food. $ $

Sabrina. Av. Getúlio Vargas, 586.
Phone: 251-1147. Meat. $

São José dos Ausentes
⊕ 54
◔ 95280-000

Useful Addresses
City Hall. Rua Professor Eduardo
Pereira, 442. Phone: 234-1100.
Bus station. Av. Ismênia Batista
Velho, s/nº.
Ambulatory. Rua do Hospital.
Phone: 234-1061.
Post Office. Rua Professor Eduardo
Pereira, 442.

Support for the Visitor
Tourist Bureau. Rua Professor Eduardo
I. Pereira, s/nº. Phone: 324-1100.
Ecotourism Local Guides.
Phone: 234-1072.

Lodging
**Pousada Fazenda Cachoeirão dos
Rodrigues.** Access via Potreirinhos
Farm, 34 km on a dirt road.
Phone: 237-233. Internet:
www.guiatelnet.com.br/
cachoeiraodorodrigues. 6 rooms.
Waterfall, horses, fire place,
dining hall. $$
Pousada Fazenda Monte Alegre.
Brasília Road, 6 km on a dirt road.
Phone: 9996-1697. 4 rooms. Cascade,
horses. $$$
Pousada Fazenda Paraíso. Access via
km 35 of BR-285 to Bom Jesus, 10 km.
Phone: 504-5002. Fax: 237-1500,
reservation: 237-1073. 2 rooms, 2 huts,
fire place. Target practice, corral,
waterfall, horses. $$$
Pousada Fazenda Potreirinhos. Access
via the road to Bom Jardim da Serra.
Phone: 9977-3482.
8 rooms, horses, fishing. $$$
**Pousada Fazenda São José do
Silveira**. Access via Silveira district.
Phone: 9972-4035.
8 rooms, heating. Corral, horses. $$$
Sítio Vale das Trutas.
Phone: 504-5693. Internet:
www.valedastrutas.com.br. 2 chalets, tv,
fire place, kitchen. Restaurant, lake,
waterfall, fish and pay. $$$

Dining
Café Serrano. Av. Ismênia, 508. Phone:
234-1072. Typical local food. $
Família Cesar. Rua Ismênia, 368.
Phone: 234-1202. Varied menu. $

Superagüi

Superagüi means "queen of the fish" in the language of the Tupi-Guarani Indians, a fitting name as the region is on an estuary with a great variety of water fauna. In the Park there are also areas covered with mangrove, riverine vegetation and pioneer formations beside the sea. Intermingled with these landscapes, there are bogs and flooded areas on the banks of rivers and lagoons where *caxetais* appear. Moisture prevails in this region, which does not have a defined dry season.

The Park is formed by the islands Peças, Superagüi, Pinheiro and Pinheirinho, as well as a continental section in the valley of Rio dos Patos, where its highest point is 575 m. The luxurious Coastal Rain Forest is composed of broad leaved and perennial tree species, covered in many vines and epiphytic plants.

The Park's ecosystem is among the most biologically diverse in the world. Species which stand out are the Brazilian Beauty leaf, the Brazilian cherry, *Guapuruvu*, Brazilian Eupatorium, *Araçá* and Assai Euterpe Palm, whose fruit feed the rich local fauna.

Mangroves occur on the flat areas, where the river and sea waters encounter. Here, trees are restricted to three main species. Apart from countless species of fish, crustacean and fowl which live in the mangrove, the environment is also visited by Crab-eating Raccoons and Water Opossums that drop by in search of food.

Animals which stand out among the region's fauna are the *Chauá* Parrot - an endangered species which chose Pinheiro

Foundation: April 1989
Area: 339,3 km²
Curitiba: 167 km; Joinville: 86 km;
Paranaguá: 20 km or three hours
by boat; Guaraqueçaba: 20 km,
three hours by boat

○
⊕ (41)
☎ 482-1262

Island as a night refuge, and the recently discovered *Caiçara* Capuchin Monkey. This is one of the most endangered species on the planet because it is restricted to a very small area and their population is no greater than 300 individuals. In the Park, there are also other species of Capuchin Monkey, Howling Monkeys, Coendous, Pacas, Peccary, Otters and some Pumas and Ocelots. Between March and April, Superagüi shelters migratory birds, such as the Long-billed Tern and the Ruddy Turnstone, which come from the northern hemisphere.

Neighbouring and within the Park there are communities who live in villages. With them, the Ecologic Research Institute (IPÊ) and the Wildlife Research Society (SPVS) develop environmental education programs. Both institutions aim at the establishment of activities focused on the protection of both the *Chauá* Parrot and the *Caiçara* Capuchin Monkey.

HISTORY · · · · · · · · · · · · · · ·

The early inhabitants of the region were fishermen and left their presence recorded in approximately 50 *sambaquis*, a kind of deposit formed by leftovers like shells, food, skeletons and other remains. Superagüi was probably inhabited by Tupiniquim and Carijó Indians, who were visited in the 16th century by Portuguese sailors. With the arrival of the *bandeirantes* from São Paulo, the indians were chased and enslaved. In the 18th century, the Jesuits arrived in the region and introduced cattle ranching. When they were expelled from the country (1767-1768), the region was nearly abandoned until the arrival of a new wave of migration from Switzerland. Their colonization declined in the 20th century and

Superagüi: the main island that compose the Park

the island received a population of *caiçara* fishermen. They are descendants of the Indians, African slaves and Europeans and live basically from fishing and on small crops which they plant for their own survival. In the 1970's, the region drew attention from ambientalists, when Superagüi Island was given the title of Natural Historic Patrimony of Paraná and, in 1985, it was attached to the Guaraqueçaba Environment Protection Area. In 1989, the National Park was created and its limits enlarged in 1997, when it came to include the islands of Pinheiro and Pinheirinho and a region known as the valley of Rio dos Patos.

Cara-roxa parrot spends the night on the islands

HIGHLIGHTS

Barra do Superagüi
The small village at the edge of the Park is the main base for those who want to stay overnight on the island.

🕊 Peças Island
It has a 7-km long beach with views of Mel Island as well as the countless mountains of Guaraqueçaba, Paranaguá and Morretes. Access is direct by boat from Paranaguá.

🕊 Pinheiro and Pinheirinho Islands
With mangroves, riverine vegetation and Coastal Rain Forest (*Mata Atlântica*). The main attraction on Pinheiro Island occurs between 4 and 5 pm, when the *Chauá* Parrots fly overhead on their return to the island to spend the night. Here, it is not permitted to go ashore.

Deserta Beach
The 37-km-long beach is inhabited by migratory fowl from March to April. The place is ideal for walks, which may take from four to seven hours.

Lagoa Trail
A flat and easy 3-km trail, from the Barra do Superagüi to Deserta beach which takes you through riverine forest.

Valley of Rio dos Patos
On the mainland. It is not open for visitation yet, but there are plans for opening up a trail through the Coastal

◀ Refuge of the *Mico-leão-da-cara-preta* (above); in the Arapira Cape, the meeting of river and sea

Rain Forest. One of the families who live in the valley still dance the *fandango*, a traditional dance which is very seldom seen today.

SURROUNDINGS · · · · · · · ·

Guaraqueçaba Ecologic Station

⊖ 30 minutes by boat from Guaraqueçaba ⊙ Six hours

An area of 136 km² composed mainly of mangroves distributed to the north of Paranaguá Bay. The ecologic station envelops parts of the islands Laranjeiras, Rabelo, Pavoçá and Sambaqui. It also includes a small area of Coastal Rain Forest and riverine vegetation. Native fauna abounds here, where the Blue Heron, the *Garça-moura*, Cormorant, Roseate Spoonbill and the *Chauá* Parrot are prominent.

Mel Island

⊖ Half hour by boat from Paranaguá
⊙ One to two days

Information: phone (41) 455-1144

Part of the island is a State Ecologic Station. The highlights of the island are deserted beaches and historic monuments. Among them, the Conchas Lighthouse, built in 1872 and the Nossa Senhora dos Prazeres Fortress, built in 1767. Access is by boat either from Paranaguá or from Pontal do Paraná (Pontal do Sul). Daily departures.

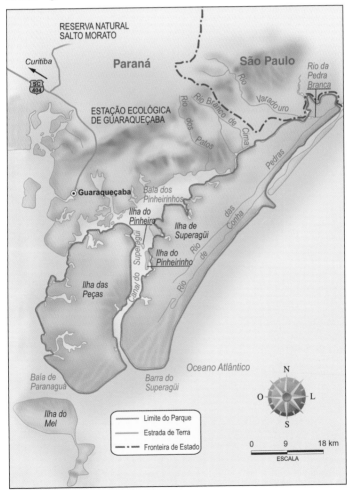

Sambaquis:
leftovers from pre-historic populations

The mounds made mainly of shells, some bones and artifacts, are records of pre-historic populations who lived in the south and southeastern coastal regions of Brazil. The *concheiros*, or "shell mounds", as the *sambaquis* are called here, have different dimensions, with heights which range from 1 to 40 m. They correspond to a dumping area of these semi-nomadic people. They lived between 1.000 and 7.000 years ago, in a social organization where men did the fishing and women, children and elderly people would gather shellfish. Apart from shells, other archaeologic traces such as the remains of fires, burial leftovers, pieces of huts and polished stone artifacts, like axes and arrow heads, are common in the *sambaquis*. This tells us that these people were skilled craftsmen. As there are skeletons in the *sambaquis*, folk-lore has them as Indian cemeteries. Other versions state that they are remains of the Great Deluge or places in which a treasure of the Jesuits have been hidden. The communities who settled down near these deposits found a good material to make mortar for the building of their houses. They could never have imagined that they were destroying important archaeologic sites.

Salto Morato Natural Reservation

⊖ 19 km from Guaraqueçaba ⏱ Four hours. Phone: (41) 482-1506. Access via PR-405 to Cacatu, on 19 km of dirt road
The reservation, which belongs to the Boticário Foundation, is near the Morato River which forms a 130-m waterfall. Take a look at the hundred-year-old fig tree which forms a natural bridge over the Engenho River. Access is by a 2-km trail. The tours must be scheduled and are led by a guide.

Quitumbé Trail

⊖ 6 km from Guaraqueçaba centre ⏱ Two to three hours
Departing from the N. S. do Bom Jesus dos Perdões church, at Cel. João Isidoro street, the 800-m trail to Quitumbê Hill takes you through native vegetation. From the top of the hill you have a nice view of Guaraqueçaba Bay and of the islands of Superagüi and Peças.

Curitiba–Paranaguá Train Trip

⊖ 110 km from the Park ⏱ Four hours. Information and ticket sales at

Sophronites: strong coloured orchids

Curitiba's Bus-Train Station, gate 8, and in Paranaguá, phone (41) 422-6882
The railroad which links Paranaguá to Curitiba was built in 1880, by order of the emperor Dom Pedro II. It cuts through an area of Coastal Rain Forest in the Marumbi region, where there is a State Park much visited by climbers and mountaineers.

To Visit

Access – Get information about the best way to visit the Park with Ibama, the government bureau for environmental affairs.
Mail Address – Rua Brigadeiro Franco, 1733, Curitiba, PR, 80420-200. Phone: (41) 482-1262. Barra de Superagüi Fishermen Village. Phone: (41) 455-1564. E-mail: parnasuperagui@onda.com.br.
How to get there – By car from Curitiba: take BR-227 up to Antonina, and then go via PR-440 and PR-405 to Guaraqueçaba. You get to Paranaguá via BR-227 and to the Park by boat. The trip takes three hours, stopping at Peças Island. By coach: The Graciosa bus company makes daily trips to Guaraqueçaba from Curitiba. Phones: (41) 482-1232 and 322-4344.
Infra-structure – There is none, but it is possible to come ashore on Superagüi and visit the Grande Beach. On other islands, as the Pinheiro, it is prohibited to come ashore

Tips

❂ Avoid visiting the Park in September and October, as it rains too much. In November, take measures against mosquitoes, which invade the region.
❂ Most caiçaras are fishermen who warmly welcome visitors.

To know more
SAINT-HILAIRE, A. **Viagem a Curitiba e Província de Santa Catarina**. São Paulo: Itatiaia, 1978.
www.celepar.br/celepar/sema/parques/diversos/supera.html

◀ There are wholly preserved mangroves on the Pinheiro Island

SERVICES

Guaraqueçaba
🌐 41
✉ 83390-000

Useful addresses
City Hall. Rua Ramos Figueira. Phone: 482-1218/1494/1441.
Bus station. Av. Ararapira. Phone: 482-1232.
Hospital. Rua Ferreira Lopes, 27. Phone: 482-1264.
Boat for Paranaguá. Phone: 482-1295.
Telephone station. Av. Paula Miranda, s/nº. Phone: 482-1297.
Post Office. Rua Ararapira, 5. Phone: 482-1276
Bank. Banestado.

Lodging
Eduardo I. Rua Paula Miranda, 165. Phone/fax: 482-1225. Internet: hoteleduardo@lol.com.br. 27 rooms, tv, minibar. Parking lot. $$
Guarakessaba. Rua 15 de Novembro, 16. Phone: 482-1273. Fax: 482-1217. 14 rooms, tv, air conditioning, minibar. $$
Pousada Bela Ilha. (beach). Phone: 455-1564. Internet. www.lol.com.br/~bellailha. 10 bedrooms. $
Pousada sobre as Ondas (beach). Phone: 9978-4213. 6 rooms. $
Pousada Centauro (beach). Phone: 9959-8426. 5 rooms. $
Pousada Costa Azul (beach). Phone: 9978-6013. 8 rooms. $
Pousada Crepúsculo (beach). Phone: 455-1564. Reservation: 9118-1637. 10 rooms. $$
Pousada Superagui (beach). Phone: 9978-9101. Reservation: 422-8468/422-2325. Internet: pousadasuperagui@lol.com.br. 5 rooms. $$
Camping Salto Morato. Road to Antonina, 19 km, reservation: 381-7000/ 9978-2140. $

Dining
Taico. Rua Luis Ramos Figueira, 144. Phone: 482-1357. Sea food. $
Barbosa. Rua Paulo Miranda, 9 (water front). Phone: 482-1248. Sea food. $
Guaricana. Rua Paula Miranda, 45. Phone: 482-1235. Sea food. $$

When sailing through the islands, it is necessary to mind the sand banks

SOUTHEAST

SOUTHEAST REGION

Clouds shroud the mountains in the Caparaó National Park

The Parks of the Southeast Region have many highlights for those who are fond of mountains. The Tijuca is in the state of Rio de Janeiro, with one of the biggest urban forests in the country and the main sources of the rivers which supply water for the city of Rio de Janeiro, besides important historical landmarks. The Park has complete infra-structure of trails, which lead the visitors past famous attractions, such as the Tijuca Forest, the Gávea Rock, and the Corcovado. The Itatiaia is near the border of the states of Minas Gerais and Rio de Janeiro; there lies the Agulhas Negras Peak, 2.787 m in height; it was there that climbing was inaugurated as a sport in Brazil, back in 1856. The Serra dos Órgãos is between the cities of Teresópolis and Petrópolis, also in the state of Rio de Janeiro, where the National Park of the same name is. The highest altitude in the

Park reaches 2.263 m, and its peaks, such as the Dedo-de-Deus, also attract climbers. The Park has many trails and waterfalls. All those Parks, mainly in their lower

São Jos do Rio F

MATO GROSSO DO SUL

Fernandópolis

Andradina

Araçatuba

Birigüi
Penápol

Pres. Prudente

Marília

PARANÁ

Ourinhos

〜〜	Rio
◉	Capital de Estado
⊙	Cidades
–·–·–·–	Fronteira de País
–·–·–·–	Fronteira de Estado
——	Estrada de Asfalto
——	Estrada de Terra

N

O — L

S

0   107   214 km

ESCALA

parts, preserve the Atlantic Forest. The Serra da Bocaina is on the border of São Paulo and Rio de Janeiro, with many waterfalls, river sources and trails which wind through the mountains. The Serra da Canastra is in the state of Minas Gerais, and it is where the source of the São Francisco River is; the river flows from that spot through 3.160 km before flowing into the Atlantic Ocean. One can walk all trails and reach all waterfalls in the Park. The Serra do Cipó is also in Minas, with dozens of waterfalls and altitude fields full of colourful flowers. The Serra do Caparaó, on the border of the states of Espírito Santo and Minas Gerais, is known mainly because of the Bandeira Peak, with its 2.890 m. The peak was considered the highest in the country, when, back in 1859, the Emperor Dom Pedro hoisted a flag on its summit. Today, it is the third highest peak in Brazil, and it is possible to ascend to the top. All the above mentioned Parks are open for visitors. On the north coast of the state of Rio de Janeiro, lies the Restinga da Jurubatiba, whose predominating topography is a plain of sandy soil which favoured the appearing of many lakes and lagoons. The Grande Sertão Veredas is in Minas Gerais and preserves a mix of Caatinga, Atlantic Forest and Cerrado ecosystems. The Cavernas do Peruaçu is near to this Park; it is full of caves and has more than 140 archaeologic sites. The spectacular Gruta do Janelão is in the Park, with huge underground spaces. These three Parks are not open for visitors at the moment.

Caparaó

The crystalline rocks that form the Caparaó Massif abruptly rise forming peaks like the Cristal (2.798 m), the Calçado (2.766 m) and the Bandeira (2.890 m). The climate is tropical and the average temperatures range from 13ºC to 27ºC. However, in the higher parts, it is sometimes extremely cold. It rains more from November to January, a time when thick fog is common. The main rivers of the Park are the São Domingos, the Caparaó and the José Pedro, whose source is up in the high lands. They flow all the way down, as if a snake winding through the fields and forests.

On the mountainside in Espírito Santo, battered by winds that blow in from the sea, a somewhat altered Coastal Rain Forest vegetation predominates. In spite of being formed mainly of secondary vegetation, in some places of difficult access, you can find species like the Scotch pine and an endangered species of Spider Monkey called *Muriqui*.

In mountainous areas, the vegetation gradually changes according to the altitude. The lower lands are dominated by forests which give way to the formation of fields according to the inclination, the wind, isolation, temperature and altitude of the terrain. In Minas Gerais, the vegetation is drier and without the influence of sea winds the woods give way to fields at lower altitudes.

In the high terrain, the rupestrian vegetation spreads over the rocky outcrops. In the lower areas Sapucaia-nut trees, Glorybushes, Cedars, Bamboos and Ferns stand out. In the high altitude fields, the flora is formed mainly by grasses and plants such as

Foundation: May 1961
Area: 318 km²
Alto Caparaó: 2 km; Manhuaçu: 40 km; Vitória: 240 km; Belo Horizonte: 340 km

○
⊕ (32)
☎ 3747-2555

the Asparagus Fern, Bromeliads, Mosses and Orchids, as well as *Canelas-de-ema* and Everlastings.

The fauna is represented by animals such as Squirrels, the Spotted Cavy, Wild Dogs, Tayras - a weasel closely allied to the Grison - , Black-billed Toucans, a species of swift called *de Coleira*, Tanagers, the Holt's Yellow Finch, the Superciliated Guan and Cuiejos, which are the most easily seen animals in the Park. Birds like *Choquinhas* dwell the heights, together with prey birds such as Hawks.

HISTORY

Located on the borders of the states of Espírito Santo, where 70% of the Park's area lies, and Minas Gerais. The Caparaó National Park stands out mainly because it encompasses the Bandeira Peak of 2.890 m. Back in 1859, it was considered to be the highest point in Brazil and the Emperor Dom Pedro ll ordered a flag to be set on the summit. This is probably the origin of the peak's name: *bandeira* means flag. Some decades later, the Bandeira Peak was beaten in terms of height by the peaks 31 de Março and the Neblina, both in the Amazon. Today, the highest peak in Brazil is the Neblina. The region of Caparaó, where the Park is located, has been occupied for many years and the native vegetation suffered severe modifications due to the action of charcoal makers and, later on, by wood cutting and fires caused by farmers and shepherds. Despite the fact that the movement for the creation of the Park had started in 1948, the conservation unit only came into being years later, in 1961. One of the curious facts which happened in the region, back in 1967, was the strategy used to arrest eight guerrilla soldiers who belonged to the Movimento Nacionalista Revolucionário (Nationalist Revolutionary Movement) and threatened the military regime: 6.000 men in camuflaged uniforms came to the Caparaó Mountain Range in order to chase them.

HIGHLIGHTS

ⓜ Aurélio Waterfall
A waterfall with pools on the São Domingos River, near Macieira.

ⓜ ✿ Bonita Waterfall
⊖ 850 m from Tronqueira
In order to get to the 80-m high waterfall on the José Pedro River, you take the dirt road and then a small trail which leads straight to the waterfall. There is a lookout and a 4-m deep pool, good for bathing.

⛺ Casa Queimada
⊖ 8 km from the Pedra Menina gate
Access is via a dirt road. It is located at an altitude of around 2.160 m at the source of the São Domingos River. There is an area for camping, rest rooms and showers.

Macieira
⊖ 3 km from the Pedra Menina gate
A 1.800-m high plateau by the São Domingos River.

Calçado Peak
On the border of the states of Minas Gerais and Espírito Santo; with 2.768 m in height; it is much visited by mountaineers.

Cristal Peak
At an altitude of 2.798 m, it is much visited by mountaineers. Check the conditions to get there at Alto Caparaó gate. Phone: 747-2565.

⚑ Bandeira Peak
⊖ 9 km from Tronqueira
🕓 Four hours
The third highest peak in Brazil - 2.890 m - is the main attraction in the Park. The ascent to the top starts with a mild walk which gets harder as you get closer to the summit. The trail to the peak is well marked. You can get mules to help carry backpacks to the foot of the peak. The Terreirão is more or less in the middle of the way and is a good place for a stop; 45 minutes more and you reach the base where the steepest part starts. From here it is 40 minutes to the top.
Another option is to go via Casa Queimada.

⚑ ⛺ Terreirão
⊖ 4,5 km from Tronqueira
🕓 Three hours
A trail, which goes along the José Pedro river, takes you to the 2.370-m high plateau. There are facilities for camping, rest rooms, visitors' shelter and fresh water where you can fill up your canteen. Take a look at Casa de Pedra.

⚑ Tronqueira
⊖ 6 km from Alto Caparaó gate
From the 1.970-m high plateau you have a nice view of the valley. It is the last point to where you can go by car.

Cristal Peak: option for experienced mountaineers

◄ Tayra: carnivorous (above); crystalline rock mountains stand out in the landscape of the Park

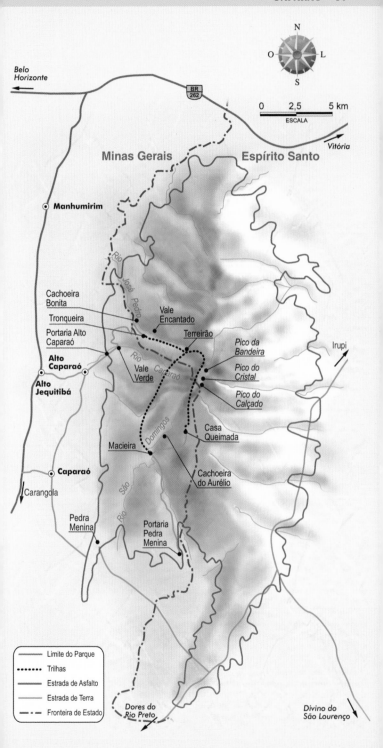

Muriqui: the biggest monkey in the Americas

The *Muriqui*, one of the Spider Monkey species, is the biggest monkey in the Americas. It is also called the *Monocarvoeiro* in Brazil and lives only in the Coastal Rain Forest, the so called *Mata Atlântica*. It used to be found from the South of the state of Bahia to the North of the state of Paraná, but today it is an endangered species not easily observed. The animals have disappeared mainly due to hunting and to the loss and fragmentation of their environment.

The *Muriqui*'s favorite environment are forests located between the altitudes of 600 to 1.800 m. They are found in groups of up to 25 individuals which use an area of around 60 ha to survive. They travel in smaller groups and spend around one third of their time roaming in the forest; the remaining two thirds, they

Muriqui: exclusive of the Atlantic Forest

spend eating and resting. Their diet is a varied one eating mainly leaves, also fruits and flowers. As most monkeys, they are active during the day. The *Muriqui* is not a territorial species, but it does tend to repel observers away by shaking branches, jumping and even by defecating on them.

⬤ 🍃 🕦 Encantado Valley

It is by the José Pedro River, with many pools for a dip and the high Bonita waterfall. Pay attention to the alteration in the landscape as the altitude changes.

⬤ 🍃 🕦 Verde Valley

Formed by the Caparaó River, it envelopes areas of the park lower than 1.000 m in altitude. The waterfall and its many pools represent a good opportunity for a cold bath.

SURROUNDINGS

⬤ 🍃 🕦 Andorinhas Waterfall
⊖ 13 km from the Park
🕓 Two hours

On the José Pedro River, which is the natural border between the states of Minas Gerais and Espírito Santo, the waterfall has a pool that is nice for a bath.

🕦 Chiador Waterfall
⊖ 27 km from the Park
🕓 Four hours

The waterfall is in the city of Espera Feliz and has a natural slide formed

by rocks, giving the nickname *Escorrega* to the waterfall. Translated this means slide. It falls into a cold water pool.

🍃 🍃 🕦 Cachoeira da Fumaça State Park
⊖ 30 km from Pedra Menina
🕓 Four hours

The Park is in the state of Espírito Santo and its main attraction is a cold waterfall where you can have a dip. It also has trails for hikes.

🍃 ⬤ 🍃 Pedra Menina
⊖ 2 km from the Park
🕓 From two to five hours

The village of Pedra Menina, near the Park's gate, has many things to do, such as river swimming, rapids and trails to hike.

⬤ 🍃 Egito Park
⊖ 15 km from the Park 🕓 Two hours

The cold and transparent waters of the Claro River and of the Egito pothole are good options for a dip. On the way you can stop by one of the region's *cachaça* distilleries. *Cachaça* or *pinga* is a typical Brazilian spirit.

Andorinhas Waterfall: pool for a bath in the José Pedro River ▶

TO VISIT

Access – Open daily. Admission fee: R$ 3,00.

Address – Rua Vale Verde, s/nº, Alto Caparaó, MG, 36836-000. Phone: (32) 3747-2555, phone/fax: 3747-2565. E-mail: parnacaparao@bol.com.br.

How to get there – The main access to the Park is from Minas Gerais: departing from BR-262, take MG-111 towards Manhumirim. From this city, go towards Alto de Caparaó (20 km), which is 2 km from the Park. From Espírito Santo, the access is via Dores do Rio Preto, on BR-482. From this city to the gate at Pedra Menina it is necessary to have a 4-wheel-drive vehicle. There are coaches departing regularly from Manhuaçu to Alto Caparaó.

Infra-structure – Roads, trails, camping areas, showers, rest rooms, picnic area and barbecuers.

TIPS

◎ The dry season is from June to September and is the best time to visit the Park.
◎ To watch the sunrise from the summit of the Bandeira Peak is a good option for those who enjoy waking up in the early hours and like to walk in the dark.

To know more
CÂMARA, I.G. **Plano de ação para a Mata Atlântica.** São Paulo: Interação, 1991.

The plateaus of the Park allow privileged views

SERVICES

Alto Caparaó, MG

🌐 32
✉ 36836-000

Useful Addresses
City Hall. Rua Luciano Bredes, 15, B. Liberdade. Phone: 3747-2532.
Bus station. Pça. da Matriz, s/nº.
Post Office. Rua Luciano Bredes, 15, B. Liberdade, Ed. Prefeitura. Phone: 3747-2532.
Hospital. Rua Conrado Emerich, 843.
Car rental. Transjeep (4-wheel-drive vehicles rental). Phone: 3747-2537.

Support for the Visitor
Tourist Bureau. Rua Luciano Bredes, 15, B. Liberdade, Ed. Prefeitura. Phone: 3747-2532.
Tour agencies. 4 x 4 Turismo. Phone: 3747-2604. Caparaó Parque. Rua Vale das Hortências, s/nº. Phone: 3747-2559.

Lodging
Caparaó Parque. Rua Vale das Hortências, s/nº. Phone: 3747-2559. Internet:www.caparaohotel.carangola.br. 30 rooms, 22 chalets, minibar, tel., tv. Swimming pool, bar, restaurant, sauna, billiard room, waterfall, playground. $$$$
Pousada do Bezerra. Av. Pico da Bandeira, s/nº. Phone: 3747-2628. Internet: www.pousadadobezerra.com.br. 32 rooms, minibar, tv. Swimming pool, bar, restaurant, sauna, waterfall, parking lot. $$$
Pousada Chalés Pico da Bandeira. Rua das Hortências, s/nº. Phone: 3747-2626, 10 chalets, minibar, tv. Swimming pool, restaurant, sauna, parking lot. $$$

Dining
Mineirão. Pça. da Matriz, 25. Phone: 3747-2604. Typical local food, meat, varied menu. $
Vale Verde. Pça. da Matriz, s/nº, Centro. Phone: 3747-2529. Typical local food, meat. $

Dores do Rio Preto, ES

🌐 28
✉ 29580-000

Useful Addresses
City Hall. Rua Pedro de Alcântara Galveias, 122. Phone: 3559-1102.
Bus station. Padaria Pico da Bandeira, 60.
Post Office. Rua Firmino Dias, 271, Centro. Phone/fax: 3559-1163.
Ambulatory. Pça. Manuel Ornelas, 48. Phone: 3359-1161.
Bank. Banestes.

Support for the Visitor
Tourist Bureau. Rua Pedro de Alcântara Galveias, 122. Phone: 3559-1102.

Lodging
Pousada Tô à Toa. Rod. BR-482, 100 m after the border of Espírito Santo and Minas Gerais states. Phone: 3359-1148, phone/fax: 3359-1101. 13 rooms. Bar, restaurant, parking lot. $

Dining
Consuelo. Pça. Manuel Ornelas, 36. Phone: 3359-1126. Varied menu, snacks, typical local food. $

Cavernas do Peruaçu

The region of the Park is located on the Bambuí Geological Province upon extensive calcareous terrain which has been eroded by the waters of the São Francisco River and its tributaries for million of years. The rivers, the rain and the sediment taken by the water dug the canyon in which the Peruaçu River flows and which harbours more than 140 cave sites. They include grottos, caves and funnel-like depressions caused by dissolution in calcareous areas or by the crumbling it produces. The climate is hot with a dry season between April and October. The region is in an ecosystem transition area between the *Cerrado* and *Caatinga*. The *Cerrado* are woods composed of stunted, twisted trees, and *Caatinga* is a type of stunted sparse forest, found in the drought areas of northeastern Brazil. The *Cerrado* vegetation is represented by fields in the lower areas and drier fields with sparse, twisted, corky bark trees atop the mountains. The Riverine forests and Buriti Palm groves occur in the moist areas. The *Caatinga* is also present with its dry woodlands, which are adapted to the alkaline soil and a lack of water. The Barbatimao Alumbark tree, the *Pau-santo*, the Fig tree, a kind of

Foundation: September 1999
Area: 568 km²
Itacarambi: 15 km; Januária: 45 km; Montes Claros: 210 km; Belo Horizonte: 645 km.

⊘
 (38)
 3621-1380

California Pepper tree called *Sertão*, Floss-silktrees, *Tinguis* - a lupine used as a fish poison -, *Muricis*, the *Cerrado* Black Rosewood, the Souari Nut tree, the Courbaril tree, *Araticum* - a tree of the genus Annona - and a species of field Cashew are among the Park's species. The fauna is represented by Deer, Armadillo, Capybara, Maned Wolf, a species of lizard called *Teiu, Mocós* - a kind of Guinea Pig -, Crested Seriemas, Zabele Red-footed Tinamous and several species of cats and rodents. The Peruaçu valley is also considered an important bird migration route and has endemic species such as the *Maria-preta* and a species of hummingbird called Saber-winged.

The collapsing of part of the ceiling allowed the sun to shine in the Janelão grotto

HISTORY

Twelve thousand years ago, pre-historic people lived in the region of the Peruaçu Valley, hunting, gathering, and recording their daily life on the walls of the caves and grottos. The rock paintings belong to distinctive styles, a fact which shows a succession of cultural influences. Later on, in the period post hunters-gatherers, the inhabitants planted tobacco, corn, manioc and beans. Then came the Xakriabá Indians, who still live in the region adjacent to the Park. The region began to change with the arrival of the bandeirantes - a colonial character from the 17th and 18th centuries who could be described as a mixture of explorer,

soldier, slave driver and prospector - who had gone in search of precious minerals. As usual, the bandeirantes left villages and descendants along their way: Itacarambi and Januária are examples, whose main economic activities today are agriculture, tanning and handicrafts. Researchers have been attracted to the many caves, the archaeologic sites, the calcareous rock formations and to the biologic diversity of the region.

Because of the researchers' findings, the government became aware of the area's importance and in 1989 created the Peruaçu Caves Environment Protection Area. Five years later, Minas Gerais created the Veredas do Peruaçu State Park, which included the Environment Protection Area. With pressure to create more conservation units, the National Park was founded in 1999.

HIGHLIGHTS

The National Park has many grottos and caves with rock paintings on their walls.

🦅 Janelão Grotto

The Peruaçu River flows through this gigantic cavern. Here you will see the world's biggest cave hall and stalactite, hanging 28 m from the ceiling. There are many parts to the cavern where there is natural illumination caused by the collapsing of the ceiling.

Rock paintings: 12 thousand years old

◀ Pampas deer (above); rocks in the *Cerrado-Caatinga* transition area

Lapa dos Desenhos

One of the many caves in the Park with rock paintings; these ones portray the corn plant from pre-historic to more recent times.

SURROUNDING

⑩ Pandeiros River Waterfalls
⊖ 48 km from Januária ⊕ Four hours
Three crystal clear waterfalls on the Pandeiros River are good points for bathing.

Januária
⊖ 45 km from the Park ⊕ Six hours
The small city on the banks of the São Francisco River has many historic buildings. From May to October beaches appear along the São Francisco River.

Veredas do Peruaçu State Park
⊖ 15 km from the Park ⊕ One day
The access to the Park is difficult, but beautiful Buriti Palm groves shelter fauna which can be easily seen.

TO VISIT

Access – It is not open for visitation. However, it is possible to visit for research purposes with permission from *Ibama*.
Address – Povoado do Fabião I, Januária, MG, 39480-000. Phones: (38) 3621-1380 and 3613-1555.
How to get there – By car from Januária, take MG-135 towards Itacarambi.
Infra-structure – There is none.

To know more
LINO, C.F. e ALLIEVI, J.
Cavernas brasileiras. São Paulo: Melhoramentos, 1980.
www.sbe.com.br
www.januaria.com.br

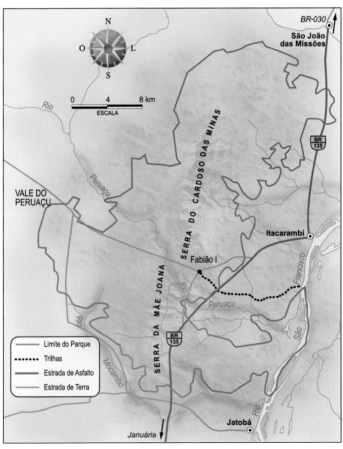

Veredas
Grande Sertão Veredas

The Park's topography is flat, with rolling hills and is located in a region composed mainly of sandstone. There is a very well defined dry season from June to September, with more intense cold in June. The Park's principal river is the river Preto and the brown water river Carinhanha is at the northern border of the conservation unit. Due to the soil's great capacity of retaining water, there are wet lands upon which Buriti Palm groves develop.

The Park is located in the *Cerrado* - an area of woods composed of stunted, twisted trees -, but there is also influence from neighbouring ecosystems with typical species from these environments: the *Caatinga* - a type of stunted forest found in the drought areas of northeastern Brazil -, and the *Mata Atlântica* - Coastal Rain Forest. The landscape is marked by fields and *Cerrados* in the dry areas, besides the *Carrasco*, a transition vegetation between the *Cerrado* and the *Caatinga*. The main species are the California Pepper tree, the Souari Nut tree, the *Araticum* - a tree of the genus Annona -, the *Pau-terra*, the *Peroba-do-campo*, the *Gomeira* - a tree of the Copaiyé family -, and species of the Curbaril tree. In the humid areas, there are riverine forests, Buriti palm groves - where a Buriti palm locally called *Bravo* (*Mauritia armata*) develops -, and *Varjões*: low grassy land bordering a stream or body of water. The fauna includes species that are common in the *Cerrado*, among which there are several endangered species,

Foundation: April 1989
Area: 840 km²
Chapada Gaúcha: 3 km; Brasília: 372 km; Belo Horizonte: 580 km
⊘
⊕ (38)
☎ 634-1132

such as the Maned Wolf, the American Ostrich, the Crested Seriema, the Scarlet Macaw, the rare Giant Armadillo, the Great Anteater, the Apar, the Curassaw, the Pampas Deer, the Mountain Lion and a species of cat called *Palheiro*.
Inhabitants of the Buriti palm groves stand out, like the Pantanal or Marsh Deer and the Scarlet Macaw, which builds its nest in the palms. The presence of endemic species - which only occur here - makes even more important the preservation of the local biologic diversity.

HISTORY

Human occupation in the region of the Park, by pre-historic peoples 11.000 years ago, is very similar to that of the valley of the river São Francisco.
Afterwards, the Caiapó Indians and the *bandeirantes* took over the region. The *bandeirantes* were armed men - explorers, slave drivers

and prospectors - who entered the backwoods in search of precious minerals and Indians to enslave, leaving pathways and villages in their wake.
The small and isolated communities have lived for decades on crops they cultivate for their own consumption - corn, bean, cassava - and cattle, which grazes in the region's fields. They live in wattle and daub houses thatched with straw, with no facilities of modern life, such as electricity, sewerage and water mains.

In the late 1970's, their land suffered pressure because of the expansion of soya bean plantations in central Brazil and because of the production of charcoal. The Fundação Pro-Natureza (Funatura) recognized the danger and, with support from both the government and the World Fund for the Environment, researched the region of the Gerais in the late 1980's: an area located in the northwestern region of the state of Minas Gerais, the west of Bahia and the southern region of the state of Piauí. Two areas were chosen, one in the state of Bahia and the other in Minas Gerais. The first one brought no results at all in terms of real action. However, the second one turned out to give origin to the Grande Sertão Veredas National Park, founded in 1989. The name is in homage to João Guimarães Rosa, the writer who wonderfully described the landscape and characters of the region. Today, the people who live in and around the Park participate in its' activities as well as cultivating and cattle ranching. They get involved with the preservation works, allying their habits and uses to the conservationists' goals.

SURROUNDINGS . . . .

Cavernas do Peruaçu National Park
⊖ 200 km from the Park
🕒 Five days
The many caves and rock paintings of the region are its main highlights.

São Francisco
⊖ 135 km from Park 🕒 One day
The main attraction of the small city on the banks of the river São Francisco is the river itself. It can be crossed by ferry and in the dry season, from May to September, white sand beaches appear on its banks where the local inhabitants enjoy the famous out-of-season Carnival.

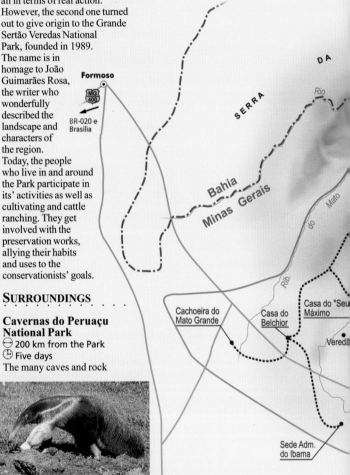

Great Anteater

◀ Swamp Deer (above); flower from the orchid family, typical of the Minas Gerais *Cerrado*

Besides being used to make wine, edible oil is extracted from the Wine palm

Araras Mountains

⊖ 50 km from the Park ⊕ Two days

Today a State Park and part of the city of São Francisco. This beautiful mountain range shelters Scarlet Macaws in its steep cliffs and attracts Catholic pilgrims every year in order to pay their promises to Santo Antônio. This festival brings around 5.000 people to the city in June. The Saint's shrine is high up and from there you can have a nice view of the region. Hire a local guide in order to visit the mountains.

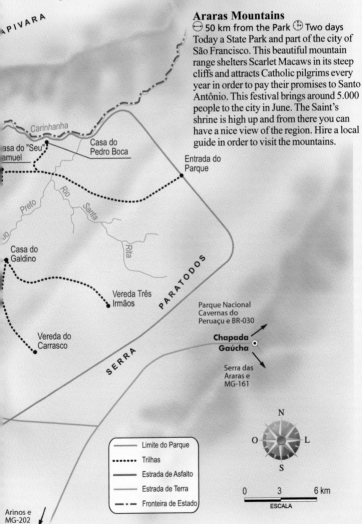

TO VISIT

Access – The Park is still not open for visitation. Information about obtaining permission to visit the Park is at Ibama's office (Ibama is the government bureau for environmental affairs).
Address – Rua Guimarães Rosa, 149, Chapada Gaúcha, MG, 39314-000. Phone/fax: (38) 634-1132.
How to get there – There are regular flights from all Brazilian capitals to Brasília. Then, if you are going by car, take BR-020 towards Salvador. Seventeen kilometers after Formosa, take GO-346 to Cabeceiras and then MG-202 up to Buritis and Arinos (dirt road). From here, go towards Chapada Gaúcha on a dirt road for 90 km. After this, it is still 20 km to the Park, on badly conserved dirt roads. It is advisable to go by four-wheel-drive vehicle. The waterfalls stand out.
Infra-structure – There is none.

TIPS

❍ One of the best things to do in the region is to chat with the natives, who have many stories to tell. Take your time to enjoy many *cafezinhos* - a small cup of coffee - offered by the house's owner: typical Brazilian hospitality.
❍ Between August and September, when the weather is drier, the sandy areas are more difficult to walk or drive on. The other months are more humid and it is better to go hiking in the open fields.

To know more
ROSA, J.G. **Grande sertão: veredas.** 38 ed. Rio de Janeiro: Nova Fronteira, 2001. www.tnc.org.br

SERVICES

Chapada Gaúcha (MG)

🌐 38
✉ 39314-000

Useful Addresses

City Hall. Rod. MG-479, km 90.
Phone: 3634-1112.
Bus station. Rua João Branco, 87.
Phone: 3634-1171.
Telephone station. Phone: 3634-1107.
Ambulatory. Rua Tancredo Neves, 480.
Phone: 3634-1255.

Support for the Visitor

Tourist Bureau. Rod. MG-479, km 90,
Ed. Prefeitura. Phone: 3634-1132.
Support for the Tourist. Ibama.

Rua Guimarães Rosa, 149.
Phone/fax: 3634-1274.

Lodging

Chapadão. Av. Antonio Montalvão,
s/n. Phone/fax: 3634-1101. 3 rooms,
bar, restaurant, parking lot. 💲
J.F. Av. Getúlio Vargas, 430. Phone:
3634-1141. 6 rooms, fan, bar,
restaurant, parking lot. 💲
Vereda. Av. Getúlio Vargas, s/n.
Phone: 3634-1111. 5 rooms, tv.
Air conditioning. Bar, restaurant,
parking lot. 💲

Dining

Ipiranga. Rua João Branco, 87.
Phone: 3634-1171. Varied menu,
self-service. 💲

Wine and mauritia palms predominate in the moist areas

Itatiaia

Itatiaia is at the border of the states of Rio de Janeiro, Minas Gerais and São Paulo, in the Mantiqueira Mountain Range, at heights which range from 700 to 2.787 m. In the ancient terrain, shaped by time, there are countless stream springs which flow down to the Paraíba do Sul or Paraná basins. December is the hottest month and July the coldest. In the highest parts, the temperature sometimes drops greatly and it may snow. The rain falls mostly between January and April while August is the driest month. In mountainous areas such as Itatiaia the vegetation changes gradually according to the altitude. In the lower areas, the Coastal Rain Forest - known in Brazil as *Mata Atlântica* - dominates the landscape, but gives way to the formation of fields as the mountain range increases in height. On the summit, rupestrian vegetation spreads amongst the rocky outcrops. Humid winds from the sea cool as they ascend the mountainsides saturating the air with vapour, which in turn precipitates as mist or rain, common in the higher parts. The Coastal Rain Forest is a perennial, broad leafed, humid, tropical forest. This is one of the ecosystems with the highest level of biologic diversity in the world, with several species that only occur in this very environment. The tree trunks are covered with a number of plants which climb or entwine on them for support in order to reach the light. Among the species which stand out in the *Mata Atlântica* there are *Jequitibás* - a tree of the Sapucaia-nut family -, Glorybushes, Cedars, Ferns and the Assai Euterpe palm, which abounds near creeks and waterfalls and from which the delicious palm heart is taken. In the higher areas, where rocky outcrops are common and the soil is not so deep, there are altitude fields. Trees and bushes disappear as the altitude increases and give way to moss, lichen, bromeliads and grasses, such as the Asparagus Fern. The species which survive are those adapted to conditions

Foundation: June 1937
Area: 300 km²
Itatiaia: 5 km; Resende: 20 km;
Penedo: 18 km; Rio de Janeiro:
175 km; São Paulo: 256 km
○
⊕ (24)
☎ 3352-1461

of intense cold, frost and the formation of ice crust. In the summer or in the rainy season, water soaks the soil and makes mud puddles.

The fauna in the lower lands is richer because the forest provides better shelters for mammals such as Squirrels, Agouti, Paca, the Coati - a tropical carnivore related to the Raccoon - and even some big sized species such as the Tapir. The Park is very rich in bird species. Among them Hummingbirds draw attention because of their diversity and quantity: Lilac-headed and Black-and-white Hummingbirds, for example, are very common. Apart from these, there are Red-breasted Toucans, colourful Calospiza Tanagers and *Guachos*, with their nests hanging on the trees. The Itatiaia Park is very important with regard to the preservation of bird species, especially large-sized frugivorous species and altitude species, as the Park is one of the few

preserved areas in the region. On the high land, small Rice Mice roam the fields and Wild Dogs are relatively common, as well as some species of Hawks.

The Prateleiras massif is 2.548 m high and overviews the Paraíba valley

Red-breasted Toucan, common in the region

HISTORY

At the beginning of the 19th century, the ancient route used to forward the gold from the Province of Minas Gerais was reputed as a hide-out of dangerous criminals. However, the bad reputation did not last long and the region began to attract the attention of adventurers and lovers of nature.

The highest peak in the region, the Agulhas Negras or Itatiaiaçu with 2.787 m, was considered for decades Brazil's tallest. It became renowned when it was first climbed by Germans in 1879. In the language of the Tupi-guarani Indians Itatiaia means "rock full of sharp ends" and is an ideal name for the furrowed peaks of the Agulhas Negras - or Black Needles. The area where the Park lies today used to be property of the Viscount of

◄ *Saíra-lengo*, a Tanager (above); the altitude fields lie in the high areas

Agulhas Negras Peak: climbing first landmark in Brazil

It is three hours hiking to get to the top

In remote times, primitive tribes used the mountains to move from one place to other. The challenge of scaling mountain summits was only taken up as an adventurous sport in Europe in the 18th century, where the great obstacle to beat was Mount White, in the Alps. Everest, the highest mountain in the world, was only reached in 1953 by a Neozealander and a Nepalese. In Brazil, climbing was inaugurated as a sport at Itatiaia in the year 1856, when Franklin Massena reached the summit of the Agulhas Negras. Since then, mountain climbing has become more and more practised in the country. The sport demands much technique, training and practice with experienced people. You need quality gear and seriousness, as a slight mistake on the top of a mountain can be fatal.

Mauá and was bought by the government in 1908. The settlers that the Emperor Dom Pedro II had brought to cultivate cold weather fruits remained in the region, but the plantations failed. As their land was not expropriated with the creation of the Park, there are still private properties within the area including farms, hotels and country places. In 1929 the land was transferred to the Ministry of Agriculture because the project to cultivate fruit failed. It became a biologic station connected to the Botanic Gardens of Rio de Janeiro, and only in 1937 the Park was created: the first national park founded in the country. Being late to join the international trend - mainly American - of creating natural protected areas, the Park received improvements which included a road, a natural history museum and lodges for researchers and mountaineers.

Véu da Noiva waterfall: easy access

HIGHLIGHTS

The Park's high region has nice views of the Mantiqueira Mountain Range and of the Paraíba Valley, and the lower part is good for hiking in the woods and to come across animals.

Rebouças Base

Base and back up for hiking visitors in the Park's high region. The hut is used by researchers, mountaineers and for military training.

Itaporani Waterfall

You get to the waterfall after a short trail in the woods; the lake into which the waterfall drops is good for a shower or bath.

Poranga Waterfall

Poranga means beauty in the language of the Tupi-guarani Indians, and this is a good indication of what you will see. The waterfall is 10 m high and there is a pool, 30 m in diameter, which is good for a dip.

Véu da Noiva Waterfall

You get to the 40-m-high waterfall after a 450-m trail by the river. This waterfall is one of the Park's post cards.

Visitors' Centre

In the Park's headquarters, at the foot of the mountain, there is a museum with information about the fauna and flora of the region, stuffed animals, library and auditorium, where several activities, such as lectures, occur.

Azul Lake

A natural lake formed by the Campo Belo River. Good place for a dip, with kiosks.

Prateleiras Massif
⏲ One day

Formed by an imposing rock block at 2.548 m above sea level. There is a nice view of the Fina Mountain Range and the Paraíba Valley, which is sometimes obscured by clouds.
It is a one-and-a-half-hour hike to the foot from the Rebouças base. If you want to climb, it is necessary to go with an experienced guide, especially if your intention is to pass over the "cat's leap", a deep crack in the rock over which is necessary to leap.

Altar Rock

A big rock formation at 2.530 m in Itatiaia's high region. There are many climbing ways up the mountainsides.

Agulhas Negras Peak
⏲ One day

2.787 m in height, it can be reached in two stages. The first is a one-hour easy hike to the foot from the Rebouças base; then, two hours of heavy ascent to the summit. It requires experience, as some parts of the climbing are only possible with the use ropes.

Maromba Pool

1.100 m above sea level, where the river forms a pool which is good for bathing.

Minas Gerais

← Resende

Rio de Janeiro

São Paulo

Portaria Planalto

———	Limite do Parque
•••••	Trilhas
———	Estrada de Asfalto
———	Estrada de Terra
–·–·–	Fronteira de Estado

N
O · L
S

0   2   4 km
ESCALA

🛑🍃🏊 Três Picos
⏱ Six hours

The hike will show you a little of the Park's two ecosystems: Coastal Rain Forest and altitude fields. It is a hard 6-km hike to the top (1.662 m). The first part, which takes one hour, is not as difficult as the second, which is a hard 1:20-hour ascent rewarded with a nice bath in the waterfall of the River Bonito.

The hike is on steep slopes with beautiful views of the Paraíba Valley and the foothills of the Mantiqueira Mountain Range.

🕕 ♨ Aiuruoca Valley
🕐 Six hours

On the side of the mountain range which lies in the state of Minas Gerais, with the freezing Aiuruoca Waterfall and the rock formation Ovos da Galinha, which means chicken's eggs. It is a moderate two-hour walk from the Rebouças base. On the way, watch for the formations Asa do Hermes and Altar Rock.

SURROUNDINGS

♨ 🏕 Engenheiro Passos
⊖ 18 km from Itatiaia
🕐 Three hours

One of the local specialties are dishes made with trout, bred in the cold waters of the region. Watch for the train station by the Dutra highway. Hikes and horse riding are also good attractions here.

♨ Garrafão Peak
⊖ 25 km from Itatiaia
🕐 Six hours

The peak is between the cities of Itamonte and Alagoa, in the state of Minas Gerais; from the top of its 1.700 m, you can have a nice view of the region. The hike to the top takes around three hours through a forest of Brazilian Pine. Notice the ruins of excavations done by the Jesuits in search of gold. In the Garrafão Valley there are also long stretches of flooded fields.

It takes 1:30 hours to go from the Rebouças base to the foot of the Prateleiras massif on an easy hike

Snow men in Itatiaia

Everybody knows that Itatiaia's high region is cold, but snowing is definitely not an expected phenomenon in the region. During the winter of 1985, the temperature reached minus 15°C and the snow dyed white the fields and sharp faces of the Agulhas Negras. In some parts the soft snow reached 1 m in depth and invited people to make snow men, as if Itatiaia were the Alps. It also snowed in 1988 when there was 40 cm of snow in the region of the Agulhas Negras.

Snow may seldom paint everything white

Papagaio Peak
⊖ 80 km from Itatiaia
⊕ One day
Located in a State Park in the city of Aiuruoca, Minas Gerais, its main attraction is the Papagaio Peak, with 2.293 m in height. It is necessary to ascend via a difficult 8-km trail which goes through forest and altitude fields. Hire a guide in Aiuruoca to lead you through the region.
Information at Casa da Cultura.
Phone: (35) 3344-1249.

❶ ⬧ Matutu Valley
⊖ 94 km de Itatiaia ⊕ Two days
The valley is in the city of Aiuruoca in the state of Minas Gerais, near the Papagaio Peak; the region has a number of trails and freezing waterfalls. There is a esoteric community which provides lodging, horse riding and guides to lead on the trails.

Visconde de Mauá
⊖ 60 km from Itatiaia
⊕ Three days
The villages of Mauá, Maringá and Maromba, neighbours to Itatiaia, have countless trails, horse riding attractions and trekkings through the Mantiqueira Mountain Range. One of the most famous treks is the Maromba-Itamonte, in Minas Gerais. You can also go horse riding in the region. There is good infra-structure of hotels and restaurants.

TO VISIT

Access – Open daily. Admission fee: R$ 3,00.
Address – Estrada do Parque Nacional, km 8,5. Itatiaia, RJ, 27580-000. Phone: (24) 3352-1461, phone/fax: 3352-1652. E-mail: pnitatiaia@resenet.com.br.
How to get there – By car via Dutra highway (BR-116): go to Itatiaia, from which it is 5 km to the Park's foothill headquarters. Access to the high region is via BR-354, which is off Dutra highway near the city of Engenheiro Passos. It is then 35 km to the dirt road which leads to the Planalto Gate (18 km more). There are coaches regularly departing to Itatiaia from São Paulo and Rio de Janeiro.
Infra-structure – Two gates, Visitors' Centre with museum, library and auditorium, rest-rooms, dirt roads, trails, picnic areas and five hotels.

TIPS

○ The best time to visit the Park is during the dry season which is between June and September.
○ Some parts of the climbing demand much technic and are only advised for experienced climbers.
○ For longer hikes, try to go with a guide and do not forget the tent as most nights are cold all year round.

To know more
GASQUES, M.V. **Caminhadas em Agulhas Negras: Parque Nacional de Itatiaia.** São Paulo: Brasiliense, 1990.
www.parquedoitatiaia.com.br

SERVICES

Itatiaia, RJ
🌐 24
✉ 27580-000

Useful Addresses
City Hall. Pça. Mariano Rocha Leão, 20, Centro. Phone: 3352-1660. Internet: www.alerj.rj.gov.br.
Bus station. Rod. Presidente Dutra, km 318,5. Phone: 3352-2144.
Post Office. Rua Oby Loyola, 32, Centro. Phone: 3352-1207. Fax: 6652-1207.
Hospital. Av. 2, s/nº. Phone: 3352-1599.
Banks. Do Brasil, Banerj, Itaú.

Support for the Visitor
Tourist Bureau. Pça. Mariano Rocha Leão, 20, Ed. Prefeitura, Centro. Phone: 3352-1660. Internet: www.alerj.rj.gov.br.
Tour agencies. F. Keller. Phone: 3352-1647.

Lodging
Aldeia da Serra. National Park, km 8, Phone/fax: 3352-1152. Internet: www.razoasocial.com.br/Itatiaia.htm. 10 chalets (up to 4 people). Minibar, fire place, tv. Natural swimming pool, sauna, waterfall, volleyball court, playground, bar, restaurant, parking lot. 🌐 $ $
Alsene. Rebouças road, km 12, Itamonte, MG. Near the Agulhas Negras Peak. Phone: (32) 9981-1217. Reservation: (35) 3363-1773. 7 rooms, 2 chalets (up to 9 people). Parking lot, bar. 🌐 $
Cabanas de Itatiaia. National Park, km 8. Phone: 3352-1228. Fax: 3352-1516. 7 rooms, 6 chalets (up to 4 people), minibar, tv. Swimming pool, sauna, billiard room, playground, bar, restaurant. 🌐 $ $
Casa Alpina. Mauá–Maromba Road, km 6, Vila Maringá. Phone/fax: 3387-1390, reservation: 3387-1125. Internet: www.a3.com/alpina. 15 rooms, tv, minibar, fire place. Swimming pool, sauna, bar, billiard room, parking lot. 🌐 $ $
Chalés Terra Nov. Access via the National Park, km 7. Phone: 3352-1458. Internet: www.chalesterranova.com.br. 10 rooms, 7 chalets, minibar, fire place, tel., tv. Natural swimming pools, sauna, bar, restaurant, billiard room, horses, fishing, playground, parking lot. 🌐 $ $ $
Donati. Parque Nacional, km 11. Phone: 3352-1509. Fax: 3352-1509. Reservation: (21) 240-9414. Internet: www.hoteldonati.com.br. 25 chalets, minibar, fire place. Heated swimming pool, natural swimming pool, sauna, bar, restaurant, billiard room, volleyball court, playground. 🌐 $ $ $
Do Ypê. Parque Nacional, km 14. Phone/fax: 3352-1453. Internet: www.hoteldoype.com.br. 8 rooms, 16 chalets (up to 4 people), 2 houses (up to 6 people), minibar, fire place, tel., tv. Heated swimming pools, sauna, bar, restaurant, multi sport court, parking lot. Chalets. 🌐 $ $ $
Fazenda da Serra. Rod. Presidente Dutra, towards RJ/SP, km 313. Phone/fax: 3352-1611, reservation: (21) 493-1737. Internet: www.paginas.rsd.zaz.com.br. 20 rooms. Natural swimming pool, sauna, lake, cascade, orchard, volleyball court, parking lot. 🌐 $
Fazenda Palmital. Rio – Caxambú Road, km 11, City of Engenheiro Passos. CEP 27555-970. Phone/fax: 3357-1108. Internet: www.easygo.com.br/~palmital. 27 rooms (up to 4 people), 3 chalets (up to 8 people), minibar, cable tv. Swimming pools, saunas, bar, restaurant, volleyball court, football field, leisure service, playground, fishing, horses. 🌐 $ $ $
Simon. National Park, km 13. Phone: 3352-1122. Fax: 3352-1230, reservation: (21) 262-8829. Internet: www.netlistas.com/hotelsimon. 60 rooms, minibar, tv, tel. Natural swimming pool, sauna, bar, restaurant, billiard room, court, tennis court, playground, parking lot. 🌐 $ $ $

Dining
Biergarten. Av. Casa das Pedras, 1017, Penedo, RJ, 12 km from Itatiaia. Phone: 3351-1303. Parking lot. $ $
Dario Frentin. Rod. Presidente Dutra, km 318. Meat, varied menu. R$ 9,00.
Pequena Suécia. Rua Toivo Suni, s/nº, Penedo, RJ. Phone: 3351-1275. Swedish food. $
Truta Viva. Access to Estrada da Fazendinha, km 4, Alto Penedo (Serra), RJ. Phone: 3351-1209. Fish. $ $

Restinga de Jurubatiba

The coastal plain where the Park is located was formed by the laying down of sediment of quaternary origin. Jurubatiba's geography is still being constantly transformed by the tides, the winds and waves. Amid long areas of sandy soil, there are brackish water lagoons, such as Paulista and Encantada, and fresh water ones, like the Comprida and Cabiúna or Jurubatiba. There are also places where the soil is wet, but they are not lagoons. However, they are rich in nutrients and attract a wealth of native fauna. The climate is tropical with a drier period between July and August.

The *restinga* and the wet land vegetation take over the landscape. Jurubatiba's most common plant species are several species of bromeliads, orchids and cacti such as the Nery melon Cactus. The Clusia, a small, thick-leafed tree which lives very well in sandy soil, reigns in areas away from the sea. The clear and dark water lagoons, rich in nutrients, attract tiny plankton, such as Copepod, which, in turn,

Foundation: April 1998
Area: 148,6 km²
Macaé: 20 km; Quissamã: 10 km;
Carapebus: 16 km;
Rio de Janeiro: 245 km

⊕ (22)
☎ 2759-4102

attract bigger organisms that feed on them.
Fish and water fowl, both sea and river
birds, have a good time in the *restinga*.
The fowl, both migratory and species
which live in the *restinga*, such as Egrets,
Ruddy Turnstones, Roseate Spoonbills,
Jacanas, American Storks, Herons and
Southern Limpkins depend on the quantity
of food in the water to survive. Common
birds easily seen in the Park are Saddle
Tanagers, Blue-grey Mockingbirds and a
species of parrot called *Chauá*. Among the
mammals which stand out among the other
species are Otters, Crab-eating Raccoons
and Wild Dogs. Reptiles are represented
by the Swamp Turtle and the Broad-
nosed Cayman

HISTORY

It is odd that the Restinga de Jurubatiba
has remained preserved, located as it is on
the north coast of the state of Rio de Janeiro, close by the city of Rio de Janeiro.

Some of the reasons are the sandy soil of
the *restinga* (a long strip of wooded land
bordering the sea coast), with its 18
lagoons, which is not adequate for
planting, and strong waves which
discourage people from swimming there.
However, in the 19th century an
engineering project threatened the
restinga: in 1844, a canal idealized by
Englishman John Henry Freese would link
the cities of Campos and Macaé. The long
canal would use the lakes and streams of
the region to provide an outlet for the

agricultural and industrial production from the north of the province to the Port of Imbetiba, where it would be exported. It took 27 years to finish. During this time, a railroad was built to link the two cities. As a result of being unable to compete against the railroad - the railroad being capable of carrying more goods - the canal was destined to failure. Today, there is a shallow canal which cuts through the Park from east to west. Since 1982, the *restinga* has been a centre for researchers interested in the region's geology, who are often delighted at the biological diversity and high rate of endemical occurrence. The results of this intense work helped to create the Park, back in 1998.

Many bromeliads are endemic to the region

HIGHLIGHTS

Campos–Macaé canal
It took 27 years to build the canal. Very shallow, it will soon be able to be used as a water way for the observation of the native fauna.

❂ Beaches
The long and clear sand beaches, beaten by a rough sea, represent 44 km of the Park's length. Today, the Visgueiro, João Francisco and Carapebus beaches can be visited.

SURROUNDINGS

❂ ❂ Feia Lagoon
⊖ 20 km from the Park ☼ Three hours

Between the cities of Quissamã and Campos, the fresh water lake is good for canoeing, windsurfing and sportfishing. It unites with the sea by the Flechas Canal.

❂ ⓪ ❂ Peito do Pombo Peak
⊖ 120 km from the Park ☼ One day
In the Sana mountain region, in Macaé, the 1.400-m-high peak can be reached by a difficult 4-hour ascending walk. The Pombo stream is on the way with its several potholes and four waterfalls. The creek by the foot of the mountain and the waterfalls are good options for a rest.

During the dry season, from June to August, the few trees from the restinga may drop their leaves

◀ Saddle tanager (above); the Carapebus lake is the largest in the Park

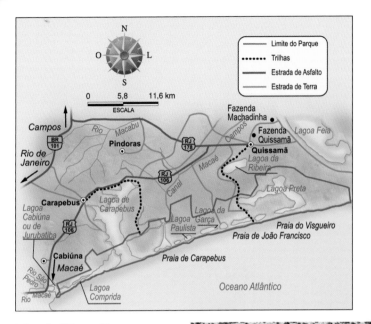

Historical Farms Tour

⊖ 20 km from the Park
⊕ Two to five hours

Fifteen farms from the 18th and 19th centuries in the city of Quissamã; they can be visited in a historical tour which portrays the Brazilian colonial epoch. Do not fail to visit the Mandiquera, Mato-de-Pipa (1777), Machadinha (1864) and Quissamã (1824) farms.

TO VISIT

Access – The Park is still not open for visitation. This depends on approval of the management plan by Ibama, the government bureau for environmental affairs.

Mail address – Parque de Exposições Latiff Mussi Rocha, Rodovia RJ-106, km 182, Barreto, Macaé-RJ. Cep: 27971-130. Email: jurubatiba@lagosnet.com.br. Phone: (22) 2772-5035.

How to get there – By car from Rio de Janeiro: take BR-101 to the north; and the RJ-182 up to Carapebus; then take RJ-178 to Quissamã, and then 14 km of dirt road off RJ-178. There are regular coaches from Rio to Quissamã.

Infra-structure – There is none.

Many of the 18 lagoons have dark waters

To know more

BECKER, M. e DALPONTE, J.C. **Rastros de mamíferos silvestres brasileiros: um guia de campo.** Brasília: Editora Universidade de Brasília, 1991.

LEME, E.C. **Bromélias da Mata Atlântica.** Rio de Janeiro: Sextante, 1997.

www.jurubatiba.com.br

Serra da Bocaina

The National Park shelters most of the Bocaina Mountain Range. This is part of the Serra do Mar Mountain Range and is located between the valley of the river Paraíba do Sul, the north coast of the state of São Paulo and the south coast of the state of Rio de Janeiro. The mountain topography has many rocky outcrops. Its main river is the Mambucaba, whose source is up in the mountains, at 1.800 m. The Paraíba do Sul's source is around the same height and at its source is called Paraitinga. The climate is tropical with a drier period between May and August. The landscape changes according to the altitude: on the lower slopes of the mountainside, towards the Atlantic Ocean, the Coastal Rain Forest, called Mata Atlântica in Brazil, dominates. Here, species like the Cow tree, the Cedar, the Anjelywood, the Pitanga or Brazil Cherry, several species of Cinnamon, the Manaca Raintree, Murici and a number of Ferns,

Foundation: February 1971
Area: 1.100 km²
São José do Barreiro: 27 km;
Bananal: 32 km; Paraty:
15 km; Rio de Janeiro: 200 km;
São Paulo: 285 km
○
⊕ (12)
☎ 577-1225

Orchids and Bromeliads are common. The Euterpe palm gives a delicious heart of palm. In the higher parts of the mountain range there are Brazilian and Scotch Pines. The higher the altitude the lower the vegetation; here, high altitude fields appear amid the rocky outcrops; there are grasses, Asparagus Fern, mountain Strawflowers, Orchids, Buttonbushes, Lichens and Bromeliads. However, many of the fields that exist in the Bocaina Mountain Range are in areas which used to be covered with the Coastal Rain Forest; the fields are a result of colonial agriculture and the coffee cycle. Animals like Brockets, Boars, Little Anteaters, Mountain Lions, Howling and Capuchin Monkeys, the endangered Spider Monkey, Holt's Yellow Finches, Red-Capped Parrots, Blue-bellied Parrots, Hawk-headed

Parrots, Red-breasted toucans and the rare Black-fronted Piping Guan stand out in the Park's fauna.

HISTORY

Centuries ago, the Guaianaze Indians blazed the pathway which was later travelled by drivers of pack animals, *tropeiros,* who went all the way down to Argentina and back doing business with cattle and mules. The term refers to the pack of animals with which they travelled: *tropa.* The pathway was then called *Trilha do Ouro* (Gold Trail). The Guarani Indians arrived later and took over the region of Bocaina, from the mountains to the coast. They used to have a semi nomadic way of life, but today they live in villages; one of them is within the Park's limits. Settlers arrived at the end of the 16th century when the *bandeirantes,* or raiders, entered the valley of the Paraíba do Sul River on raiding expeditions in search of minerals and Indians to enslave. At that time, the main economic activity along the coast was the cultivation of sugar-cane. The economic cycle of gold came at the end of the 17th century. Troops of the Crown transported the precious metal from the province of Minas Gerais, which means "general mines", through the Bocaina Mountain Range to the port of Paraty. In the 18th century, the economic cycle of coffee took over the Paraíba Valley fostering the development of many urban centres such as Bananal, São José do Barreiro and Areias. When the German naturalists Von Spix and Von Martius travelled through the region, they described it as an area of forest intermingled with large areas of cultivation. At the end of the 19th century the coffee plantations were substituted by cattle ranching and in the 20th century, the country's largest economical axis – São Paulo, Rio de Janeiro and Minas Gerais – had its wealth increased by industrialization of the region.

The Serra da Bocaina National Park was founded in 1971, on the border of the states of Rio de Janeiro - with 62% of the Park's area - and São Paulo. It envelopes land which used to belong to Central do Brasil railroad; the regions are called Horto Florestal and Mambucaba. In the following year, the borders of the Park where altered to the area held today. This includes mountain regions stretching up to the sea near the city of Trindade, at the border of São Paulo and Rio de Janeiro, and also includes a coastal island.

View from the highest part of the Park

◀ Orchid (above); mountainous topography, typical of the Serra do Mar

HIGHLIGHTS

São Izidro Waterfall

It is located 1,4 km from the Park's entrance; its 80-m falls and its cold pools are good options to cool down during the hikes.

Posses Waterfall

Its 30-m fall invites to take a dip in the cold waters. It is a good place to camp during the crossing of the Ouro trail.

Veado Waterfall

Both falls that form the waterfall drop from a height of 200 m. On the second day of the Ouro trail trek, the pond formed by the fall invites to take a bath.

Mambucaba River Source

The source of the Park's main river is in the mountains at 1.800 m; it flows to Angra dos Reis.

Tira Chapéu Peak

⊖ 6 km from the Park

A hike leads to the summit of Bocaina's highest peak at 2.088 m in altitude. From the top you can enjoy a nice view of the rolling hills and the coastline.

Ouro Trail

⊖ 63 km from the Park ⊕ Two or three days, depending on the starting point

The trail which leads to the village of Mambucaba on the coast used to be travelled by *tropeiros* - pack animals traders - who transported gold from the General Mines Province - today the state of Minas Gerais - to the port of Paraty. It takes three days to walk the trail at a moderate pace; you will walk past the waterfalls São Izidro, Posses and Veado. On the way, take note of the pavement built by slaves back in the 19th century, the farms, stretches of forest, logs or planks across streams called *pinguelas,* and banana plantations.

SURROUNDINGS

Bananal

⊖ 32 km from the Park ⊕ One day

The city reached the height of its development during the coffee boom and still has rows of colonial houses. Visit the train station built back in 1889, the Pharmácia Popular - an old chemist's shop - and the historical farms of the region. Among them, the Resgate, the Independência and the Três Barras, which took in Emperor D. Pedro I on his way to Ipiranga, where he declared the independence of Brazil from Portugal in 1822.

Usina Waterfall

⊖ 3 km from São José do Barreiro
⊕ One hour

Very near the city; its 15-m fall gives good showers and baths in its cold waters.

Bananal Ecologic Station

⊖ 20 km from Bananal ⊕ Four hours

Located in a stretch of preserved Coastal Rain Forest, the São Paulo State Environment Bureau's station has trails and a part of the Sete Quedas Waterfall.

Paraty

⊖ 15 km from the Park
⊕ One to three days

The small colonial town, which had 250 sugar mills working simultaneously, has been declared Cultural Patrimony of Human Kind and its buildings are a nice example of Brazilian colonial architecture. A cultural and artistic centre, it has more than 50 islands surrounded by a transparent sea. You can't miss the *pinga* festival in August. If you still do not know this typical Brazilian spirit, it is a kind of raw, white rum also called *cachaça.*

◀　The two falls from the Veado waterfall are 200 m high

🐾 Pedra Redonda Peak

🚶 8 km from São José do Barreiro

🕐 Five hours

You can either walk or go horse riding the way up to the peak. If you decide to walk, it is a moderate slope. It is 7 km to the top, where you will find a buddhist monastery and an ecologic park.

Legenda:
- ——— Limite do Parque
- ••••••• Trilhas
- ▬▬▬ Estrada de Asfalto
- ——— Estrada de Terra
- –·–·– Fronteira de Estado
- ⊢⊢⊢⊢⊢ Ferrovia

TO VISIT

Access – Open from 8 am to 6 pm.
Free of charge.

Address – Rod. Estadual da Bocaina
(SP-221), km 0, São José do Barreiro,
SP, 12830-000. Phone/fax: (12)
577-1225. E-mail:
pnsb@fastnet.com.br.

How to get there – From São Paulo or
Rio de Janeiro: take Via Dutra
(BR-116) up to Queluz, then take SP-066
up to São José do Barreiro. It is 27 km to
the Park's entrance via SP-221 – a dirt
road in bad condition. There are coaches
traveling regularly from São Paulo and
Queluz to São José do Barreiro.

Infra-structure – Reception with
information about the Park, parking lot
and rest rooms. Trails for the waterfalls
and dirt roads.

TIPS

◗ The Park can be visited all year
round. It rains more in summer, from
December to March. In winter, from
June to August, it is colder and drier.
◗ If you intend to walk the Ouro trail,
prepare the trip at least a fortnight before,
because the Park requires previous
reservations. Look for a tour agency or
experienced guide for the trek.

To know more
SPIX, J.B.V. e MARTIUS, C.F.P.V.
Viagem pelo Brasil: 1817-1820.
Vol. 1. Belo Horizonte: Itatiaia/Edusp,
1981. www.paraty.com.br/pnsb.htm

SERVICES

São José do Barreiro, SP
⊕ 12
◔ 12830-000

Useful Addresses
City Hall. Rua José Bento Teixeira, 45, Centro. Phone/fax: 577-1288. Internet: www.citiesite.com.br/valehistorico/sjbarreiro.
Bus station. Av. Fortunato Lobão, s/nº.
Post Office. Pça. Prof. José de Marins Freire, s/nº, Centro. Phone/fax: 577-1135.
Hospital. Rua Virgílio Pereira, 6. Phone: 577-1252.
Bank. Nossa Caixa.

Support for the Visitor
Tourist Bureau. Rua José Bento Teixeira, 45, Ed. Prefeitura, Centro. Phone/fax: 577-1288. Internet: www.citiesite.com.br/valehistorico/sjbarreiro.
Tourist Information Service. Ibama (the government bureau for environment affairs) office at S. José do Barreiro. Phone: 577-1225.
Tour agencies. MW Trekking. Pça. Cel. Cunha Lara, s/nº, Centro. Phone/fax: 577-1178. Internet: www.mwtrekking.com.br.

Lodging
Conde d'Eu. Access via Estrada Serra da Bocaina, km 25, next to the National Park's entrance. Phone: 853-4480. 11 rooms. Reservation: 985-4331. Restaurant, sauna, horses.Ⓢ Ⓢ Ⓢ Ⓢ
Fazenda São Francisco. Estrada São Francisco, km 6. Phone: 577-1264. Fax: (21) 286-1736, reservation (21) 286-9763. Internet: www.citiesite.com.br/valehistorico/sjbarreiro/saofrancisco. 6 chalets (up to 7 persons). Restaurant, lake, waterfall, corral, football field, volleyball court, fishing, horses, parking lot.Ⓢ Ⓢ Ⓢ Ⓢ
Porto da Bocaina. Access km 260 of SP-068 road towards Areias. Phone: 577-1102. Fax: 577-1303. Internet: www.hoteisdabocaina.com.br. 35 rooms, air conditioning, minibar, tel., tv. Swimming pool, sauna, bar, restaurant, launch, dock for boats, kayaks, tennis court, volleyball court, football field, horses.Ⓢ Ⓢ Ⓢ Ⓢ
Pousada Vale dos Veados. Estrada da Bocaina, km 42. Phone: 577-1102. Fax: 577-1303. Internet: www.hoteisdabocaina.com.br. 8 rooms, 1 chalet (up to 5 persons), fire place, heating. Lake, sauna, waterfall, restaurant, horses.Ⓢ Ⓢ Ⓢ Ⓢ

Dining
Regis. Av. Fortunato Lobão, s/nº. Phone: 577-1184 Ⓢ
Sabor da Terra. Rua Capitão Antonio Gomes, s/nº. Phone: 577-1119. Typical local food, varied menu. Ⓢ

Bananal, SP
⊕ 12
◔ 12850-000

Useful Addresses
City Hall. Av. Bom Jesus, 93, Centro. Phone/fax: 576-1224.
Bus station. Pça. Dona Domiciana, s/nº. Phone: 576-1274.
Post Office. Av. Bom Jesus, s/nº, Centro. Phone: 576-1298.
Ambulatory. Av. Bom Jesus, 134, Centro. Phone: 576-1293.
Banks. Do Brasil, Banespa.

Support for the Visitor
Tourist Bureau. Rua Manoel de Aguiar, s/nº, near the main church. Phone: 576-1648.

Lodging
Castor. Rua Pedro Humberto Bruno, 123. Phone: 576-1229. Fax: 576-1579. 14 rooms, tv. Swimming pool, bar, restaurant, parking lot. Ⓢ Ⓢ Ⓢ
Fazenda Boa Vista. Tropeiros road (SP-068), towards Barra Mansa, km 327. Phone/fax: 576-1539. Internet: www.bananal.com.br/hotelfazendaboavista. 16 rooms, minibar, tv, tel. Swimming pool, sauna, restaurant, bar, billiard room, lake, corral, football field, tennis court, courts, horses, fishing. Ⓢ Ⓢ Ⓢ
Fazenda Casa Grande. Road to Bocaina, km 1. Phone/fax: 576-1543. 12 rooms, minibar, tv. Swimming pool, bar, restaurant, billiard room, football field, playground, horses, parking lot. Ⓢ Ⓢ Ⓢ
Fazenda Independência. Road SP-064, towards Barra Mansa, km 324. Phone/fax: 576-1110. 10 rooms, minibar, tel., tv. Swimming pool, sauna, bar, restaurant, waterfall, corral, horses. Ⓢ Ⓢ Ⓢ Ⓢ

Dining
Chez Bruna. Estrada da Bocaina (Rod. SP-247), km 28. Phone: 576-1520. Brazilian food. Ⓢ Ⓢ
Dona Licéia. Fazenda Caxambú, Rod. dos Tropeiros (SP-068), km 23. Typical local food, varied menu, Brazilian food. Ⓢ Ⓢ Ⓢ
Recanto do Espigão. Rua Manuel de Aguiar, 66. Phone: 576-1375. Varied menu, typical local food. Ⓢ Ⓢ

Canastra
Serra da Canastra

The Park's mountainous terrain shelters two major outcrops: the Sete Voltas and the Canastra Mountain Range, where the highest peak in the area (1.496 m) and the Serra Brava are located. But the Chapada to the northwest and the Cemitério to the south are mountains which also make up part of the Park's topography. Here, summers are rainy, mainly between January and February, and winters are dry; the local temperatures are mild, with monthly averages between 17ºC and 23ºC. The vegetation is typical of the *Cerrado* - woods composed of stunted, twisted trees - with spots which reveal a transition between this kind of vegetation and the Coastal Rain Forest, or Mata Atlântica as it is called in Brazil. Fields - here called *campos limpos* - are common in the higher parts, forest areas in the low lands and rupestrian vegetation upon the mountains' rocks. In this scenery, it is possible to

observe typical species of the Cerrado, such as the Nightshade, the Holywood Lignum Vitae, the Lixeira and the Tabernaemontana. In the forests, whose canopies can reach up to 25 m in height, there are Cedars, Porcupine Podtrees, Cinnamons and Floss-silk trees.

The rupestrian field landscapes are composed of a low vegetation which grows on the rocky outcrops at heights greater than 800 m. Many species that occur at those places are endemic. Among the common plants there are Canelas-de-ema, Mountain Arnicas, Orchids and Bromeliads. In the more humid areas, moss and lichen take over the rocks, painting them orange and green.

As it is located in a region which has been occupied for many years, the Park's area has suffered several anthropic alterations such as the cutting of the forest and mining. These actions ended up impeding

Foundation: April 1972
Area: 715 km²
São Roque de Minas: 8 km; Araxá: 90 km; Sacramento: 60 km; Franca: 125 km; Belo Horizonte: 370 km

◯
⊕ (37)
☎ 3433-1195

the fauna and reduced the animal population. However, due to the open formation of the fields, low and homogeneous vegetation, the animals are easily observed. With a bit of luck, you will be able to see the Great Anteater, the Maned Wolf, the Wild Dog and the 9-striped Armadillo. The rare Giant Armadillo, despite being an endangered species, can still be seen at dawn or in the evening, roaming about the Cerrado in search of food. The most common birds are the Crested Seriema, the Holt's Yellow Finch, the American Ostrich, Partridges, Quails and flocks of Toco Toucans, which dye orange the blue heavens of the Canastra Mountain Range. Near the water courses it is possible to watch King Fishers, Cormorants and Egrets.

São Francisco River: its source is here; it flows through five states before getting into the Atlantic

HISTORY

The region of São Roque de Minas was inhabited by the Cataguaze Indians, who were probably annihilated by Lourenço Castanho in 1675. Today, there are only a few battered objects left to tell the story. Later, runaway slaves from the neighbouring farms used the fertile land on the banks of the São Francisco River, established hide-outs called *quilombos*. These *quilombos* were real communities, sometimes as big as villages. But in the middle of the 18th century, by order of the governor of the province of Minas Gerais, they were defeated in bloody battles. At the same time, the neighbouring mining centres exhausted their mineral reserves and the population began to move to the region where today the conservation unit is. Nowadays, enveloped by the Park are the ruins of the first house which belonged to Florêncio Rodrigues and the *senzala*, or slave quarters, of an 18th century farm which had an area of 190 km². At the beginning of the 19th century, St. Hilaire - the first naturalist who visited Brazil as an official guest - travelled through the mountain range and highlighted its landscape as an asset, extolling the Casca d'Anta Waterfall. The mountain range's name is due to its shape, which reminds one of a large chest (*canastra* is an old word for chest) when seen from far away. An interesting legend from the local lore is one about the *zagaia*. They say that a wooden wheel with spikes in it - the *zagaia* - was hung on the ceiling of one of the bedrooms of a farm whose owners used to take travellers in. When the guests settled in their quarters the owners of the farm - actually a gang of criminals - would let the *zagaia* fall in order to steal the poor devils' belongings.

Farms witness the wealth of the past

◀ Toucan (above); high cliffs and sparse trees of the *Cerrado*

Canastra: Old Chico's source

The São Francisco River is known as the "river of national unity" and its importance is acknowledged by all Brazilians, although mainly by the 14 million who depend on the water from its basin. It is difficult to believe that the small source in the Canastra Mountain Range is the origin of a river which flows for 3.160 km through five Brazilian states until it reaches the Atlantic between the states of Sergipe and Alagoas. On its way, during the floods, it fertilizes the arid soil of the dry regions allowing the farmers to plant beans, potatoes and rice on its banks. The Três Marias and Sobradinho dams, in the state of Minas Gerais, produce electricity for a great part of the population. However, in the last decades the São Francisco suffered serious aggression, such as the cutting of trees on its banks and the action of illegal miners prospecting for diamonds. One of the reasons for the creation of the Canastra National Park was to protect the river's source. Today, Old Chico is responsible for 60% of the water reserve for the Brazilian northeast, a region often subject to severe droughts and which might suffer serious water supply problems, if the river is not preserved.

The water falls from a height of 186 m, forming the Casca D'anta Waterfall

HIGHLIGHTS

The best form to get to know the Park is by walking. Take advantage of the inter-city road which cuts through the conservation unit, providing easy access to the main attractions.

🌑 Casca d'Anta Waterfall

It can be observed in all its might, both from the top and from the foot. It falls off a cliff of 186 m. A great thing to do is to go up to the pool above the falls.

🌑 🌊 Rolinhos Waterfall

Access is via a short trail with a 15 minutes walk off the main road. The waterfall can be seen from the lookout. Its cascades fall into the transparent waters of the Azul Lake and are good for taking a bath. It is the second most visited waterfall in the Park.

Curral de Pedras

The name means "stone corral" and it is actually the ruins of a farm where there are vestiges of old stone corrals. The source of the São Francisco River is 6 km ahead, via the main road.

Cândidos and Garagem das Pedras Farms

Cândidos farm is located on the border between the Canastra and Babilônia plateaus, where it is possible to enjoy a view of the mountains. Access is via an inter-city road which starts at the Casca d'Anta gate.

Fazenda Zagaia

It is located near the Sacramento gate, in a less visited corner of the Park, and is of difficult access. Many Rattle snakes are found in the area. People say that the farm was owned by a gang of criminals.

São Francisco Source

Access is via the Park's main entrance, São Roque de Minas gate. After 6 km by road you get to the river's source without much difficulty; the source is in a small riverine forest.

Retiro das Pedras

It has ruins of the *senzala*, or slaves' quarters, of one of the old farms of the upper São Francisco region. It is near the São João Batista gate.

Torre Brava

The highest peak in the Park, with 1.480 m. Its name means angry tower and it can be appreciated from the main road, near Garagem de Pedras.

🏊 🌑 Casca d'Anta Trail
🕐 Five hours

The Park's most famous trail leads to the upper part of the waterfall of the same name. In order to get there you should depart from the Casca d'Anta gate and go up the trail for 4 km on a two-hour walk. From the highest point of the trail you have a nice view of the Canastra and Babilônia outcrops. It takes only one hour to descend.

SURROUNDINGS

🏊 🌑 Babilônia Mountain Range
⊖ 30 km from São Roque de Minas
🕐 From three to eight hours

The mountain range divides the waters of the São Francisco and Paraná basins and it has a number of trails and waterfalls of transparent waters. From the top, you have a nice view from the Canastra Mountain Range. You can walk the trail, go horse riding or take a 4-wheel-drive vehicle.

	Limite do Parque
•••••••	Trilhas
	Estrada de Terra

ⓘ ⓒ ⓢ ⓓ Capão
Forro Waterfalls
⊖ 5 km from São Roque de Minas
⊕ Three hours

The five waterfalls are near the São Roque de Minas gate. The first one is 80 m high. Here, you can go canyoning and rappelling. The trails that take to the other waterfalls are short and easy. All the waterfalls are good for bathing.

ⓘ ⓒ ⓢ ⓓ Nego Waterfall
⊖ 10 km from São Roque de Minas
⊕ Five hours

Located within the farm of the same name, it is a private area with three waterfalls in a row. The pools are good for bathing and the falls are up to 40 m high; good for canyoning and rappelling.

ⓢ Fernandes Gorge
⊖ 10 km from Casca d'Anta Waterfall
⊕ Four hours

40 m high at the creek with the same name, it is a good place to go rappelling. During the dry season, the creek dries up and the descent is made on the dry cliff.

The São Francisco River

ⓢ ⓘ ⓖ Cerradão
Waterfall Ecological Park
⊖ 6 km from São Roque de Minas
⊕ Four hours

Located on private property, there is a trail to the waterfall on the Cerradão Creek with good opportunities for watching the native fauna. Here you can go on a 30-m *tirolesa* which falls into the lake. Information at Tamanduá Ecoturismo. Phone: (37) 3343-1126.

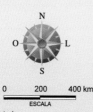

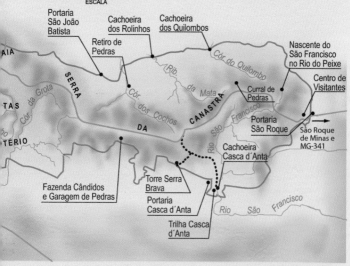

TO VISIT

Access – Open daily from 8 am to 6 pm. Admission fee: R$ 3,00. The fee to camp in the Park is R$ 6,00 per day.

Address – Rua Tancredo Neves, 498, São Roque de Minas, MG, 37928-000. Phone/fax: (37) 3433-1195.

How to get there – The easiest access is via São Roque de Minas: on the MG-050 road, go towards Piumhi on MG-341, which leads to São Roque de Minas, 8 km from the Park's entrance. There are coaches regularly departing from São Paulo and Belo Horizonte to Pumhi.

Infra-structure – Four gates, Visitors' Centre with information on the Park, camping ground at Casca d'Anta, roads and trails to the main attractions, including the source of "Old Chico".

TIPS

❂ The best time to visit the Park is from April to October, when it rains less.

To know more
CALDAS, J. e SOUTO, N.G. **Parque Nacional da Serra da Canastra.** Rio de Janeiro: Paper Mill, 2001.
SAINT-HILAIRE, A. **Viagem às nascentes do rio São Francisco.** Belo Horizonte: Itatiaia/Edusp .
www.canastra.com.br
www.serracanastra.com.br
www.sacramento.com.br

SERVICES

São Roque de Minas, MG

☎ 37
✉ 37929-000

Useful Addresses

City Hall. Pça. Alibinedeis da Costa Faria, 10. Phone/fax: 3433-1199.
Bus station. Pça. da Matriz, s/nº, Centro. Phones: 3433-2020 and 3371-1310.
Post Office. Rua 15 de Novembro, 177. Phone/fax: 3433-1236.
Bank. Bemge.
Hospital. Av. Getúlio Vargas, 490. Phones: 3433-1122/1236/1188.
Car rental. Tamanduá Ecoturismo. Av. Pres. Tancredo Neves, 15. Phone/fax: 3343-1126 and (11) 270-5947.

Support for the Visitor

Tourist Bureau. Pça. Alibinedeis da Costa Faria, 12. Phone/fax: 3433-1199.
Tourist Information Service. Ibama's office at São Roque de Minas. Pres. Tancredo Neves, 498. Phone: 3433-1191. Central de Reserva Serra da Canastra. Phone/fax: 3433-1126.
Tour Agencies. Tamanduá Ecoturismo. Av. Pres. Tancredo Neves, 15. Phone/fax: 3343-1126 and (11) 270-5947. Internet: www.serracanastra.com.br.

Lodging

Chapadão da Canastra. Rua Benjamin Constant, 10. Phone/fax: 3433-1267/3433-1226. Internet: www.serracanastra.com.br. 24 rooms, minibar, tv, fan. Natural swimming pool, parking lot. [$][$]
Pousada Barcelos. Av. Vicente Picardi, 189. Phone: 3433-1216. Reservation: (31) 3223-0084. Internet: www.serracanastra.com.br/barcelos. 18 rooms, minibar. Swimming pool, sauna, bar. [$][$]
Pousada da Limeira. (rural lodging) Vargem Bonita–Casca D'Anta road, km 7, Vargem Bonita, MG. Phone: 3435-1118. Reservation: 9106-9705. Internet: www.pousadadalimeira.com.br. 2 rooms, 6 chalets (up to 4 people), 2 houses (up to 10 people). Natural swimming pool, waterfall, corral, volleyball court, horse riding, fishing. [$][$]
Recanto da Canastra. Exit to Vargem Bonita, km 30. Phone: 3435-1108. Fax: 3371-2080. Reservation: (16) 9992-7706. Internet: www.recantodacanastra.com.br. 2 rooms, 10 chalets. Swimming pool, waterfall, multi sport court, horse riding, parking lot. [$][$][$][$]
Toca do Picardi. Rua Miguel da Costa Pereira, 17. Phone/fax: 3433-1351. Internet: www.serracanastra.com.br. 8 rooms, tv, hiking in the mountains, trekking, rappelling, parking lot. [$]

Dining

Paredão. Av. Padre Murilo, 456. Phone: 3433-1264. Typical local food. [$]
Zagaia. Av. Tancredo Neves, 10. Phone: 3433-1323. Typical local food. [$]

Delfinópolis, MG

☎ 35
✉ 37910-000

Useful Addresses

City Hall. Pça. Manuel Leite Lemos, 115, Centro. Phone: 3525-1020.
Bus station. Rua Cel. Melo Santos, s/nº. Phone: 3525-1042.
Port/Wharf. Road to Cássia, km 8. Ferry continuously working to Cássia (15 minutes to cross). Phone: 9981-4523.
Post Office. Rua José Abrahão Pedro, 330. Phone/fax: 3525-1162.
Bank. Bemge.
Hospital. Av. Padre Ivo Soares de Matos, 193. Phone: 3525-1122.
Car rental. Off Road. Av. Torquato José de Almeida, 794. Phone: 3525-1073.

Support for the Visitor

Tourist Bureau. Pça. Dr. Lafaiete Soares, s/nº. Phone: 3525-1020.
Tourist Information Service. Centro Atendimento ao Turista. Pça. Dr. Lafaiete Soares, s/nº. Phone: 3525-1020, r. 331.
Tour agencies. Carioca Passeios de Lancha. Phones: 3523-1783, (37) 9983-9252.

Lodging

Pousada Jardim da Serra. Rua das Flores, 184. Phone/fax: 3525-1256. Reservation: (16) 3610-9972. E-mail: jardimserra@cassianet.com.br. 6 rooms, minibar, fan. Parking lot. [$][$]
Pousada Rio Grande. Rua Torquato José de Almeida, 794. Phone: 3525-1073. Internet: www.pousadariogrande.com.br. 22 rooms, tv, minibar, fan. Parking lot, shuttle for tours. [$][$]

Dining

Tempero Mineiro. Rua Torquato José de Almeida, 865. Phone: 3525-1242. Typical local food and meat. [$]

Serra do Cipó

The Espinhaço Mountain Range (espinhaço is Portuguese for backbone), which envelopes the Serra do Cipó, rose 600 million years ago. It divides two important Brazilian river basins: the São Francisco and the Doce. Formed mainly by quartzite, it also has calcareous rocks where fossils from other ages are preserved. Sharp rocks outcroping westwards from the soil can be seen all over Cipó. They are quartzite formations which were formed due to the high pressures and temperatures resulting from tectonic movements; these occurred from east to the west distorting the earth's crust. The climate of the mountain range is characterized by mild summers and a well defined dry season, which goes from April to September. The rain falls mainly from October to March. In the high lands the temperature may reach

Foundation: September 1984
Area: 338 km²
Belo Horizonte: 100 km; Cardeal
Mota: 4 km; Confins: 50 km

⊕ (31)
☎ 3683-5226

0°C, and the corrupiana - a thin drizzle blown by the east wind - is also common. Many species, adapting in order to survive the poor soil conditions and difficult climate, have become endemic. Rupestrian fields with many rocky outcrops dominate the landscape above 900 m. They are covered in grasses, dotted here and there with small bushes and trees which look like bonsais. But the greatest highlights are the flowers which paint the scenery with different shades as the year advances. Everlastings are typical here, as well as Bromeliads, Orchids. Canelas-de-ema stand out: there are some gigantic ones here - up to 6 m high, one hundred years old or more. The fields are intermingled with riverine forests and groves of trees, which are like islands of thicker vegetation in the mountainous parts. The fauna is composed mainly of Deer, Allouata Howling Monkeys, Saki Monkeys,

Crested Seriemas and many endangered species such as Maned Wolves, Mountain Lions, Wild Dogs, Ocelots and Great Anteaters. You will easily come across Iguanas, small lizards, Calospiza Tanagers, Hummingbirds, Brazilian Siskins, a species of toad called De Pijama and even families of Capybaras.

The Mascate River has eroded the rocky terrain for thousands of years, forming some canyons

◄ Sauim or tamarim (above); the Grande Waterfall is outside the Park

HISTORY

Pre-historic men who portrayed their daily lives in rock paintings, which can still be seen today, inhabited the calcareous caves of the Cipó Mountain Range. Peter Lund, a Danish palaentologist, first noticed the importance of the region in terms of archaeology. It was he who found the remains of the Lagoa Santa Man, who is believed to have lived in the area 10.000 years ago.

The Espinhaço Mountain Range, which envelopes the Serra do Cipó, was first explored by the *bandeirantes* back in the 17th century. The men were explorers who went to the backwoods in search of precious minerals and Indians to enslave. When gold and precious stones were discovered in the state of Minas Gerais, the mountain range was used as the route for the outflow of the production of diamonds. Later, the name of the mountain range was changed to *Cipó*, the Portuguese word for "vine", probably being due to the winding river.

In the 19th century, the region drew the attention of Brazilian and foreign naturalists for the wealth of its flora and fauna. For almost two centuries, scientists researched the region discovering some endemic species. The creation of the National Park was a natural answer to the need of preserving its biologic diversity.

The rupestrian fields without trees are a symbol of the region

Everlastings, Cipó's abounding flowers

The dwellers of the Cipó Mountain Range have always plucked the small flowers which abound in the fields in order to adorn their houses. When they dry, they remain with the same look they had when alive. After the discovery of this phenomenon, the flowers were intensely gathered and sold to big cities in order to adorn brides' bouquets and vases. It is estimated that more than a billion flowers are picked per year from the rupestrian fields of the Cipó Mountain Range. The trade in everlasting flowers only diminished when the National Park was created. However, bunches and bunches of illegally picked everlastings are sometimes seized.

Clusters: used in decoration

HIGHLIGHTS

There are enough attractions for you to spend many days in the Cipó Mountain Range exploring the more than 55 waterfalls, mountains and canyons of the Park and its surroundings.

ⓜ ❧ Farofa Waterfall
🕐 Four hours

It has seven falls in a row; the lowest is 270 m high and it falls in three levels to a pool, which is easily reached and much visited. On the way, you will see the Comprida Lagoon in a valley from which it is possible to see a rocky outcrop, the Paredão. Access to the Farofa de Cima waterfall is via a more difficult trail, which requires the expertise of a guide.

ⓜ ❧ Lagoa Dourada Waterfall
⊖ 15 km from São José da Serra
🕐 One day

Located where the vegetation colour ranges from shades of gold and red, on the Park's southern border. The trail to the waterfall is a hard walk, so many visitors would prefer to go by horse. The waterfall and the landscape repay the effort.

ⓜ ❧ Braúnas Waterfall
⊖ 40 km from the Park 🕐 Three days

The waterfall above the Bandeirinhas Canyon is difficult to reach. It is necessary to go via a trail which goes by the upper part of the Bandeirinhas Mountain Range. It starts at Travessão and passes Tatinha's house - a renovated colonial house, which is now used to lodge researchers.

ⓜ ❧ Congonhas Waterfall
⊖ 24 km from the Park 🕐 One day

The two 30-m waterfalls on Congonhas Creek can be reached via the same trail to Travessão, going to the right at a fork in the road. Seventeen out of the 24 km to the waterfall must be travelled by foot.

ⓜ Gavião and Andorinhas Waterfalls
⊖ 18 km from Cardeal Mota
🕐 One day

They can be seen on the same trail, which starts at the Alto Cruzeiro lookout, in Cardeal Mota, and goes to Bocaina Stream. It is 9 km by car plus 6 km on foot up to the Gavião Waterfall; 3 km more to the Andorinhas Waterfall.

ⓜ ⓜ ❧ Bandeirinhas Canyon

A 12-km walk: in the part where the Bandeirinhas Creek narrows, its width is around 80 m and has many cascades, waterfalls and pools one after the other. On the way, it is necessary to cross Mascates Creek, whose bottom is covered with slippery rocks. At the waterfall, climb the rocks as high as you can. With a permit from the government bureau for environmental affairs, Ibama, you can go canyoning.

ⓜ Travessão
⊖ 27 km from the Park 🕐 One day
17 km by car via MG-10 towards Conceição do Mato Dentro up to km 112; you must then walk the remaining 10 km

This is probably the most impressive landscape in the Park with the formation of two canyons; it divides the river basins of the São Francisco to the west and the Doce to the east. Here too the Peixe and Capão Rivers have their sources, 200 m away from each other. It is one of the most difficult hikes in the Park, with many ups and downs.

SURROUNDINGS

ⓜ Pedreira Hill
⊖ 10 km from the Park 🕐 Two hours

Four calcareous rocky cliffs with more than 130 sites for climbing. The hill is also good for cave exploration: there are 25 small grottos that have never been visited.

ⓜ ❧ Véu da Noiva
⊖ 10 km do Parque 🕐 Two hours

It is a 60-m high waterfall located in the camping grounds of the YMCA. The grounds, which pack with visitors on holidays, have a swimming pool, courts and rest rooms. It is possible to go rappelling, but only for the experienced.

ⓜ Lapa da Sucupira
⊖ 15 km from the Park 🕐 Two hours

A calcareous rock zone with a number of rock paintings which date back to 8.000 years ago.

ⓜ Lapa do Gentio
⊖ 14 km from the Park 🕐 Two hours

The Paredão do Gentio, an important archaeologic site, has records of the people who inhabited Cipó 10.000 years ago.

🌑 Lapinha Grotto

🚗 13 km from the Park   🕐 Three hours
Open daily from 9 am to 4:30 pm
This 551-m long grotto is one of the few in the region with facilities for the visitor. It also has 12 halls with stalactites and stalagmites. The Lapinha Archaeologic Museum, founded in 1972, has precious pre-historic objects from the region.

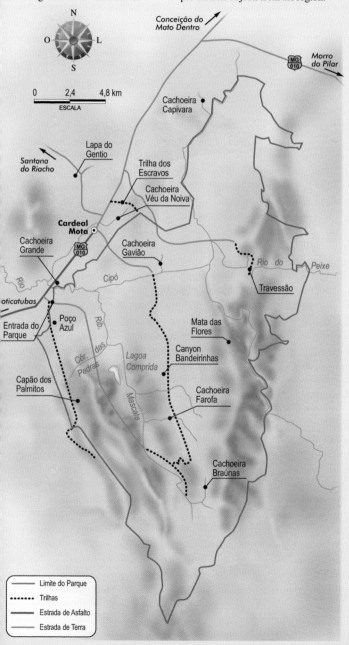

Conceição do Mato Dentro

Morro do Pilar

MG 010

Cachoeira Capivara

N
O   L
S

0   2,4   4,8 km
ESCALA

Lapa do Gentio

Santana do Riacho

Trilha dos Escravos

Cachoeira Véu da Noiva

Cardeal Mota

Cachoeira Grande

MG 010

Cachoeira Gavião

Rio do Peixe

Cipó

Travessão

Rio

oticatubas

Entrada do Parque

Poço Azul

Mata das Flores

Canyon Bandeirinhas

Rib. das

Cór.

Pedras

Lagoa Comprida

Capão dos Palmitos

Mascate

Cachoeira Farofa

Cachoeira Braúnas

———— Limite do Parque
●●●●● Trilhas
———— Estrada de Asfalto
———— Estrada de Terra

TO VISIT

Access – Open daily from 8 am to 5 pm. Admission fee: R$ 3,00. You can rent horses and bicycles. The Park has two Jeeps to take visitors to some attractions; it costs R$ 10,00. There is no camping ground, but those who are on a trekking expedition of three or four days with a guide may camp. It is necessary to previously obtain a special permit with Ibama

Address – Rod. MG-010, km 96, Distrito de Cardeal Mota, Santana do Riacho, MG, 35847-000. Phone: (31) 3683-5226. E-mail: parnacipo@uol.com.br.

How to get there – By plane, landing at Pampulha Airport (Belo Horizonte): walk for ten minutes to Av. Antonio Carlos where the bus which goes to the Park stops. By bus: there are regular departures from Belo Horizonte to Conceição do Mato Dentro or Morro do Pilar. Get off at km 94 at MG-010 road. By car from Belo Horizonte: take MG-010 towards Conceição do Mato Dentro up to Cardeal Mota district (km 94), and 4 km more of dirt road to the Park.

Infra-structure – Visitors' Centre with exhibition hall, information about the Park, rest-rooms and auditorium. Snack bar and souvenir shop. There are licensed guides in Cardeal Mota and tours on which you must go with a guide. There is a Laboratory and lodge for researchers.

TIPS

◗ The best time to visit the Park is between April and July, as the drought is not so intense, the waterfalls are still full, it rains little and the temperature is mild.
◗ Do not walk off the trails in wintertime, which is the time of the ticks' reproductive cycle. The micuim, a kind of tiny tick, abounds in the Park's low area. Tuck your pants into the socks and take sulfur soap in case you get infested.
◗ Take care with heavy rainfalls on the head of waters of rivers and waterfalls as they have been known to overflow quickly, because it is a region of canyons.

To know more
CARTELLE, C. **Tempo passado: Mamíferos do Pleistoceno em Minas Gerais.** Belo Horizonte: Palco, 1994. www.serradocipo.org.

SERVICES

Santana do Riacho, MG
🌐 31
✉ 35847-000

Useful Addresses
City Hall. Rua Alfredo Domingos de Melo, 44, Centro. Phone/fax: 3718-6127.
Bus station. São José de Almeida. Phones: 3683-5116/3683-5244.
Post Office. Rua dos Engenhos, s/nº, Centro.
City Hospital. Rua José Azevedo Filho, 55. Phone: 3718-6165.
Car rental. Calango Ecoturismo (off road). Rod. MG-0101, km 97. Phone: 9136-8032. E-mail: calangocipo@globo.com.

Support for the visitor
Tourist Bureau. Rua Alfredo Domingos de Melo, 44, Ed. Prefeitura, Centro. Phone/fax: 3718-6104. Guides Association.
Phones: 9971-4467, (31) 3486-6771.
Tour agencies. Calango Ecoturismo. Rod. MG-0101, km 97.
Phone: 9136-8032. E-mail: calangocipo@globo.com. Cipoeiro Expedições. Phone: 9146-5762. Monsyerra. Phone: 9971-4467.

Lodging (in Cardeal Mota)
Camping Véu da Noiva. Young Men Christian Association.
Phones: 3274-2749 and 3799-1177. Internet: www.acm.mg.com.br. 4 chalets (up to 5 persons), minibar, complete kitchen. Hot showers, bar, restaurant, swimming pools, court. 💲💲💲💲 (chalets), 💲 (camping).
Pousada Canto das Águas. MG-010 road, km 95,5. Phone: 9986-1836. Reservation: 3482-5202. 10 rooms, minibar, tv. Swimming pool, sauna, bar, parking lot. 💲💲💲
Pousada Canto Verde. MG-010 towards Serro, km 95. Phone: 3213-2444. Reservation: 9972-5962. 8 rooms, horses, parking lot. 💲💲
Pousada Chão da Serra. MG-010 road, km 99,5. Phone: 9986-1512. Reservation: 3482-5202. 13 chalets (up to 4 people), minibar, tv. Swimming pool, bicycle, volleyball court, parking lot. 💲💲💲
Pousada das Pedras. MG-010 towards Serro, km 100. Phone: 3344-8238. Reservation: 9952-8238. 8 rooms, minibar, tv. Swimming pool, bicycle, horse, volleyball court,

The pau-de-santo flower stands out in the flora

parking lot. 💲💲💲
Pousada Ipê. MG-010 towards Serro, km 95. Phone: 3799-1151. Fax: 3291-4911. Reservation: 3291-4791. 10 rooms, minibar, tel., tv. Swimming pool, sauna, billiard room, court, parking lot. 💲💲💲
Pousada Pedra do Elefante. MG-010 road, km 113, Alto da Serra do Cipó. Phone/fax: 3681-3896. Reservation: 9974-0878. 7 rooms. Natural swimming pool, bar, restaurant. 💲💲💲
Pousada Sempre Viva. MG-010 towards Serro, km 95. Phone: 9946-2375. Reservation: 3681-1327. 6 rooms. kayak, horse, parking lot. 💲💲💲
Pousada Serra Morena. Road to Val da Lagoa, km 5, Fazenda Cornélio, access via MG-010, km 105. Phone: 9977-1421. Reservation: 3486-1421. 6 rooms Bar, Restaurant, waterfall, parking lot. 💲💲💲
Pousada Varandas da Serra. MG-010 towards Serro, km 99,5. Phone: 9986-0305. Fax: 3273-8400. Reservation: 3481-6806. 7 rooms, minibar, tv. Swimming pool, sauna, parking lot. 💲💲💲

Dining
Panela de Pedra. Rod. MG-010, km 97. Phone: 9903-4400. Varied menu. Traditional cooking of Minas Gerais. 💲
Banana Cipó. Rua Vacaria, s/nº, Centro. Phone: 9957-4667. Varied menu. Traditional cooking of Minas Gerais. 💲

Serra dos Órgãos

The area of the Serra do Mar mountain range between the cities of Petrópolis and Teresópolis is known as Órgãos Mountain Range where the predominant rocks are granite and gneiss. High peaks with steep mountainsides stand out in the landscape. Altitudes range from 400 to 2.263 m at Sino Rock.

The mild mountain climate may reach temperatures below 0°C in winter, during the months of June and July, which is also the driest time of year. Four main rivers flow through the Park: Soberbo, Paquequer, Beija-flor and Roncador. At the foot of the mountain range, the Coastal Rain Forest, which in Brazil is called *Mata Atlântica*, takes over the landscape and gives way to the formation of fields as the altitude increases. On the mountain side facing towards Rio de Janeiro, the Coastal Rain Forest also dominates, with perennial broad-leafed plants and a rich fauna. Despite the exuberance, a great part of the Park's vegetation is secondary, i.e. a kind of vegetation which was exploited and/or cut in the past. However, the original forest still exists in parts where access is more difficult. In the Park, it is possible to observe bromeliads and orchids hanging on trees all over. *Jequitibás* - a tree of the Sapucaia-nut tree family - "pierce"

Foundation: November 1939
Area: 118 km²
Petrópolis: 18 km;
Teresópolis: 1 km; Magé: 40 km;
Rio de Janeiro: 91 km
○
⊕ (21)
☎ 2642-1575

the canopy in a scenery of green painted
with beautiful shades by flowers of
Tabebuias - also called Yellow Ipe trees
-, Glorybushes, and *Canelas-santas*.
In the higher parts of the mountain range, realm of the altitude fields, rocky
outcrops do not allow the development
of deep soil. Trees and bushes give way
to creeping vegetation. Only species
adapted to conditions of intense cold,
frost and the formation of ice crust can
survive. During the rainy season -
between December and March -, water
from the rain forms puddles and bogs.
There are riverine forests with small
sized trees, down in the valleys. In the
fields the most common species are
grasses such as the Asparagus Fern,
bromeliads, moss, lichen and orchids.
Above 1.800 m, it is possible to find an
endemic species, the *Cravina-do-
Campo* of the Grass Pink family.
The fauna is richer at the foot of the
mountain, as the forest provides more
shelter for animals as Coatis - a tropical
cousin of the Raccoon -, the Agouti,
Squirrels, Little Anteaters and Howling

Monkeys. The biggest Primate of the
Americas also lives here: the *Muriqui*, an
endangered monkey. There are many bird
species in the Park too: Calospiza
Tanagers and Hummingbirds draw the
visitor's attention because of their colours
and diversity. Some endangered species
are also present in the Park: Hawk-headed
Parrots, Finches of the Oryzoborus genus
and Black-fronted Piping Guans.

HISTORY

In 1817, the German naturalists Von Spix and Von Martius arrived in Rio de Janeiro to explore the regions which were little known in the country. On their trip through Brazil, they crossed the Mar Mountain Range towards the states (then provinces) of Minas Gerais and São Paulo. On the way, they collected species of the flora and fauna and marvelled at the beauty they came across. In the Órgãos Mountain range, Von Spix described the grandness of nature without knowing "what to admire most, the shapes, the colours or the animals' voices". The region has attracted many visitors who become fascinated for some time by its features. In 1830, Dom Pedro I - the Portuguese prince who was raised in Brazil when, fleeing from Napoleon, the court settled down in the country - bought land in the region. Later, he became the emperor of the new country by declaring the independence of Brazil from Portugal. The city of Petrópolis, named after the emperor, harboured his summer palace and to this day has the charming atmosphere that originally attracted the Brazilian royal family. Together with them, the presidents Getúlio Vargas and Juscelino Kubitschek were also charmed by the mountain range and often visited it. It was Getúlio Vargas who signed the decree for the creation of the National Park, the second biggest in the country. Teresópolis, which was also named after the royal family - the last empress was called Dona Teresa Cristina -, is the city which is home to the National Park headquarters. The name of the mountain range, which translates as "organs", is due to the fact that the peaks are named after parts of the human body. The most famous of these peaks, and also a great challenge for climbers, is the Dedo de Deus Peak - 1.692 m -, a needle-like peak whose name means "Finger of God".

Cone-like rock formations reach up to 10 m in height

◄　Muriquis are common (above); it is possible to overlook Teresópolis from the Park

The Serra do Mar mountain chain encircles all the valley

Spix and Martius: naturalists in love with Brazil

An expedition of European scholars of several areas was organized to explore Brazil after the agreement of marriage between D. Pedro de Alcântara - the future emperor of Brazil - and Dona Leopoldina - daughter of the Emperor of Austria Francis I. Five scientists from Austria and one from Italy came over in charge of natural sciences. In April 1817, they departed from Triest and arrived in Rio de Janeiro in July of the same year. The group ended up being split in the trips through the country. Zoologist Von Spix and young botanist Von Martius began to explore the forests of Rio de Janeiro and its outskirts. Spix and Martius were amazed as every step they took they came across new species. The explorers made notes on the fauna, flora, the ethnography and uses of the Brazilian Indians, collecting a rich set of material which to this day is a reference for biologists all over the world. Spix and Martius travelled for almost three years visiting the regions where today the states of São Paulo, Minas Gerais, Bahia, Pernambuco, Piauí, Maranhão, Pará and Amazonas are. Martius drew a map of Brazil, dividing it in five provinces on the basis of the vegetation: Naiades, Oreades, Napaeae, Hamadryades and Dryades. The last province corresponds with the Coastal Rain Forest, where the Serra dos Órgãos National Park is. This is what they wrote about the region: "Solemn, mild, tranquillity hovered in these pleasant sites, which seem to have been created for the enjoyment of the serene and secluded contemplation of nature".

HIGHLIGHTS

Base 4
200 m from the Sino Rock
Phone: 2742-0811
It was renovated with a kitchen and has capacity for 30 people.

🌀 🔆 Andorinhas Waterfall
Ten minutes from the Véu da Noiva Waterfall. The 15-m fall and pool below invite you to take a dip.

🌀 🔆 Véu da Noiva Waterfall
A 35-m high fall, one of Dom Pedro's favorites. You get there via an easy trail of loose pebbles which starts in Petrópolis.

Nossa Senhora da Conceição Chapel
Built in 1713, is a historic monument near the Guapimirim headquarters.

🌀 Cenário Verde Visitors' Centre
Information about the Park, with panels, pictures and models.

Von Martius Visitors' Centre
The centre is in an old farm house and has original works such as paintings and maps collected by the botanist Von Martius.

Dedo de Deus
With 1.692 m in height, it is one of the most coveted peaks for climbing. It requires experience and previous permission by the Park's management. The hike to the foot of the rock is a difficult one.

🔆 Dedo de Nossa Senhora
A hike of moderate difficulty, via a trail in the woods which leads to the foot of the rock. The peak is 1.406 m in height and, with previous permission of the Park's management, may be climbed with an experienced guide.

🔆 Açu Rock
The Açu formation or Açu Castle, on the top of the mountain range, is composed of a sequence of huge rocks of around 10 m in height. The trail starts at the Bonfim Valley, a district of Correas, Petrópolis. It is a hard 7-km hike. After ascending for four hours, you may, if the weather helps, have a beautiful view of Guanabara Bay. Take note of the stone

piles along the trail used to mark the way. The trail can be used as part of the Pedra do Sino-Teresópolis trek, which adds 22 kilometers to the hike and requires a good sense of direction. A guide is essential for the Pedra do Açu–Pedra do Sino trail.

🌀 🔆 Sino Rock
🕐 12 km from the Park's headquarters
🕐 One day
The highest peak in the mountain range, with 2.263 m. The hike starts at the headquarters in Teresópolis, at 1.100 m. The first part is steeper, going through forest via a trail whose pavement dates back to the times of the empire. The two waterfalls along the way are good options for a rest. The ascent becomes more difficult, but the effort is repaid by the views of the Órgãos Mountain Range. The best climbing in Brazil is done here, but it is necessary to obtain permission from the Park's Mountain Activities Sector.

🔆 Preguiça Pool
Another good option for bathing; it is 15 minutes away from the Guapimirim headquarters.

🔆 Verde Pool
Excellent place for a dip; it is 30 minutes on foot from the Guapimirim headquarters.

Beija-flor Trail
The 3-km trail through the forest is full of Hummingbirds (beija-flor) flying through it.

🔆 Primavera Trail
This is an easy trail with informative signs along the way; for people of all ages, it takes 15 minutes to walk. You may go with a guide if you happen to visit the Park on a holiday or weekend.

🔆 🐾 Mozart Catão Trail
It is an easy 40-minute walk to Alexandre Oliveira lookout. From the top you can see Teresópolis. The trail and the lookout are named after two climbers from the city who were killed back in 1998 while trying to climb Mount Aconcagua from the southern side.

SURROUNDINGS

☕ Paraibuna River Rapids
⊖ 40 km from Petrópolis ⏲ Six hours
Information: Aventur
Phone: (24) 255-8125
At the city of Três Rios, there are rapids of levels III and IV, ideal for rafting. The tour is 20 km and includes still and white water areas. You can also try the night rafting, a shorter tour on full moon nights.

☀ Soberbo Lookout
⊖ 1 km from the Park's headquarters
⏲ Thirty minutes
On the BR-116 highway, with a nice view of Guanabara Bay and the National Park and its peaks. From left to right, respectively: Escalavrado, Dedo de Nossa Senhora, Dedo de Deus, Cabeça de Peixe, Santo Antônio and São João.

Petrópolis
⊖ 18 km from the Park ⏲ Two days
The city has a number of attractions, but the Imperial Museum (1834) is something you can not miss: among the pieces on exhibition there are coaches and the emperor's crown and cloak, made out of toucan feathers. The Crystal Palace, the Rio Negro Palace, the Botanic Gardens, which was designed by the architect Oscar Niemeyer and Santos Dumont's house - the Brazilian who invented the first airplane - are other options. The city has good hotels and restaurants, mainly in the region of Itaipava.

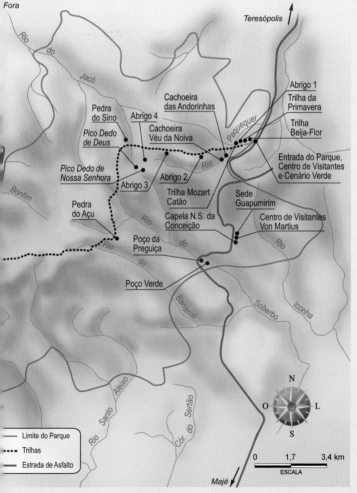

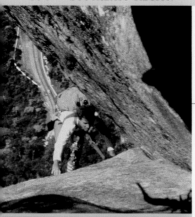

TO VISIT

Access – Open daily except Mondays, from 8 am to 5 pm. Admission Fee: R$ 3,00 (visitors under 10 and over 60 do not pay). The fee for camping is R$ 6,00 per day per person. Parking lot: R$ 5,00 (cars) and R$ 3,00 (motorcycles).

Address – Av. Rotariana s/n°, Alto Teresópolis, Teresópolis, RJ, 25960-602. Phones: (21) 642-1575, 642-2374, 2742-0811 and 9221-9147. Fax: 642-4460. E-mail: parnaso1@terra.com.br.

How to get there – From Rio de Janeiro by car: take BR-116 towards Teresópolis. At Soberbo lookout (roundabout to Teresópolis), take Rotariana Avenue, which leads to the Park's entrance. The access from Petrópolis is via União – Indústria road, in the Correias/Bonfim district.

Infra-structure – Visitors' Centre with information about the Park, historic documents and pictures. Rest-rooms, trails, swimming pool, guided visits on weekends. The Park also has a suspended trail, the mountaineer's house, a wall for climbing, huts used as bases, camping ground and a hall for parties.

TIPS

◗ The dry season is from June to September and best time to visit the Park.
◗ Hire an experienced guide for the Petrópolis–Teresópolis trek. Forks on the pathway, tall grasses and the many ways amongst them tend to puzzle the hiker.
◗ Take care with bathing in the region's rivers, mainly the Soberbo River. Its waters rise fast and there is risk of accidents.
◗ The Dedo de Deus - 1.692 m in height - stands out in the trail that links Petrópolis to Teresópolis.

To know more
SPIX, J.B. von e MARTIUS, C.F.P. von. **Viagem pelo Brasil: 1817-1820 / Spix e Martius.** Belo Horizonte: Itatiaia/Edusp, 1981.

◀ **Dedo de Deus Peak, between Teresópolis and Petrópolis**

SERVICES

Teresópolis, RJ

🌐 21
✉ 25953-000

Useful Addresses

City Hall. Av. Feliciano Sodré, 675, Centro. Phone/fax: 2742-3352.
Bus station. Rua 1° de Maio, 170. Phone: 2742-3352, extension 4036.
Post Office. Av. Lúcio Meira, 259, Centro. Phone/fax: 2742-0258.
Hospital. Rua Judith Maurício de Paula, 40, B. Alto. Phone: 2642-1062.
Banks. ABN/Real, Banerj, do Brasil, Bradesco, Caixa Econômica Federal, HSBC, Itaú, Sudameris, Unibanco.
Car rental. Mespasa. Phones: 2742-0078/2742-6870.

Support for the Visitor

Tourist Bureau. Terminal Turístico Tancredo Neves. Av. Rotariana (Soberbo Roundabout). Phone: 2742-3352, extension 2106.
Tourist Information Service. Pça Olímpica, s/nº. Phone: 2742-3352, r. 4082. Internet: ww.terenet.com.br.
Tour Agencies. Vila Nova. Phone: 2742-5320.

Lodging

Alpina. Av. Pres. Roosevelt, 2500, exit to Petrópolis, km 4. Phone/fax: 2742-5252. E-mail: alpina@terenet.com.br. 68 rooms, air conditioning, minibar, tv, tel. Swimming pool, heated swimming pool, sauna, restaurant, bar, bicycles, billiard room, parking lot, valet service. $$$
Pousada Center. Rua Prefeito Sebastião Teixeira, 245. Phone: 2742-5890. 18 rooms, minibar, tv, tel. Bar, parking lot. $$
Pousada Chamonix. Rua Gonçalo de Castro, 757, B. Alto. Phone: 2642-3230. Fax: 2642-3260. Internet: www.terenet.com.br/~tirol. 22 rooms, 3 chalets, minibar, tv, tel. Heated swimming pool, sauna, bicycles, parking lot. $$$$
Pousada Monte Oliveira. Rua Cecília Meireles, 174, B. Alto. Phone: 2642-6404. 24 rooms, minibar, tv. Bar, parking lot. $$
Pousada Villa Tiroleza. Rua Dona Mariana, 144, B. Bom Retiro. Phone/fax: 2742-7337/2642-3230. Internet: www.terenet.com.br/~tirol. 13 rooms, minibar, fire place, complete kitchen, tv. Swimming pool, sauna, bar, parking lot. $$
Camping Quinta da Barra. Rua Antônio Maria, 100 - exit to Petrópolis, km 3. Phone: 2643-1050. Restrooms, swimming pool, sauna, restaurant, multi-sport court, parking lot. $
Mundo de Mato. Turismo de Aventura and Refúgio de Montanha. Rua Major Carvalho, 55, Várzea. Phone: (21) 2742-0811. E-mail: mundodemato@ig.com.br. $

Dining

Camponesa da Beira. Rua Heitor de Moura Estevão, 22. Phone: 2742-1993. Portuguese cookery. $$
Cremérie Genève. Rod. RJ-130 p/ Nova Friburgo, km 16. Phone: 2644-6250. French cookery. $$
Dona Irene. Rua Tenente Luis Meireles, 1800. Phone: 2742-2901. Russian cookery. $$
Fattoria Di Teresa. RJ-130 road to Nova Friburgo, km 12, B. Vargem Grande. Phone: 2644-6110. Italian cookery. $$
Manjericão. Rua Flávio Bortoluzzi de Sousa, 314. Phone: 2642-4242. Pizza, varied menu. $$
Margô. Rua Heitor de Moura Estevão, 259. Phone: 2643-1175. German cookery, varied menu. $$
Tutu-terê. Pça. dos Namorados, s/nº. Phone: 2642-5020. Minas Gerais cookery, varied menu. $$

Petrópolis

🌐 24
✉ 25620-000

Useful Addresses

City Hall. Av. Koeller, 260, Centro. Phone: 2246-9320. Internet: www.petropolis.rj.gov.br.
Bus station. Rua Dr. Porciúncula, 75, Phone: 2237-0101.
Post Office. Rua do Imperador, 350, Centro. Phone: 2242-1447. Fax: 2242-3200.
Hospital. Av. Portugal, 236, B. Valparaíso. Phone: 2237-6262.
Banks. ABN/Real, Bandeirantes, Banerj, Banespa, do Brasil, BCN, Boavista, Bradesco, Caixa Econômica Federal, HSBC, Itaú, Mercantil/SP, Sudameris, Unibanco.

Tijuca

Tijuca

The Tijuca National Park is part of the Mar Mountain Range, upon mountainous crystalline terrain, which harbours the Tijuca Monolith. The lowest part of the conservation unit is just behind the Botanic Gardens and the highest at the Tijuca Peak (1.021 m). Hot and humid, the climate has favoured the re-forested area, which grew quickly to its present day aspect. The dry season corresponds to the months of July and August. The Park is an important area for the sources of many rivers, which are responsible for a great part of Rio de Janeiro's water supply. Its main rivers are the Trapicheiro, the Comprido, the Carioca, the Cabeça, the Macaco, the Jacaré, the Joana, the Maracanã and the Cachoeira. The lushness of the Coastal Rain Forest, humid, high and dark, dominates the mountainsides, and almost makes us

Foundation: July 1961
Area: 32 km²
Niterói: 20 km; São Paulo: 400 km; Vitória: 520 km

⭕
🌐 (21)
☎ 2492-5407

forget that the area is not a primary forest. Among the species, there are *Angicos* - a tree of the Mimosa family -, Red Quebrachos, Cinnamons, Tabebuias, *Jequitibás*, Brazilwood trees, Glorybushes and *Sapucaias*. In the flowering season, they paint the green of the forest with lively colours. Among the animals there are Coatis - a tropical cousin of the Raccoon -, several species of Capuchin Monkeys, Opossums, Crab-eating Raccoons, Armadillos, Wild Dogs, as well as *Jararaca* Vipers, Coral and Vine Snakes. Among the birds, the most common are Toucans, Aracaris, Wood Rails, Bellbirds with their metallic voices, Hawks, Budgerigars, Calospiza Tanagers, Juriti Doves and Hummingbirds.

HISTORY

Before the Portuguese arrived in Rio de Janeiro, the forests and beaches of the region were already inhabited by Indians spread amongst at least 22 villages around the bay of Guanabara. The city of São Sebastião do Rio de Janeiro was founded in 1565, when thick forests grew upon the mountainsides and amid the rocky outcrops which dominate the landscape.

The Wonderful City was seen by eyes that marvelled at the natural beauty: Charles Darwin, Auguste de Saint-Hilaire, Spix and Martius, J. Batiste Debret, Rugendas, Wied-Neuwied and Jean de Lery, to name a few, were some of the people who wrote about and painted the charms of the natural scenery from the 16th to the 19th centuries. Many of the trails in the Park are historic and all those travellers, as well as the Brazilian imperial family, walked upon them. The occupation of the city, which has dominated the mountains for centuries, caused the cutting a great part of the forest. Coffee, sugar-cane plantations and smaller farms spread throughout the mountains, contributing to the cutting of the native vegetation. Emperor Dom Pedro II decided to re-forest the region in order to avoid losing the sources of the city's water. The Tijuca Forest was seen as an area to be preserved and the emperor nominated an officer in charge of the operation. But after the proclamation of the Republic, the forest was forgotten. Declared as National Patrimony by the Institute of the National Historic and Artistic Patrimony (Iphan) in 1960, the area became a National Park in the following year, with the name of Rio de Janeiro National Park. In 1967, the name was changed to Tijuca National Park, because of confusion caused with

Tarmac eases bikers' ascent

two other national Parks in the state of Rio de Janeiro: Itatiaia and Serra dos Órgãos. In 1999, Ibama - the government bureau for environmental affairs - and the City of Rio de Janeiro Council, set an agreement to joint-manage the Park.

Portuguese tiles map the Park

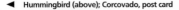

◄ **Hummingbird (above); Corcovado, post card**

The biggest urban forest

Vista Chinesa: one of the lookouts

At the beginning of the 20th century, coffee plantations destroyed the native forests of the Tijuca outcrop. Emperor Dom Pedro II, worried as he was with the city's water supply, decided to protect the area and to foster re-forestation. Since the middle of the 17th century, people knew how important the water sources were for the city. Due to a particularly severe drought back in 1844, there were propositions to expropriate private properties and to re-plant trees in the area. Thus, the Paineiras and the Tijuca Forests were created by Dom Pedro II in 1862. He nominated Major Archer to coordinate the re-forestation, who worked with only six slaves at the beginning of the works. Later, his team was increased to 22 workers, who planted 100.000 seedlings of native trees in 13 years. Between 1874 and 1887, more 30.000 seedlings were used to recompose the forest. The huge work was conceived by the emperor at a time when care for nature was not a much considered subject. The re-forestation with many plant species was the first in Latin America.

HIGHLIGHTS

The Tijuca National Park has three distinctive sectors with around 150 trails and 130 historic and archaeologic sites within them: the Tijuca Forest, the Gávea Rock – Bonita Rock area and the Carioca Mountain Range (Corcovado, Paineiras and Trapicheiro). The Lage Park should soon be attached to the Park.

Caveira

The site is where the Caveiras farm used to be; the farm was one of the first to be expropriated by the empire in order to create the Tijuca Forest. Today, there are only ruins of the construction, which was inhabited until the 1970's.

Andaraí Maior

The mountain, whose sides was once covered with coffee plantations, was re-forested at the same time as the Tijuca Forest. The peak is 861 m high. There are legends about treasures hidden in secret places.

Barracão

The big hut, as the name has it, is at 474 m in altitude; the old building harbours historic pieces collected by researchers, from the coffee boom era.

🍂 Bico do Papagaio
🕙 Five hours

There are two trails which lead to the 989-m-high peak. Both start from Largo do Bom Retiro and fork on the way. Both are difficult, taking between 1 hour and 30 minutes to 2 hours. The longest goes through the Serrilha way, although you can ascend by one and descend by the other, seeing the city from the top.

Bom Retiro

The largo do Bom Retiro is in the Tijuca Forest zone, at the end of the Park's paved road. Here is the place where many trails which cut the forest start from.

Mayrink Chapel

The chapel in the Tijuca Forest was built in the 19th century and has just been renovated. The belfry is new, as well as the panels painted by the famous modernist painter Cândido Portinari. Mass is celebrated on the last Sunday of each month, at 12 o'clock.

Taunay Cascade

Just after the Floresta gate, it was named after the French painter Nicolau Taunay, who had a property in front of the cascade.

Corcovado

Rua Cosme Velho, 513. Admission fee: R$ 20. Phone: 558.1329. Open daily from 8 am to 6:30 pm.

At 704 m in altitude, it harbours one of Rio de Janeiro's main symbols, the statue of Christ the Redeemer. Dom Pedro I, who first climbed the rock around 1824, ordered it to be one of the first trails blazed. Around 150.000 people visit the Corcovado every year. To get there, you can take the train, go by car or walk the trail which starts at Lage Park - a difficult 1:45-hour hike.

Manacás Garden

The favorite place of Empress Leopoldina; it is said that she used to have tea here with the ladies-in-waiting, back in the 19th century. Besides the garden, surrounded by Manaca Raintrees,

another attraction is the Wallace fountain, made in 1872 of cast iron, in France.

Emperor's Table

One of Dom Pedro's favorite places for his luncheons outside the palace, with a nice view of the Atlantic Rain Forest. It is also on the Vista Chinesa road.

Andaime Pequeno Lookout

On the top of the mountain range, it has a nice view of the Rodrigo de Freitas Lake.

Bela Vista Lookout

Unlike the other lookouts, this one does not face the ocean

but the back part of the Carioca Mountain Range.

Excelsior Lookout

Excelsior is also the name of the road, a tribute to the mountaineer and poet Longfellow.

Dona Marta Lookout

It was named after the mother of Rio's General Vicar and former owner of the Quinta São Clemente, today known as Botafogo. The lookout is at 364 m and has a nice view of the city. It is on Paineiras road.

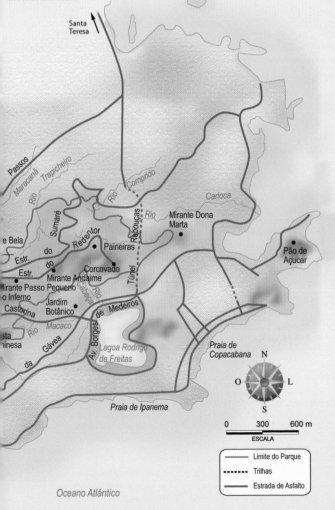

Satellite picture shows in green the vegetation in Rio de Janeiro, most of it within the Park

☀ Passo do Inferno Lookout
Near the Andaime Pequeno Lookout, it has a nice view of the forest with the ocean in the background.

Paineiras
Paineiras Road, between the Hotel Paineiras and the Sumaré/Paineiras fork. Access for vehicles is not permitted on weekends, holidays and at night. Besides being a nice area for hikes, climbing practice and bicycle riding, there is a beautiful view of Rodrigo de Freitas Lake with the sea in the background. The Paineiras circuit is 4,6 km long and has informative signs about exercises along the way.

Bonita Rock
The trail which leads to the top of the 696-m rock is well marked. It is possible to practice mountain climbing and has a hang-gliding ramp. The access is via Canoas road.

Gávea Rock
With its 842 m, it has been a landmark for sailors since the 16th century. There are three different trails through the Coastal Rain Forest and a nice view of Rio from the top.

Tijuca Peak
With its height of 1.201 m, it is the highest peak in the Park. To reach the top you have to walk for 1 hour and 30 minutes from the Largo do Bom Retiro. You will enjoy a nice view from the

trail, used since the 19th century. Take a look at the stairway, built in 1928 when the King of Belgium visited the city.

Ciganos Dam
The old water reservoir still supplies water for the district of Jacarepaguá.

Tijuca Mirim
It is neighbour to Tijuca Peak and can be reached from it. It is 917 m in height.

☀ Grutas do Morro Archer Trails
It goes past natural cavities in the rock, including the Paulo and Virgínia Sucuri, Bernardo de Oliveira, Solitária, Morcego, Eleuthério, Belmiro, Perdida and Luís Fernandes grottos. The first two are easier and advised for beginners.

A mire or a way to the sea?

The name Tijuca is Tupi, a language used by the Indian nation of the same name, but the origin of the name changes according to the author. Some of them assure that it means mire or marsh, thus the origin of the name is the mire where today the district of Jacarepaguá is and the marsh ended by naming a beach, a city's district and the mountain range behind it. However, others state that the word means "way which leads to the sea".

Vista Chinesa

A homage to the Chinese, who introduced the cultivation of tea to the country at the beginning of the 19th century. The building, of an eastern style, was build in the 1930's and is on the road of the same name.

◑ Vista do Almirante

One of the lookouts on the Floresta da Tijuca road, with nice views of the city's southern part.

SURROUNDINGS

Botanic Gardens
⊕ Four hours

The more than 7.000 plant species of the Botanic Garden make it one of the most important in the world. It was created at the beginning of the 19th century by Dom João VI, the king who fled with his court from Portugal to Brazil when Napoleon's troops invaded the country. At the beginning it was a garden to aclimatize spice plants from the East, then it became a Royal Garden and received species from all over the world. Take a look at the huge Imperial Palms.

⑩ Açude Museum
⊕ Two hours

On the Açude road, it used to be Castro Maya's house, the man who managed the Tijuca Forest back in the 1940's. Very fond of the forest and of Rio, he renovated many trails and historic buildings in the Park. The museum is decorated with Portuguese and Dutch tiles and also has a nice collection of furniture and sculptures.

Lage Park
⊕ Three hours

Between the Park and the Lake, it was property of the family of Rodrigo de Freitas for more than 200 years. It has well tended gardens and woods, apart from the Visual Arts College at the old Henrique Lage manor. The area has been preserved since 1965 and became a Park in 1976.

Sugar Loaf and Urca Hill
⊕ Two hours (Sugar Loaf) and 40 minutes (trail to Urca). Cable car: Ticket R$20. Children between 6 and 12 pay half the fee. Open from 8 am to 10 pm

The bay of Guanabara is another post card of the city. The hike to Urca hill is not a difficult one and some parts of it go through the forest.

Cidade Park
⊕ Three to five hours

Also called Gávea Park, it was the property of many people and had its name changed many times. In 1933, it became property of the Federal Government and was transformed into a public area. The old farm headquarters became the City Museum, with around 20.000 pieces, including drawings by Debret and the throne of Dom João VI. There are some trails which cut through the Park, one of which leads to the Horto Florestal.

TO VISIT

Access – Open daily from 8 am to 6 pm.
Address – Rua Major Rubens Vaz, 122, Gávea, Rio de Janeiro, RJ, 22470-070. Phones: (21) 2492-2253 and 2492-5002.
How to get there – The Park has three distinctive sectors spread through the city. Its main gates are: Cascatinha and Açude da Solidão (Tijuca Forest); Canoas, Seridó, Sorimã roads and ways which lead to Barra da Tijuca and Furnas road (Gávea Rock – Bonita Rock); Macacos gate – Dona Castorina, Passo das Pedras roads – Vista Chinesa, Sapucaias roads – Cristo Redentor; Caboclas roads – Almirante Alexandrino and Sumaré streets – Sumaré road (Cariocas Mountain Range).
Infra-structure – Visitors Centre with auditorium, library, exhibition room and information about the Park, hang-gliding ramp, picnic areas, paved trails, bicycle path, 61 km of trails with informative signs, wall for climbing practice and gym gear (Paineiras), train tour (Corcovado), helipad (Dona Marta lookout), parking lots, restaurants, shops, snack bars and coffee shop.

TIPS

❍ If you want to hike in the Park and explore nice views, hire a guide at Projeto Guia Legal.
❍ For hang-gliding off Bonita Rock, talk to Super Fly – (21) 3322-2286 and 9982-5703 –, or Rio Tandem Flight – (21) 2422-6371 and 2493-4324.
❍ Waterfall and bathing in the river are not permitted within the Park. The only exceptions are in the area Paineiras, Bacia dos Macacos and the Primatas waterfall.

To know more

BANDEIRA, C.M. **Parque Nacional da Tijuca.** São Paulo: Makron Books, 1993.
MACHADO, J. de P. **Parque Nacional da Tijuca.** Rio de Janeiro: Agir, 1992.
MENEZES, P. da C. **Trilhas do Rio.** Rio de Janeiro: Salamandra, 1996.
SAINT-HILAIRE, A. **Viagem pelas províncias do Rio de Janeiro e Minas Gerais.** Brasília: Brasiliana, 1938.
SPIX, J.B. Von e MARTIUS, C.F.P. Von. **Viagem pelo Brasil: 1817-1820** / Spix e Martius. Belo Horizonte: Itatiaia/Edusp, 1981.
www.sapnt.org.br
www.terrabrasil.org.br
www.rio.rj.gov.br/smac/

SERVICES

Rio de Janeiro

🌐 21
✉ 20000-00 to 23799-999

Useful Addresses

City Hall. Rua Afonso Cavalcanti, 455, Centro, Phone: 2503-3000. Internet: www.rio.gov.br.
Bus station. Rua Barão de São Félix, 165. Phone: 2233-7819. Mariano Procópio bus station. Praça Mauá, 5. Menezes Cortes bus station. Rua São José, 35. Novo Rio bus station. Av. Francisco Bicalho, 1. Phone: 2291-5151. Subway. Information. Phone: 2483-5357.
Airport. Rio de Janeiro International Airport (Galeão/Tom Jobim). Av. 20 de Janeiro, s/nº, Ilha do Governador, RJ. Phone: 3398-5050. Santos Dumont Airport. Praça Senador Salgado Filho, s/nº. Phone: 3841-7070.
Port/Wharf. Administração Marítima/ Capitania dos Portos (sea passengers' station). Rua Alfred Agache, s/nº, Pça. XV de Novembro. Phone: 3870-5320.
Hospital. State Hospital Getúlio Vargas. Av. Lobo Júnior, 2293, Penha. Phone: 2290-2121. City Hospital Sousa Aguiar. Praça. da República, 111, Centro. Phone: 2296-4114 (general), 2221-2121 (Ambulatory). Santa Casa. Rua Santa Luzia, 206, Centro. Phone: 2297-6611.

Support for the Visitor

Tourist Bureau. Rua da Assembléia, 10, 9° floor. Phone: 2217-7575. Fax: 2531-1872. Email: riotur@pcrj.riotur.com.br.
Tourist Information Service. Riotur. Rio de Janeiro International Airport. Phone: 3398-2246. Centro. Av. Princesa Isabel, 183. Phone: 2542-8080. Novo Rio bus station. Rua Equador, s/nº, exit ward. Phone: 2291-5151, r. 197.

Lodging

Albergue da Juventude do Rio de Janeiro (Youths Hostel). Rua Gal. Dionísio, 63, Botafogo. Phone: 2286-0303. Fax: 2286-5652. 60 beds (up to 6 people per room), sheets and blankets, breakfast. Reading room, tv room, bar. $
Praia Linda. Av. do Pepê, 1430, Praia da Barra da Tijuca. Phone: 2494-2186. Fax: 2494-2198. 60 rooms, air conditioning, minibar, safe, tv, tel. Restaurant, parking lot. $$$$
Rio Internacional. Av. Atlântica, 1500, Praia de Copacabana. Phone: 2546-8000. Fax: 2542-5443. Reservation: 0800 211-559. 117 rooms, air conditioning, minibar, safe, tv, tel. Swimming pool, sauna, bar, restaurant, gym, business center, valet park, paid parking lot, panoramic view. $$$$
Scorial Rio. Rua 2 de Dezembro, 135, Catete. Phone: 2556-9119. Fax: 2285-5080. Internet: www.scorialriohotel.com.br. 57 rooms, air conditioning, minibar, safe, tv, tel. Sauna, bar, restaurant, parking lot. $$$$
Sol Ipanema. Av. Vieira Souto, 320, Praia de Ipanema. Phone: 2525-2020. Fax: 2247-8484. Reservation: 0800 110-098. Internet: www.solipanema.com.br. 90 rooms, air conditioning, minibar, safe, tv, tel. Swimming pool, bar, restaurant. $$$$

Dining

Floresta. Estrada do Bom Retiro, s/nº, Floresta da Tijuca. Phone: 2492-5358. Varied menu, feijoada on Saturdays. $$
Gattopardo. Av. Borges de Medeiros, 1426, Lagoa Rodrigo Freitas. Phone: 2219-3133. Pizza. $$
Mostarda. Av. Epitácio Pessoa, 990, Lagoa Rodrigo Freitas. Phone: 2522-1999. Varied menu, vegetarian, salads. $$
Mosteiro. Rua São Bento, 13/15, Centro. Phone: 2233-6478. Portuguese cooking. $$
Natraj. Av. Gal. San Martin, 1219, Leblon. Phone: 2239-4745. Indian cooking. $$$
Pato com Laranja. Rua do Ouvidor, 16, Centro. Phone: 2221-8905. Varied menu. $$
Porcão. Rua Barão da Torre, 218, Ipanema. Phone: 2522-0999. Meat. $$
Quadrifoglio. Rua. J.J. Seabra, 19, Jardim Botânico. Phone: 2294-1433. Italian cooking. $$$
Sushi Leblon. Rua Dias Ferreira, 256, Leblon. Phone: 2274-1342. Japanese cooking. $$$
Typhoon. Av. Armando Lombardi, 800, shop C/D, Barra da Tijuca. Phone: 2493-5970. Thai cooking. $$$
Umas & Ostras. Rua Barão de Mesquita, 235, Tijuca. Phone: 2568-7128. Sea food. $$$

CENTRE WEST

CENTRE WEST REGION

The Centre-West Region has the Chapada dos Veadeiros and the Chapada dos Guimarães. Both Parks are visited by ecotourists, specially by those who are fond of hiking in the *Cerrado*, with chances to go for many dips. The topography of the Chapada dos Veadeiros - located in the Planalto Central, in the state of Goiás - is formed by a huge block of quartz crystal and its rough shape favours the formation of waterfalls, such as the Salto do Rio Preto, 120 m in height. The Chapada dos Guimarães, in the state of Mato Grosso, stands out for the beauty of the sandstone cliffs and the waterfalls. One of its most famous waterfalls is the Véu da Noiva, 75 m in height. The Brasília National Park is one of the main leisure areas of the city. The Cerrado and its landscape variations predominate in the Park, which is cut through streams that form pools, ideal for a bath. The Emas Park, in the state of Goiás, preserves a big area of Cerrado and it is famous for its more than 2,5 million termite mounds that exist in the Park. The two Parks that are not yet open for visitation in the Centre-West Region are in the states of Mato Grosso and Mato Grosso do Sul, respectively. The Pantanal Park preserves areas of the Pantaneira Plain that are likely to be flooded. The Serra da Bodoquena Park, founded in 2000, harbours areas of the Cerrado, Pantanal and Atlantic Forest ecosystems. In the Park lie the sources of the crystal clear rivers which form aquariums of colourful fish in the region of Bonito.

AMAZONAS

Panelas

Aripuanã

RONDÔNIA

BR 174

Cáce

BOLÍV

Sunset at Pantanal in Mato Grosso state

Formoso River, in the Emas National Park

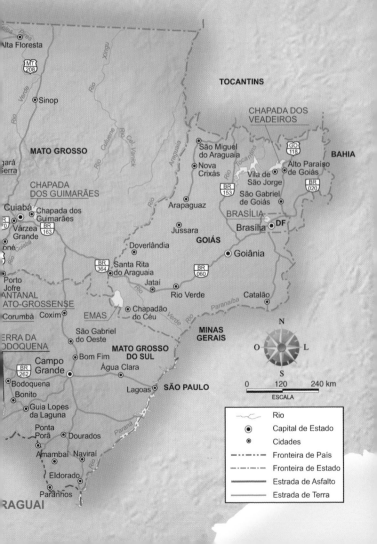

AMAZONAS

TOCANTINS

CHAPADA DOS VEADEIROS

MATO GROSSO

BAHIA

Alta Floresta

Sinop

São Miguel do Araguaia

Nova Crixás

Vila de São Jorge

Alto Paraíso de Goiás

São Gabriel de Goiás

CHAPADA DOS GUIMARÃES

Chapada dos Guimarães

Arapaguaz

BRASÍLIA

Brasília ⊙ **DF**

Cuiabá

Várzea Grande

Jussara

GOIÁS

Doverlândia

Goiânia

Santa Rita do Araguaia

Jataí

Rio Verde

Catalão

Porto Jofre

PANTANAL MATO-GROSSENSE

Corumbá Coxim

EMAS

Chapadão do Céu

MINAS GERAIS

SERRA DA BODOQUENA

São Gabriel do Oeste

MATO GROSSO DO SUL

Bom Fim

Água Clara

Campo Grande

Bodoquena

Bonito

Lagoas ⊙ **SÃO PAULO**

Guia Lopes da Laguna

Ponta Porã

Dourados

Amambaí Naviraí

Eldorado

Paranhos

PARAGUAI

N
O — L
S

0   120   240 km
ESCALA

～	Rio
⊙	Capital de Estado
⊙	Cidades
-------	Fronteira de País
--·--·-	Fronteira de Estado
——	Estrada de Asfalto
——	Estrada de Terra

Brasília

Foundation: November 1961
Area: 300 km²
Brasília: 10 km; Goiânia: 205 km;
Belo Horizonte: 714 km.

○
⊕ (61)
☎ 465-2013

The Brasília National Park altitude is around 1.000 m and there are three main geographical occurrences: the Contagem Plateau, the Paranoá Depression and the Contagem Mountainside. The climate can be described as cold and dry in the winter - very dry, mainly between June and September - and hot and humid in summer - mainly from November to March. All the streams that flow through the Park have their source in the Park's area and contribute to the formation of the three main Brazilian Basins: Paraná, Tocantins and São Francisco. The region is extremely important for the city of Brasília because its sources supply the Santa Maria dam, which contains 20% of the water used by the city. The *Cerrado* and its wide range of landscapes compose the scenery: grasslands - locally called *campos limpos* - take over the Park; in the *Campos Sujos* and *Cerrados* more bushes and trees gradually appear. Here the Wolf tree, the *Canela-de-Ema*, the Yellow and Pink Ipe Trees, the Souari Nut Tree, the *Murici* (a tree of the genus Byrsonima), the Barbatimao Alumbark Tree and the *Pau-Terra* are common. The vegetation is composed of mature riverine forest, Moist Fields, Tussock fields and Buriti Palms, where palms arranged in semicircles adorn the banks of the water courses. In the woods around the pools, Curassows and Capuchin Monkeys are so common that they have become a pest, for they knock down garbage bins looking for leftovers.

Wild Dogs, Crested Seriemas, Caracaras (hawks), Jays and Armadillos can be seen with a bit of luck. The number of bird species is over 300. Among them the *Soldadinho* - endemic in the *Cerrado* - stands out. As the Park is located in an urban area, it has problems such as hunting, fishing, fruit gathering, the capture of animals and fires which spread from neighbouring farms. Animals which were introduced in the region also compete with the native species. Packs of stray dogs, for instance, roam in the area killing the local fauna. In order to solve these problems, projects for the handling of these species have been created in the Park.

HISTORY

Around 10.000 years ago, primitive peoples in the dry *Cerrado* - woods composed of stunted, twisted trees - used favorable areas near the water courses for living. Indians, who planted in the fertile grounds of forest areas, came after them. They were followed by small farmers who used a farming system called *roça* inherited from the indians: deforestation of the area, sowing and, later, abandoning of the land in order to look for another area for the next *roça*. For this reason, it is believed that the Park's forests are all secondary, recovered after 250 years of woods clearance for the planting of traditional *roças*.

The Poço Azul at APA Cafuringa is formed by quartz rocks

◀   Pampas flicker in the nest (above); Old Pool, leisure structure of the Park

During the Gold Cycle - from 1750 to 1760 - the gold prospected in Goiás and Mato Grosso was taken to the ports via the Estrada Real (Royal Road), which according to the description of the Count of Lumiares, governor of the Capitânias das Minas de Goiás went across the Park near the Santa Maria dam. Those Capitânias, in colonial Brazil, were a jurisdictional division corresponding to a province.

In 1858, Pedro José de Alcântara - an emperor's namesake - claimed to be the owner of the Torto and Bananal farms, whose area corresponded to 80% of the Park's area and all the Pilot Plan. After him, the land was divided and several smaller proprietaries came to live in the region. In the 19th century, a expedition to explore the region - led by Luiz Cruls, a Belgian director of the National Observatory - went to the region in order to stake out the future Federal District. In 1961 the Park was founded: an attempt to compensate and to try to stop the devastation caused by the construction of Brasília. The Piscina Velha area, for instance, was used to extract quartzite blocks. Pebbles and sand were also extracted in large amounts from the conservation unit. Today the Água Mineral - the name that the people from Brasília use to refer to the Park - is one of the main leisure areas of the city.

HIGHLIGHTS

🔵 Visitors' Centre

There is a nice model of the Park, a museum with native fauna and flora exhibition, an auditorium and rest rooms. Environment education courses organized by the Park's staff association are held here.

⚫ Meditação Island

One can reach the island via a 150-m-trail which starts at the Visitors' Centre. It is a good place to relax for there is no noise from the city, only the singing of birds which live there. Tapirs sometimes also go to the island.

🔵 🟢 Pool 1

Also known as Piscina Velha (Old Pool), has transparent mineral water flowing through it. Cold in winter, it is a good option to cool down in Brasília's summer heat. Look for the Capuchin Monkeys, but take care as they are used to "fighting" for food. There are bars, rest rooms and kiosks for picnics. It closes on Mondays for cleaning.

🔵 🟢 Pool 2

The Piscina Nova (New Pool), also with flowing transparent water, is bigger than the Old Pool but with less vegetation on its banks which is good for those who want to go sun bathing. It has good facilities such as snack bars, rest rooms and kiosks for picnics. It closes on Tuesdays and Wednesdays for cleaning.

🟢 Cristal Água Trail

It is 5 km long, with a circular shape: at the first fork in the trail there is the Rego Stream riverine forest and at the second, near the eucalyptus, you should take the way to the right. It is a dirt road which goes across a part of the *Cerrado*. In the middle of the trail there is a good place for bathing in the Rego stream. In the riverine forest it is possible to see Holt's Yellow Finches and other Finches of the genus Oryzoborus, Tyrant-Flycatchers, Great Kiskadees and, with a bit luck, Tamarins jumping from one tree branch to another or a pack of *Catetos* (a kind of Brazilian wild pigs). In the *Cerrado*, look for Crested Seriemas and Wild Dogs. On the floor, small quartz crystal appear on the surface.

🟢 Capivara Trail

It is a 1,3-km-fenced trail which goes through a riverine forest area and a small stretch of *Cerrado*. Look for song birds and for iguanas in the *Cerrado*. It takes 20 minutes to walk the trail and it is much used by people who go jogging.

SURROUNDINGS

Buraco das Araras

⊖ 126 km from Brasília
🕐 Three to four hours

In the city of Formosa, the hole is a large calcareous formation where the underground terrain crumbled (50 m in diameter and 40 m in depth). At the bottom there is a forest with huge ferns and two caves.

Corumbá de Goiás

⊖ 119 km 🕐 One to two days. Access is by BR-070

The region at the base of the Pireneus Mountain Range has waterfalls and river beaches. The Corumbá falls - with drops of up to 80 m - are on the road to Cocalzinho de Goiás (BR-414). The main attraction of the region is the Ecos Cave, which is 1.5 km long in Girassol city. The visit to the cave takes around 5 hours.

Crested seriema: adapted to the *Cerrado*

Mumunhas and Poço Azul
⊖ 40 km from the Plano Piloto
🕑 Two hours

The Poço Azul is formed by quartz rock and is inside the Cafuringa Environment Protection Area. A 3-km walk leads to the Mumunhas waterfall, with pools where one can go swimming. There are nine caves and pits in the area.

Riacho Fundo Wild Life Sanctuary
⊖ 10 km from Plano Piloto 🕑 Two hours

It is next to the zoo and it has almost untouched woods, with clear water streams where several animal and plant species exist. It is run by Funatura, an environmental non-government organization.

Itiquira Fall
⊖ 124 km 🕑 Half a day
Price: R$ 5,00 Access by GO-040, 34 km from Formosa 🎏 🚻

Besides the 180-m falls on the Paraná River, you can also visit the Grande and Tranqüilidade wells, the Túnel waterfall, the Lourdes cascade and the Felicidade fall. The facilities are good and include a restaurant, paved trails, drinking fountains and rest rooms. A few kilometers down the falls there is a club with chalets, swimming pools, sauna and a camping area under the trees.

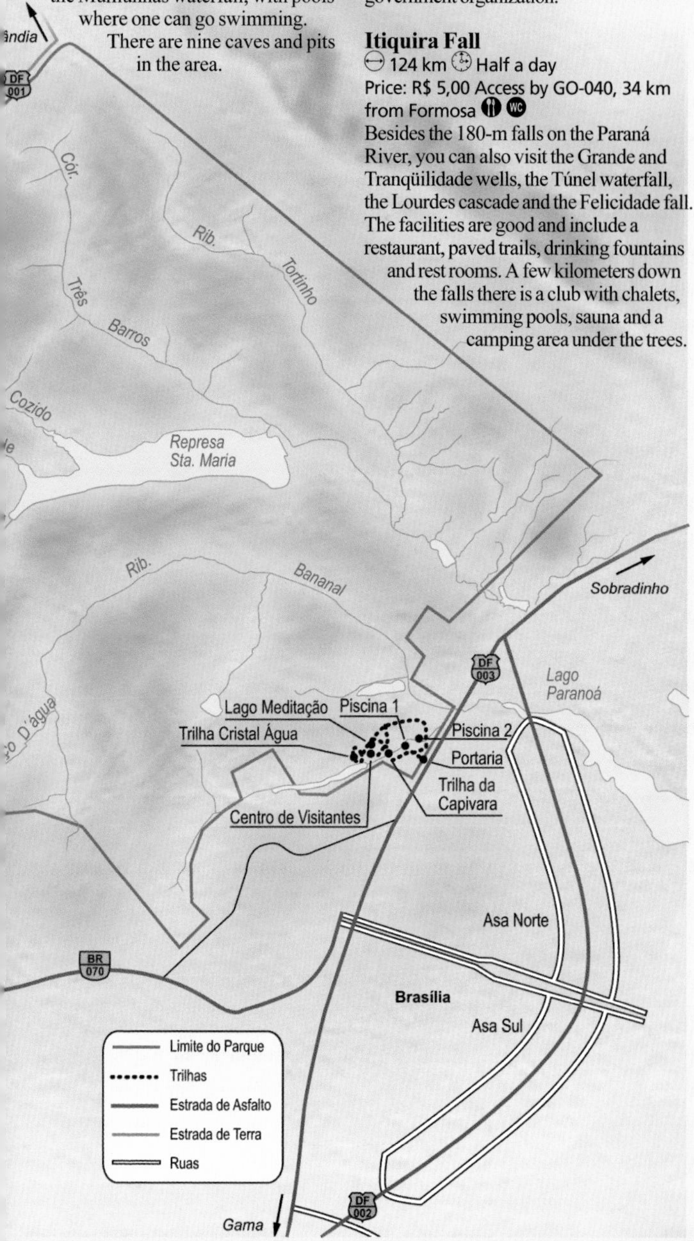

Map labels:
- andia
- DF 001
- Cór.
- Rib.
- Três
- Barros
- Tortinho
- Cozido
- Represa Sta. Maria
- Rib.
- Bananal
- ro D'água
- Sobradinho
- DF 003
- Lago Paranoá
- Lago Meditação
- Piscina 1
- Trilha Cristal Água
- Piscina 2
- Portaria
- Trilha da Capivara
- Centro de Visitantes
- Asa Norte
- BR 070
- Brasília
- Asa Sul
- DF 002
- Gama

Legend:
- Limite do Parque
- Trilhas
- Estrada de Asfalto
- Estrada de Terra
- Ruas

TO VISIT

Access – Open daily from 8 am to 4 pm. Price: R$ 3,00.

Address – BR-040 SMU, Brasília, DF, 70700-000. Phones/fax: (61) 465-2013, 465-2016 and 465-2085.

How to get there – If you are going from Brasília, take the Estrada Parque Indústria e Abastecimento (Epia) from the Asa Norte or from the west zone of the Plano Piloto. There are regular flights and daily coaches from all capitals of the country to Brasília.

Infra-structure - Rest rooms, dressing rooms, snack bars, kiosks for picnics, natural swimming pools, parking lot and visitor's centre. On weekends, volunteers engage in the task of environmental education and awareness for visitors.

TIPS

⊙ When planning your trip to Brasília, choose the months from October to May, when the weather is not so dry and the relative humidity of the air is still reasonable. Do not fail to visit the attractions near the city, specially the Salto Itiquira.

⊙ Do not leave your rubbish in the Park, even in a plastic bag, mainly in the area of the Piscina Velha. The Capuchin Monkeys have learned how to open the bags and, besides eating people's food, they spread the garbage throughout the place.

To know more
ANTAS, P.T.Z. e CAVALCANTI, R.B. **Aves comuns do Planalto Central.** Brasília: Editora UnB, 1988.
FROTA, L.C. **Frutas nativas do Cerrado.** Brasília: Embrapa, Centro de Pesquisa Agropecuária dos Cerrados, 1994.
www.mre.gov.br/ndsg/textos/turbra_p.htm

SERVICES

Brasília, DF
🌐 61
✉ 70000-000

Useful Addresses
City Hall. Setor Comercial Norte, quadra 4, bloco C. Phone: 327-5000.
Bus station. Plano Piloto. Plataforma Térreo Norte, room 25. Phone: 327-4631
Bus and railroad station. Phone: 363-2281.
International Airport. Presidente Juscelino Kubitschek. Phones: 365-1224, 364-9041, 364-9036.
Telephone Station. Telebrasília. Super Quadra Sul, on the corner of quadras. 407/8. Phone: 443-1587.
Post Office. Phone: 327-8868.
Hospital. SMHS, quadra 1, bloco A. Phone: 325-5050.
Banks. Bradesco, Unibanco, Itaú, do Brasil.
Car Rental. Avis. Phones: 365-2782/2344; First. Phone: 345-8212; Hertz. Phone: 0800-147-300; Localiza. Phone: 0800-312-121; Unidas. Phone: 0800 121-121; Via DF. Phone: 322-3181.
Tour Agencies. Buriti Turismo. Comércio Local Sul, 402, bloco B, lj. 33. Phone: 225-2686; Casablanca Turismo. SEPS 705/905, building B, room 117. Phone: 244-1026; Fenatur. Setor Comercial Sul, quadra 3, Planalto building, bloco B, shop 50. Phone: 321-4830; Formtur. Comércio Local Norte, 403, bloco E, shop. 51. Phone: 226-5117; Janot Turismo. Setor Comercial Norte, quadra 1, bloco E, Central Park building, shop 70. Phone: 327-2020; MS Turismo. EQS 102/103, bloco A, shops 4-22. Phone: 224-7818.

Support for the Visitor
Serviço de Informações Turísticas (Tourist Information Service). SDC, Centro de Convenções Ulisses Guimarães, 1st floor, Ala Sul. Phone: 325-5730.

Lodging
Bittar Plaza. Setor Hoteleiro Norte, quadra 2, bloco M. Phone/fax: 328-7077. Internet: www.hoteisbittar.com.br. 88 rooms, tv, air conditioning, minibar. Restaurant. $$$$
Bristol. Setor Hoteleiro Sul, quadra 4, bloco F. Phone: 321-2690. 141 rooms, tv, air conditioning, minibar. Swimming pool, restaurant, bar, gym. $$$$
Casablanca. Setor Hoteleiro Norte, quadra 3, bloco A. Phone: 328-8586. 58 rooms, tv, air conditioning, minibar, tel., restaurant. $$$$
Continental. Setor Hoteleiro Norte, quadra 3, bloco J. Phone: 225-7071. 35 rooms, tv, air conditioning, minibar. Restaurant. $$$$
Diplomata. Setor Hoteleiro Norte, quadra 2, bloco L. Phone: 328-8675. 44 rooms, tv, air conditioning, minibar, tel. $$$
Hotel das Américas. Setor Hoteleiro Sul, quadra 4, bloco D. Phone: 321-3355. Fax: 321-1972. Internet: www.hoteldasamericas.com. 149 rooms, tv, air conditioning, minibar. Restaurant, bar. $$$$
Hotel das Nações. Setor Hoteleiro Sul, quadra 4, bloco I. Phone: 322-8050. Fax: 225-7722. Internet: www.hoteldasnacoes.com.br. 120 rooms, tv, air conditioning, minibar. $$$$
San Park. Setor de Armazenamento e Abastecimento Norte, quadra 3, bloco D, km 8. Phone: 361-0077. Fax: 361-0088. 56 rooms, tv, air conditioning, minibar. Restaurant, bar. $$$
St. Paul. Setor Hoteleiro Sul, quadra 2, bloco B. Phone: 317-8400. 243 rooms, TV, air conditioning, minibar, tel. Restaurant, conference room, beauty parlor, sauna, swimming pool, convenience shop. $$$$

Dining
A Capitu. Comércio Local Sul, quadra 403, bloco D, lote 20. Phone: 223-0080. Varied menu. $$
Alice. Setor de Habitações Individuais Norte, quadra 11, cj. 9, casa 17, Lago Norte. Phones: 368-1099 and 577-4333. From Tuesday to Saturday, dinner only. It is necessary to make a reservation. Varied menu. $$$
Le Bateau Ivre. Setor de Habitações Individuais Sul, QI 23, cj. 8, casa 20. Phone: 366-3153. French. $$$
Le Bistrô. Setor de Clubes Esportivos Sul, trecho 4, cj. 5, lote 1-B. Phone: 316-6358. French. $$$
Trem da Serra. Second roundabout to the Núcleo Rural Sobradinho II, follow ads until the dirt road which leads to the restaurant. Phone: 387-0304. Typical food from the state of Minas Gerais. $$$

Chapada dos Guimarães

The Chapada dos Guimarães is on one of the most ancient tectonic faults, dated at around 500 million years old. It was covered in ice during one of the great glaciations and 200 million years later it became sea floor.

When the mountains that comprise the Andes appeared, the region of the Pantanal sank and the plateau rose. Today, the landscape is marked by orange-reddish sandstone cliffs, with canyons and caves. Dinosaur bones and fossilized shells have been found in the archaeologic sites of this region.

The erosion provoked by water and wind during millions of years carved grottos and natural sculptures; and streams dig out the cliff rims and become huge waterfalls, thus creating the *Chapada*'s scenery. The Park protects the source of some of these rivers, such as the Aricazinho, the Coxipó and the Mutuca, all tributaries of the Cuiabá and Pantanal Rivers. Because the plateau is 800 m in height, the altitude helps to make the temperature mild. In the lower neighbouring areas the temperature may reach up to 45°C. The rainy season is from October to April and the dry season

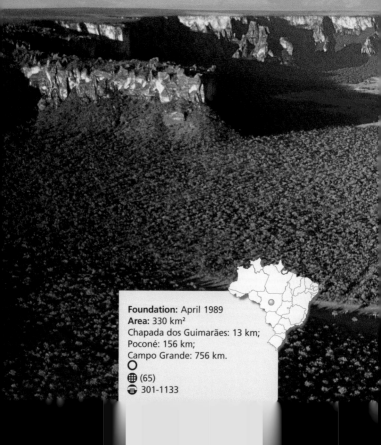

Foundation: April 1989
Area: 330 km²
Chapada dos Guimarães: 13 km;
Poconé: 156 km;
Campo Grande: 756 km.

○
⊕ (65)
☎ 301-1133

from September to May, when the Ipe tree dyes the *Cerrado* landscape yellow. The scenery ranges from the *Campo Limpo* (open grassland) - where grasses dominate - to the *Cerradão*, where bigger trees are commonly found. This range changes according to the amount of trees in the fields; it includes the *Campo Sujo* (grasslands with some small trees), the *Campo Cerrado (*grasslands with medium sized, twisted trees*)* and the *Cerrado (*grasslands with herbs, shrubs and twisted trees with corky bark*).* The vegetation is also composed of dry woodlands and humid areas. Among the tree species, the most common are the Sweet wood, the Souari Nut tree, the Barbatimao, the *Pau-santo*, the Alcornoco and the *Cumbaru*. The mountainsides of reddish sandstone are painted green by bromeliads and orchids. In the woods there are mainly *Paus-d'óleo* (a tree from which a medicinal oil is extracted*),* several species of Cinnamon, Courbaril trees and Pink Ipes.

In the fields, grasses and low vegetation are very common

The fields, with their low and homogeneous vegetation, make animal watching easier. With a bit of luck, mammals like the Armadillo, the Maned Wolf, the Wild Dog, the Pampas Deer and the Great Anteater can be spotted. Among the most common birds there are Crested Seriemas, American Ostriches, Scarlet Macaws, Toco Toucans and noisy Pega Jays.
On the plateau's mountainsides, look for Cayenne Swifts and Aracaris which shelter under the waterfalls.
In spite of being small, some insects also draw the visitor's attention due to the size of their houses: one-meter-high termite moulds appear in the middle of the fields. Besides feeding Anteaters, they allow the soil to be identified, for their colour changes according to the sub-soil's.
In the humid areas, near the rivers, there are distinct landscapes, such as the Mature Riverine forest, Moist Fields and Buriti Palm groves, where it is easy to find Tapirs, Whitelipped Pecaries and Pampas Deer.

HISTORY

The first dwellers of Guimarães Plateau 12.000 years ago were a pre-historic people who inhabited caves and rock shelters. They left their mark - ceramics chips and rock paintings - in the 50 archaeologic sites that have already been studied. Following them came Indians of different ethnic groups, such as the Paiaguás, the Caiapós and the Guaicurus. In 1720, the explorer Antônio de Almeida Lara went to the plateau from Cuiabá in search of land to form a ranch, where - so it is said - a miraculous *pinga* was made, capable to cure malaria. *Pinga* is a distilled Sugar cane alcohol.
Around 1750, Jesuits also arrived at the place and founded Mato Grossos' first mission: Vila Santana de Chapada. Because of a law, it was renamed as Chapada dos Guimarães in 1872. The Russian Expedition to South America, led by the famous German explorer Georg Heinrich von Langsdorff (1773 - 1852), also went through the area between 1821 and 1829. Adrian Taunay - one of the expedition's draftsmen - portrayed the Véu

◄   Toco toucan (above); orange-reddish cliffs form the Park

The cold that frightened Langsdorff

Despite the region's usually stable annual temperature - around 25°C -, extreme temperatures, ranging from -1°C to 41°C, also occur. Because of the variation in the north-south air streams between the Andes and the Brazilian Plateau, cold winds from the South blow in winter over this area on their way to Ecuador, causing a sudden drop in the temperature, locally called *friagem*, which could be more or less translated as 'coldness'. It sometimes happens five times a year, but in other years, may not arrive. On may 1st 1827, some members of Langsdorff's Expedition, as the Russian Expedition is known, went to Vila de Guimarães from Cuiabá. Hercules Florence wrote in his diary: "We sometimes feel a very hard - really hard - cold during our stay in Guimarães, worsening when the wind blows from the South and the sky is cloudy. The fog is so thick that

Haze: typical of the cold weather

we can not know what lies 15 footsteps from where we are. It is totally humid around us; moisture affects everything: furniture and the clothes locked in trunks. It is possible to believe that the cold in the plateau is sometimes so strong that it freezes, as in Russia".

da Noiva Waterfall and the Bororo Indians. The early ideas and efforts to preserve the region date back to the 19th century. At that time the attentions were drawn to the protection of the main springs and sources of Cuiaba's rivers, which are located in the plateau. In the late 1970's, alternative communities in search of peace and love moved to the place. Because it is located in

South America's geodesic centre - the equidistant point between the Atlantic and the Pacific Oceans -, the plateau has attracted mystic people who believe that the place emanates a strong energy. At that time, the campaigns for the area's preservation intensified, a local community's proposition was accepted and the Park was created in 1989.

The action of the water and the wind has shaped the rock formations

HIGHLIGHTS

⑩ Namorados Waterfall
⊖ 50 m from Cachoeirinha
This waterfall drops as a 8-m mantle off the cliff from which it originates.

⑩ Véu da Noiva Waterfall
⊖ Located just a few minutes from the Park, where the Coxipó River falls from the *Chapada* ⊙ Two hours
It is possible to see it from the lookouts along the trails that take you to the waterfall. But it is better to walk 30 minutes in a thick forest up to a place that reveals an extremely interesting angle of the waterfall. It takes 40 minutes to return. This part of the trail is presently restricted.

⑩ ⑪ Cachoeirinha
The 18-m waterfall is very good for a bath as it falls into a pool surrounded by a small beach. There are restaurant, snack bar and rest rooms.

Caminho das Pedras and São Jerônimo Hill
⊖ 15 km from the Casa de Pedra Grotto to the beginning of the trail and 8 km through the *Cerrado*
⊙ One day
Hiking goes past interesting sandstone formations, such as the stone Cayman, the stone altar - a cup-like stone - and the whitish sandstone Mushroom. From the Mushroom to the Sacrifice Table it is 2 km more. The table is a flat formation - 15 km in width by 12 m in height, where it is possible to find fossilized shells. On the way to the Table it is possible to see a huge stone wall known as Pedra Furada (Perforated Stone), where there is an archaeologic site with a rock painting. At the end of the Pathway of Stones lies São Jerônimo's Hill, the highest peak of the *Chapada* with an altitude of 836 m. You can also get to the hill via a 8-km dirt road, but it is advisable to use a 4-wheel-drive vehicle on the road.

Casa de Pedra
⊙ Two hours
It is a very clear and ventilated grotto, also known as the Esconderijo do Riacho Independência. There is a 40-m² room carved in the sandstone, where a small creek flows through. Next to the grotto, there is a waterfall where it is possible to take a dip.

⑪ ⑭ Visitors' Centre
At the Park's entrance. It supplies information on the Park. It has an auditorium, rest rooms, restaurants and pay phone.

Cidade de Pedra
Here it is possible to walk on rock formations, carved by wind and water, at an altitude of 350 m. The place looks like a stone city. The access is via a road that links the *Chapada* to the Água Fria district. It is 24 km to go from one place to the other.

⑩ Waterfalls Circuit
⊙ Six hours
Also known as the Complexo das Cachoeiras (Waterfall Complex), this 3-km trail starts after a small bridge and a 700-m walk in the *Cerrado*. There are seven waterfalls in a row; the first one is the Sonrisal, with a 4-m fall. The lateral trail that leads to Sonrisal takes 15 minutes to walk. Back to the main trail - the Araras Trail - you will get to the Pulo - with an 8-m fall; difficult access, but with a nice lake for a dip - Degrau, Andorinhas and Independência or Arco-Iris, within a Mature Riverine forest. Look for swifts on the cliffsides. To return, it is necessary to take another trail up to a fork on the path: to the left you take the waterfalls trail, which leads you back; to the right you take the Degrau Trail, which leads you to the waterfalls.

Cuiabá

Paredão do Eco
⊖ 15 km from the Chapada dos Guimarães ⊙ Two hours
The region's natural lookout, is formed by a huge sandstone cliff at the summit of the plateau. The access is via a road that leads from Água Fria (5 km) to a small road which goes into the Park.

⑩ Portão do Inferno
The canyon is 85 m in depth and can be seen from the road that links Cuiabá to the *Chapada* (MT-25). From the canyon it is possible to see the Cidade de Pedra.

Riolândia

N
O   L
S

0   1,7   3,4 km
ESCALA

Cidade de Pedra

Cór. Porteira

Claro

Rio Salgadeira

MT 251

Rio

Rio

xipó

Rio

Coxipozinho

Portão do Inferno

Cór. da Mata Fria

Cachoeira
Véu da Noiva

Chapada dos
Guimarães

MT 251

Buriti

Casa
de Pedra

Centro de
Visitantes

Complexo
de Cachoeiras

Chapada dos
Guimarães

Rio Coxipó

Mirante da
Geodésia

Morrro de
São Jerônimo

Limite do Parque
Trilhas
Estrada de Asfalto
Estrada de Terra

Maned-wolf: common in the *Chapada*

SURROUNDINGS

❶ Martinha's Waterfall

⊖ 40 km from the Park
towards Campo Verde
⊕ Six hours

The greatest water volume
in the *Chapada* is concentrated
in this waterfall. The access is
by car, via a 150-m trail which
takes to five falls in the Casca
River. Be careful when walking
on the rapids.

❷ Geodésio's Lookout

⊖ 8 km from Chapada
dos Guimarães city
⊕ One hour. Access via
8 km of dirt road on the
way to Campo Verde

The lookout is South
America's central point. It is
located at an altitude of 797 m
and forms a plateau, 150 m in
diameter. The meeting of the
Pantaneira plain with the
Chapada is a wonderful view.

Fish, fruit and liqueurs: *Chapada*'s cookery

The local cookery includes dishes such as the tasty piranha chowder which may look odd for those who are not natives. Fish are Mato Grosso's main food: *Pintados*, *Pacus*, *Piraputangas*, *Curimbatás*, *Dourados*, and others, cooked in many different ways. Try side dishes such as a very spicy fish *pirão* (fish gravy thickened with manioc meal), or a banana *farofa* (cornmeal fried in butter).

Main dishes are the *ensopadão cuiabano* (stew from Cuiabá) - a stew of beef ribs with manioc, potato, kale, corn and green banana - and the *galinhada de panela* (pan chicken). As for desert, try fruit like cashew, guava and *mangaba*, washed down with the region's most traditional drink: souari nut liqueur. There are also other drinks made of fruit like *mangaba*, *jabuticaba* and lime.

◀ The Corixó River falls 75 m and forms the Véu da Noiva waterfall

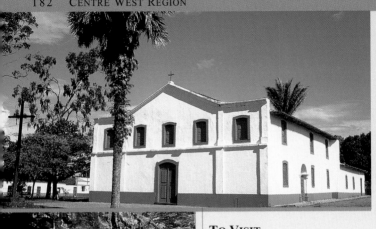

TO VISIT

Access – Open daily from 8 am to 5 pm. Price: R$ 3,00.
Address – In Cuiabá: Av. Rubens de Mendonça s/nº, CPA/IBAMA/MT, Cuiabá, MT, 78055-500. Phone/fax: (65) 644-1200. In the Park: Rod. Emanuel Pinheiro (MT-251) km 56. Phone: (65) 301-1133.
How to get there – By plane: there are regular flights from the rest of the country to Cuiabá. The Park is 56 km from Cuiabá via MT-251, totally paved. There are two coach companies (Viação Rápido Chapadense and Expresso Rubi) with several daily departures to the Chapada.
Infra-structure – Restaurant at the Visitor's Centre and at Cachoeirinha. Rest rooms at the Park's headquarters, Véu da Noiva Waterfall and at the Visitor's Centre, which also has a exhibition room and an auditorium for 40 people. It is not permitted to stay overnight in the Park. There are 35 km of roads within the Park which lead to the main highlights

TIPS

◗ The best time to visit the *Chapada* is between May and July, when flower blossoms and the water volume at the falls is at its height. During the rainy season, from December to April, the trails are dangerous and the administration of the Park closes some of them. However, the natives consider it the most beautiful time of year as the vegetation is most exuberant.

To know more
Philips Guides Pantanal and Bonito. **São Paulo: Horizonte Geográfico, 2000.**
www.chapadadosguimaraes.com.br

SERVICES

Chapada dos Guimarães, MT
🌐 65
✉ 78195-000

Useful Addresses
City Hall. Rua Tiradentes, 166, Centro. Phone: 301-1570.
Bus station. Rua Cipriano Curvo, s/n°, Centro. Phone: 301-1280.
Post Office. Rua Fernando Correia, 848, Centro. Phone: 301-1333.
Hospital. Santo Antonio. Rua Sto. Antônio, 106, Centro. Phone: 301-1116.
Banks. Bradesco, Banco do Brasil.

Support for the Visitor
Tourist Bureau. Rua Quinco Caldas, 47, Centro. Phone: 301-2045. E-mail: sind.chap@vsp.com.br.
Arca. Association for the Environment's Recovery and Conservation. Phone: 301.1313. E-mail: arcamt@terra.com.br. Asconvi. Chapada's Guides Association. Phone: 301-1687.
Tour agencies. Atimã Turismo. Rua Quinco Caldas, 333, Centro. Phones: 301-3391/3392; Aventuras e Caminhos. Rua Tiradentes, 28, Centro. Phones: 301-1836/2404. E-mail: actur@vsp.com.br; Eco Turismo Cultural. Pça. do Wunibaldo, 464, Centro. Phone: 301-1393, Fax: 301-1639. E-mail: ecotur@terra.com.br.

Lodging
Candial Margarida. Av. Rio da Casa, s/n°. Phone: 301-2053. 13 rooms Bar. 💲
Chácara Pousada Santa Rosa. Rua dos Jurunas, 184, Aldeia Velha. Phone: 301-1405. 4 chalets, tv, fridge, stove. 💲💲💲
Chapadense. Rua Ver. de Souza Neves, 534/535. E-mail: peaguda@vsp.com.br; Phone: 301-1117. Fax: 301-1718. 11 rooms, tv, air conditioning, minibar. Restaurant. 💲💲
Laura Vicunha. Rod. Manuel Pinheiro, km 62. Phone: 301-2313. Fax: 301-2631. Internet: www.pl.vicuna.com.br. 12 rooms, 3 chalets, tv, air conditioning, minibar. Swimming pool, restaurant, bar, billiard room, buggy, football field and court. 💲💲💲
Pousada Bom Jardim. Pça. Bispo Dom Wonibaldo, 641, Centro. E-mail: bomjardim@chapadadosguimaraes.com. 19 rooms Phone/fax: 301-1244. 💲💲

Pousada da Chapada. Rod. Emanuel Pinheiros, km 63 (exit to Cuiabá, 1,5 km). Phone/fax: 301-2332. E-mail: pousada@terra.com.br. 35 rooms, tv, air conditioning. Swimming pool, sauna. 💲💲💲
Pousada Florada da Serra. Rua Frei Canuto, s/n°, Centro. Phone: 301-3193. E-mail:deoade@ig.com.br. 4 chalets, tv, minibar. Swimming pool, restaurant, bar. 💲💲
Pousada Penhasco. Av. Penhasco, s/n°, Sítio Taipinha. Phone/fax: 301-1555. Internet: www.penhasco.com.br. 28 rooms, tv, air conditioning, minibar. Swimming pool, restaurant, bar. Hiking to the cliff, convention room, tenis court, football, billiard room. 💲💲💲
Pousada Piquezeiro. R. Homero Mousar, 1447, Centro. Phone: 301-3333. Internet: www.pousadapiquezeiro@bol.com.br. 10 rooms, tv, air conditioning, minibar. Swimming pool, restaurant. 💲💲💲💲
Rios. Rua Tiradentes, 333, Centro. Phone: 301-1126. 25 rooms, air conditioning, minibar. Snack bar. 💲💲

Dining
Felipe. Rua Cipriano Curvo, 598, Centro. Phone: 301-1793. Varied Menu. (à la carte) (self-service, Monday to Wednesday) 💲
Miaus Espetinhos. Rua Quinco Caldas, 55 A, Centro. Phone: 301-2049. Meat. 💲
Mistura Fina. Rua Quinco Caldas, 50, Centro. Phone: 301-2240. Pizza. 💲
Montanha. Rua Dr. Penn Gomes, 524, Centro. Phone: 301-1495. Typical local food. 💲💲
Morro dos Ventos. Av. Rio da Casca, km 1. Varied Menu (lunch only). Phones: 301-1030/1440. E-mail: mventos@vsp.com.br. 💲
Nutriquilo Rezende. Rua Cipriano Curvo, 729, Centro. Phone: 301-1149. Varied Menu. 💲💲
Nívios Tour. Rua Ver. José de Souza Neves, 54. Phones: 301-1206/1284. Typical local food. 💲
O Mestrinho. Rua Quinco Caldas, 119, Centro. Phone: 301-1118. Fax: 301-1599. E-mail: mestrinho@vsp.com.br. Varied Menu. 💲💲
Penhasco. Av. Penhasco, s/n°, Centro. Phone: 301-1844. Varied Menu. 💲
Trapiche. Rua Cipriano Curvo, 580, Centro. Phone: 301-2629. Varied Menu. 💲

Chapada dos Veadeiros

The huge quartz crystal block of the Veadeiros Plateau has been sculpted for millions of years. Rock walls and canyons, with their steep cliffs, are a result of this long, everlasting, process which designs the landscape. On the top of this rugged plateau, rivers of dark waters - dyed with iron oxide - appear and flow through it until they drop in 150 waterfalls, some only showing up during the floods. The seasons are marked by a rainy time - mainly from November to March - when the flowers bloom and the rivers brim. In dry season, the vegetation becomes brownish and the air is full of dust. In July and August, apart from the low humidity of the air, the cold mistreats the *Chapada*.

The Park is located in the *Cerrado* of the Brazilian Plateau, whose main feature is the great landscape variation. In the open grassland you will find several types of grasses; in the fields locally called *campos sujos* and in the *Cerrado* you will see more trees and bushes. Because fires are common, the trees tend to be twisted and covered in a thick layer of cork. On rocky outcrops in the fields, flowers like the *Canela-de-Ema* and the small *Compostas*, of the Daisy family, grow. In the areas near the rivers, there are moist fields, riverine forests and Buriti Palm groves - flooded regions where the Buriti palm predominates. In the dry season, moist areas supply shelter for the fauna, being very important for the maintenance of ecosystem biological

Foundation: 1960
Area: 2.350 km²
Vila São Jorge: 3 km; Alto Paraíso de Goiás: 33 km; Goiânia: 460 km; Brasília: 260 km
O
⊕ (62)
☎ 446-1570

diversity. The *Babaçu* Palm - highly prized for several products - is also part of the Park's lowlands landscape. In the riverine forests, there are trees such as the Copal, the California Pepper and the Pricklyash. In September, the yellow Ipes paint the scenery. On the *Chapada*'s mountain sides there are Orchid species which are typical of Brazil's Central Plateau. Animal watching is easiest in the vegetation of the fields. Look for mammals like Wild Dogs, Great Anteaters, and 9-banded Armadillos. There used to be more Maned Wolves, Giant Otters, Pampas Deer, Giant Armadillos and Jaguars but today they are only seldom seen. Among the birds that you will easily see are Crested Seriemas, American Ostriches, Ibis, Scarlet Macaws, Toucans, several species of Hawk and the noisy Pega Jays. The Royal Vulture,

a threatened species, is still common in the Park where it is easy to see them. Along the riverine forests and the Buriti Groves it is possible to find animals such as Capybaras, Pampas Deer and Whitelipped Pecaries. Despite their size, some small animals attract our attention because of their houses: 1-m high termite mounds in the middle of the fields are common.

Poço Encantado: waterfall near the road to Cavalcante

HISTORY

At the end of the 16th century, the first explorers arrived in search of gold. They met with the Goiazes Indians, who - as most tribes - had a sad end in the hands of the *bandeirantes* (explorers who entered the backwoods hunting for Indians to enslave or searching for precious metals and stones). In the middle of the 18th century, the main economic activities in the Veadeiros Plateau were coffee plantations and cattle ranching. The region's name - veadeiro would translate as a deer hunter – is due to the great quantity of deer which used to roam here.

The village of São Jorge, today the Park's entrance gate, was founded at the beginning of the 19th century. In 1912, the village became important when quartz crystal was discovered on its outskirts. Because of the quartz crystal mining, the population grew and the new economic activity left its marks throughout the place: they used to dig holes of up to 5 m in diameter in order to extract the mineral.

Brasília's construction, in the early 1960's, drew the country's attention to the Central Plateau and the idea of creating an area to protect the plateau's fauna and flora arose. Tocantins National

◄ Papalantus, known as chuveirinho (above); Baleia hill, near the entrance of the Park

Chapada: quilombos' land

Kalunga dwellers from Vão das Serras

At the beginning of the 18th century, the wealth of the Minas dos Goiazes Province drew the attention of miners who moved to and populated the region which today is the state of Goiás. With the miners, thousands of African slaves also came. For decades, the mines prospered, digging treasures out of the heart of the earth. Between 1796 and 1807, there was a city near the *Chapada* called Cavalcante, which supplied labour for the mines. After this period, taxes increased and it was more difficult to keep slaves. In order to fool the government and not to pay the taxes, the miners hid some of the slaves. At the same time, the *quilombo* (a hiding place of runaway slaves, sometimes as big as villages) movement increased and spread throughout the country. The slaves abandoned the mines and hid in the mountains and valleys founding *quilombos*. The Kalungas have occupied the Vão das Serras region, 80 km from Cavalcante, since then. Around a thousand descendants of slave families live there, yet ironically their land ownership has never been declared.

Park was founded in the same year as Brasília's construction. However, local farmers disagreed with the limits of the Park and it was staked out again. As a result, the Park's area today corresponds to only 10% of the original area, and was renamed as Chapada dos Veadeiros. On September 27, 2001, the Federal Government enlarged the area to 2.350 km². In the last few decades, the mysticism which involves crystals has attracted people to the region of Alto Paraíso de Goiás. According to them, the Chapada emits a powerful cosmic energy because it is the highest point in the Central Plateau and because it is located on a huge crystal layer.

The landscape of Veadeiros mixes Cerrado, fields and riverine forest along the rivers

Preto River falls: the water course falls 120 m

HIGHLIGHTS

Hikes and animal watching are the *Chapada*'s main activities: get ready for a trip through the Brazilian *Cerrado*. Old miners' routes are now being used by the visitors.

🄼 River Preto Waterfall

It falls 80 m into a natural pond, 300 m in diameter. The water is dark due to iron oxide.

🄼 Canyon 1

It is one of the many canyons formed by the narrowing of the River Preto. It can only be visited during the dry season.

🄼 Canyon 2

It is the Park's most beautiful precipice. This is a 20-m cliff where the River Preto narrows.

Baleia Hill

One of the Chapada's peaks, it is 1.501 m high and it is located 20 km from the Park's gate. During the flood season a waterfall drops from here. The access is not allowed.

SERRA
Rio Preto

Pedreiras
Cachoeira do Rio Preto
Cachoeira Cariocas
Cânion 2
Salto II do Rio Preto
Cânion 2
Entrada do Parque
São Jorge ◉
Niquelândia
Mirante São Jorge
Rio São Miguel
Vale da Lua
Salto do Rio Raizama
Cachoeira Morada do Sol

——— Limite do Parque
••••••• Trilhas
——— Estrada de Asfalto
——— Estrada de Terra

Pampas deer

Pedreiras

As stated in the name, the region is an old quarry with many natural ponds among the rapids of the River Preto. In fact, they are like a natural hydro massage.

 River Preto II Waterfall

At the end of an old mining trail, you will see a rock wall with a 120-m waterfall. There is a very steep path to descend. Bathing in this waterfall is not permitted.

Canyon 2 Trail and Cariocas Waterfall

This is a 10 km hike. It takes 1:30 hour to go up and its not very steep. The first destination is Canyon 2, where you can have a bath.

From this point there are two options to get to Cariocas Waterfall: one is to take the trail which leads away from the river into the *Cerrado*; it is easier but not as interesting; the other is to go along the river rocks, more difficult but not really that hard. You go down to the waterfall by a quartz cliff; it takes 10 minutes to get there and it is a bit difficult, however the view of the waterfall repays the effort.

 🏊 River Preto and Pedreiras Waterfalls Trails

This is a 11,5-km trail in total length; it takes 3:30 hours, two of which you take to go up
Preto River Waterfall is the first destination, a 5-km slippery and rocky trail. Then, through a 1-km lateral path you get to Rio Preto Waterfall, where it is possible to go swimming. The view is outstanding: the river drops 80 m into an immense lake. It is 4 km plus some shortcuts to return by the same path.

SURROUNDINGS

Água Fria Waterfall
⊖ 15 km from Alto Paraíso ⊕ Six hours. Price: R$ 50,00. Access via GO-118, towards Teresina de Goiás, plus a 6-km walk. Phone: (61) 552-3151
Located in an old mining zone, today it is private property. There are two levels of rappel: one for beginners - a 40-m descent -, and another for more experienced ones - 90 m. A group of at least four people is necessary.

Morada do Sol Waterfall
⊖ 9 km from São Jorge ⊕ Two hours. Access via the road to Colinas
The 1-km trail leads to the waterfall on São Miguel River. There are some steep parts up the trail. At the end there are small waterfalls and ponds good for bathing.

Waterfall on the Cristal River
⊖ 7 km from Alto Paraíso de Goiás ⊕ One hour. Price: R$ 3,00. Access via GO-118 towards Teresina de Goiás
The waterfall, in a private property, is formed by a series of waterfalls and rapids on the Cristal River.

São Bento Farm
⊖ 10 km from Alto Paraíso de Goiás ⊕ Three hours
By car you can get as close as 500m from the São Bento waterfall: It is a 6-m waterfall into a dark water pond. It is also possible to visit the Almacegas waterfall, which is a bit further: 4 km by car up to the hill and a 700-m trail to the Almacegas lookout, at the top of the first waterfall, which is 60 m. The second waterfall, is 8 m in height, and is 2 km away by car. Access via the São Jorge road.

Igrejinha Grotto
⊖ 10 km from Alto Paraíso in Goiás ⊕ Two hours
The grotto was carved out by slaves in the 19th century to shelter a small chapel to where the gold was taken to be blessed. The trail starts at the Moinho Lookout, which you can reach via GO-118.

São Jorge Lookout
⊖ 100 m from the entrance gate ⊕ Thirty minutes
It is next to the Park's entrance, on a 1.400-m high hill. The spot is much appreciated to enjoy the sunset.

Hills known as "lady's breasts"

🜨 Buracão Hill
⊖ 20 km from Alto Paraíso de Goiás
🕐 Three hours

A steep 2.5-km trail, barely marked, takes to a 1,576-m-high lookout from which you can overlook the region. The hill is in a private property and access is difficult. It is better to hire a guide. Access via the road to São Jorge.

🄓 🜨 Solarion Park
⊖ 18 km from Alto Paraíso de Goiás
🕐 Four hours. Price: R$ 5,00

The hike in the village of Moinhos takes you to the Arcanjo (10 m) and Anjo (7 m) waterfalls on the Pretinho River. The trail is sometimes steep but well marked. You walk 1 km to a fork in the path and then 300 m more to the Arcanjo Waterfall. Be careful not to slip.

From the fork in the trail to Anjo Waterfall you go down via a 150-m track. Both trails take 20 minutes to walk and are in a private property.

🄓 🜨 🄖 Raizama River Waterfall
⊖ 5 km from São Jorge   🕐 Six hours

It takes 40 minutes to walk the 2-km trail along the river to the 40-m waterfall. It is 2-km on a good trail to go up the canyon. Access is via the road to Colinas do Sul. Good for canyoning.

Vale da Lua
⊖ 6 km from São Jorge, 600 m of trail   🕐 Four hours. Price: R$ 3,00

The greyish rocks through which the São Miguel River flows looks like the moon landscape. Craters 2-m deep with crystals on the surface are remeniscent of the moon.

TO VISIT

Access – Open from Tuesday to Sunday. Admission from 8 to 12 am and exit until 5 pm; during summer time admission from 9 am to 1 pm and exit until 6 pm. Visits are only permitted with a guide (around R$ 50,00 a day for group of ten people). Price: R$ 3,00.
Address – Rod. GO-239, km 33, Zona Rural, Alto Paraíso de Goiás, GO, 73770-000. Phone/fax: (61) 646-1570 and 508-3388.
How to get there – By car: from Brasília, take BR-020; in the city of Planaltina, take GO-118. Alto Paraíso is after you go past São Gabriel and São João da Aliança. In Alto Paraíso, take the dirt road to São Jorge – 33 km away – to where the Park's entrance is. By bus, there are daily departures from Goiânia and Brasília to Alto Paraíso de Goiás.
Infra-structure – A gate at São Jorge and a visitors'centre with information about the Park.

TIPS

❍ For those who enjoy adventure sports, it is possible to go mountain bike riding on the Boa Vista road, which goes down towards the Mata farm and ends 8 km from São Jorge. It is possible to go canyoning after a 2 km walk on the waterfall of the Raizama River, while on the Água Fria waterfall, in an old mining area, you can go rappelling.
❍ The best time to visit the Park is between April and May when the flowers bloom in the fields, there is little rain and the water volume in the rivers is still good.
❍ It is only permitted to visit the Park with licensed guides. Hire one at the Associação de Condutores de Visitantes da Chapada dos Veadeiros (Chapada dos Veadeiros Visitors' Guides Association) or at Servitur. Phone 646.1690.

To know more
ANTAS, P.T.Z. e CAVALCANTI, R.B. **Aves comuns do Planalto Central.** Brasília: Editora UnB, 1988. DAVID, I. **Chapada dos Veadeiros.** São Paulo: DBA, 2000. www.altoparaiso.com/chapada

◀ Cerrado landscape with the Baleia hill in the background

Services

Alto Paraíso de Goiás, GO

🌐 62
✉ 73770-000

Useful Addresses

City Hall. Pça. do Centro Administrativo, 1, Centro. Phones: 646-1255/1249.
Bus station. Pça. Boa Vista, s/nº. Phones: 646-1359/1861.
Hospital. Rua São José Operário, s/nº. Phone: 646-1450/1103. Fax: 646-1450.
Bank. Banco do Estado de Goiás.
Car rental. Transchapada. Rua dos Cristais, 7, sl. 1, Centro. Phones: 646-1345 and 9961-8444. Internet: www.transchapada.com.br

Support for the Visitor

CAT. Av. Ari Ribeiro Valadão Filho, 1100, Centro. Phone: 646-1156. Internet: cataltoparaiso@aol.com
Tourist Bureau. Pça. Do Centro Administrativo, 1, Centro. Phone: 646-1255, extension 34.
Chapada dos Veadeiros Visitors' Guides Association. Av. Ari Ribeiro Valadão Filho, 100, Centro. Phone/fax: 646-1690.
Servitour. Rua da Palha, 260, Centro. Phone: 9904-8810.
Tour agencies. Alpatur. Rua Nascente, 129, Centro. Phone: 646-1820. Fax: 646182. Internet: www.altoparaiso.com. Travessia Ecoturismo. Av. Ari Valadão Filho, 979, Centro. Phone/fax: 646-1595. Internet: www.travessiatur.com.br. Transchapada Turismo. Rua dos Cristais, 7, Centro. Phone/fax: 646-1345.

Lodging

Chácara Anos Luz. Av. João Bernardes Rabelo, chácara 8, Centro. Phone: 646-1315. Internet: www.tba.com.br. 5 rooms, tv, minibar, 18 bedrooms, bed, bathroom. 1 chalet, oven, tv, fridge. Meditation area, lectures, zen garden. $ $ $
Europa. Rua Um, qd. 7, lote 1, Setor Planalto. Phone/fax: 646-1558. Internet: www.hoteleuropa.com.br. 17 rooms, tv, minibar. Restaurant, bar. $
Fazenda dos Anões. Rod. GO-118, km 144. Phones: 508-3232/3333 and 508-3434. Internet: www.pousadadosanoes.com.br. 1 room, 24 chalets, communitary fridge. Natural swimming pool, restaurant. 2 waterfalls, cave, 35 km of trails. $ $
Fazenda Osho Lua. Caixa Postal 15. Phone: 646-1613. E-mail: institutolua@aol.com. 5 chalets, communitary bathroom. Restaurant. $ $
Fazenda São Bento. Rod. GO 327, 6 th km on the road to São Jorge. Phone: 508-3000/997-88265. Internet: saobento@pousadasaobento.com.br. 20 rooms. Restaurant, bar, 4 waterfalls, horses, buggy. $ $ $ $
Paralelo 14. Rua Três, qd. 52, Setor Novo Horizonte. Phones: 9953-8025, 646-1137 and 242-6825. Internet: www.persocom.com.br/paralelo14. 8 double chalets (2 rooms en suite each), minibar. Bar. $
Pousada Alfa & Ômega. Av. Joaquim de Almeida,15, Centro. Phone: 646-1225. Fax: 646-1935. Internet: www.veadeiros.com.br. 12 rooms, tv, minibar. Termic swimming pool, sauna, meditation room , VCR, library. $ $ $
Pousada do Alto. Rua São Miguel, 15, Centro. Phone: 646-1515. Fax: 646-1500. E-mail: pousadadoalto@ig.com.br. 5 rooms tv, minibar. $ $
Pousada do Mirante. Rua Três, qd. 4, lote 13/15, Estância Paraíso. Phone/fax: 646-1494. Internet: www.chapadaecologia.com.br/mirante. 10 rooms, minibar. Lookout, internal garden. $ $
Camping Portal da Chapada. Rod. GO-118, 327, km 9. Phone: 9978-9398. Internet: www.tba.com.br/pages/prtchapada. Electricity, barbecue, kiosk, hiking trail, waterfall, bar, snack bar. $

Dining

Casa da Mamma. Rua São José Operário, 305, Centro. Phone: 646-1362. Pasta. $
Casa Nostra. Av. Ari Ribeiro Valadão Filho, 952, Centro. Phone: 646-1686. fax: 646-1857. Pasta. $
Churrascaria Espeto do Sul. Rua 1, qd. 7, lote 1, Setor Planalto. Phone: 646-1729. Barbecued meat. $
Clube da Esquina. Av. Ari Ribeiro Valadão Filho, 1032, Centro. Phone: 646-1926. Varied menu and natural. $ (Kg).
Jambalaya. Rua 7, qd. 6, lote 1, Estância Paraíso. Phone: 646-1456 and 9973-5501. Varied menu. $ $
Kahuna Café. Av. Ari Ribeiro Valadão Filho, 1035, Centro. Phone: 646-1790. Varied menu. $ $
Oca Lila. Rua João Bernardes Rabelo, 449, Centro. Phone: 646-1773. Snacks and pizza. $ $

Emas

Located in the Highland region of Goiás, the park is on sandstone formations with more recent soils upon them. The plateau's highest point is 900 m, and its lowest point, which forms part of the moist valleys below the highlands, is 750 m.

With regard to the climate, there are two well defined seasons: the dry season, from May to September, and the rainy season, from October to April. At the beginning of the rainy season, lightning, predicting the rain falls is very common. Lightening strikes are responsible

Foundation: January 1961
Area: 1.318 km²
Mineiros: 85 km; Chapadão do Céu: 27 km; Goiânia: 550 km; Cuiabá: 585 km.

○
⊕ (62)
☎ 224-2441

for fires, which are always present in the *Cerrado*. In order to avoid catastrophic fires, the park is divided into 12 "blocks" which are separated by a 25 to 100-m strips of land without vegetation (firebreaks; localy called *aceiros*). The firebreaks prevent the fire from spreading from one block to another.

The landscape of the *Cerrado* in the Emas (American Ostrich) Park ranges from open grasslands to the *Cerrado* itself, with more bushes and trees. Apart from these two ecosystems, the vegetation is also composed of dry woodlands, riverine forests, moist fields and Buriti palm groves.

Christmas lights in the Park

Termite moulds get "bioluminescent"

It is estimated that there are more than 2.5 million termite moulds in the Park. They are land marks at Emas, built by termites, and may reach a height of up to 2 m. Besides being a house for their builders, they shelter many other animals such as Striped Owls, Budgerigars, Snakes, Armadillos, Conepates and more than 15 species of ants. However, it is another insect which draws the visitor's attention when it moves to the termite moulds. From September to October, at the beginning of the rainy season, the termite moulds shelter larvae of a beetle species which gives off an intense greenish light, thus transforming the night landscape into real "Christmas tree fields". It is a bio-luminous phenomenon, when thousands of beetles try to attract prey with their light.

Fields of arrow grass are dominant, however, the *Guabiroba*, the *Cajuzinho* and the *Murici* are also common in these fields. As the quantity of bushes and trees increase in the *Cerrado* other typical species show up: the Alumbark tree, the Souari Nut tree and the yellow Ipe tree, which blossoms at the end of the dry season. At the river sources and along the water courses there are riverine forests and Buriti palm groves, which are extremely important for the maintenance of ecosystem biologic diversity as they shelter fauna during the dry season.

Among the easy-to-see species are the American Ostrich, which gives its name to the Park; the Pampas Deer, which roams the burnt fields looking for sprouts; the Wild Dog and the Striped Owl. Several threatened species, such as the rare Giant Armadillo, the Maned

Cervo-do-pantanal, or Swamp Deer, offspring; endangered herbivorous mammal

◄ American ostrich (above); rapids in the Formoso River, in the south of the Park

Wild-dog, night lonesome animal

Wolf, the Jaguar and the Marsh Deer, also inhabit the Park and with a bit of luck, may be seen.

Researchers have recorded 360 bird species, among them the Crested Seriema, the Partridge, the Quail and the Ibis, which is common in the fields.

HISTORY

The Brazilian Central Plateau was cold and arid 10.000 years ago. During that time it was home to peoples who survived on hunting and gathering. Centuries later, when the weather became similar to what it is today, human occupation spread through the fertile valleys.

During the 17th century gold rush, the Portuguese and Spanish conquerors invaded the region and met with the Caiapó and Bororo Indians. However, during the next few centuries, the area was not extensively occupied by Europeans, except for a few white settlers whose main economic activity was cattle ranching. In the 1970's the *Cerrado* (bush land) became the main goal of border expansion within Brazil as a result of increasing growth in agriculture and cattle ranching. The foundation of Brasília and the improvement of roads also turned Brazil's centre-west region into one of the main destinations for migrants, further increasing pressure on the environment. The idea of creating a protected area in the region arose during a hunting trip, when a hunter from São Paulo noticed the wealth of native fauna. He told his idea to a local farmer who passed the suggestion on to a senator from Goiás and the Park was created in 1961. This area, which was used as grazing land, is now the most important *Cerrado* reserve in the country.

Wine palms sparse in the Cerrado landscape at Emas

HIGHLIGHTS

Guarda do Tamanduá Circuit
⊖ 50 km from the Park ⊕ Seven hours
Most of the way is done by car and it
goes through stretches of open
grasslands, moist fields, *Cerrado*
and mature riverine forest. From
the Tamanduá Gate, go via the road to
the left which takes you to Glória.
Observe the Mature Riverine forest
which grows along the Formoso River.
Next stop is at the Park's headquarters.
From here, a short walk takes you to
the Formoso River bridge. Again by
car, drive towards the gate; after
4 km, take the road to the left
which goes to Capivara lagoon.

Jacuba Circuit
⊖ 54 k m from the Park ⊕ Six hours
It starts at the Jacuba Gate, and most of
the way is done by car. The first stop is
the Jacuba's forest. During the dry
season, tuck your pants into your socks
in order to avoid ticks. The way conti-
nues through the *Cerrado* on a road
which goes along the highland's edge.
There are views to the valleys which
drain the river sources and stream
tributaries of the Jacuba River.
The road goes to the Jacuba Gate,
which is the end of the circuit.

Glória
The Glória Stream is located on the
Park's southwest border, in a open
grassland region, with Riverine forest
and Buriti palm groves along the water
course. To get there, it is necessary to go
through a *Cerrado* with an area of tall
vegetation. Look for packs of
Whitelipped Pecaries and for Great
Anteaters. Here, it is only possible to go
during the dry season.

Jacuba Woods
Is the only area of dry forest in the Park
which is permitted to visit, there is a trail
which goes through the vegetation for
around 1 km. Here, with a bit of luck, it
is possible to see Howling Monkeys,
Capuchin Monkeys, Brockets and Coatis.

Formoso River Bridge
The wooden bridge allows visitors to observe one of the clear water rivers which
flow through the Park, besides the path
by the Buriti Torto stream and the
Formoso's lowland. Look for animal
footprints on the road, easily seen in this

moist soil zone. The Marsh Swallow-
tailed Chatterer and the Yellow-
Rumped Marsh Bird are common in
the low grassy land bordering the
river and Scarlet Macaws are easily
seen in the Buriti palm groves.

Jacuba Gate
This is the Park's entrance which is
mostly used by those who come from
Mineiros. It gives access to the
Jacuba woods and to a 50-km trail.
There are rest rooms here.

Tamanduá Gate
This is the Park's entrance for those
who come from Chapadão do Céu.
It is located 5 km from the Park's
headquarters and gives access to
the airstrip, to the Formoso River
and to Glória Stream. There are
rest rooms here.

SURROUNDINGS

Sucuriú Canyon and Falls
⊖ 40 km from Chapadão do Céu
⊕ Six hours
Also known as *Requeijão*, it
is reached by a 2-km trail
which passes by the rivers'
canyons and takes you to
other falls and cascades. Good
for a bath. It is advisable to go
with a guide.

Pinga Fogo and Formiguinha Complex
⊖ 50 km from Mineiros and 135 km
from the Park ⊕ One day
There are many rock formations, such
as the Aparada Rock and uncountable
river springs which spray an endless
drizzle on the cliffs. The Portão do
Céu has big hills which are good for
hiking, mountain bicycle riding and
plant and animal watching. The
Chapada da Lua completes the
scenery with its natural
aquariums.Use a local guide.

Serranópolis
⊖ 81 km from Chapadão do Céu
⊕ One day
Is considered one of Brazil's largest
complexes of archaeologic sites and
its rock paintings date back 10.000
years. The sandstone caves are also a
highlight. Access is via the 75-km
road to Itumirim, where there are
many waterfalls good for a dive.

SERRA

Pacaás
Novos

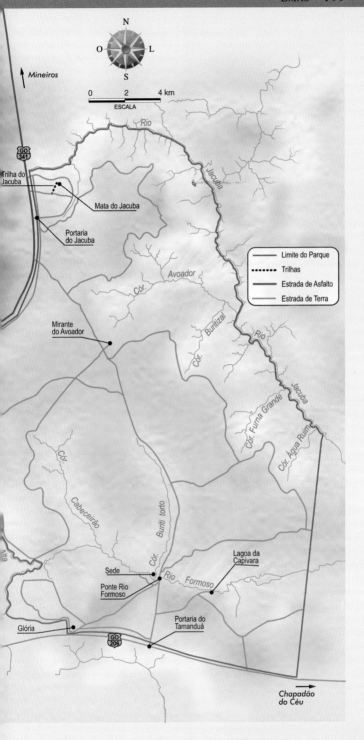

TO VISIT

Access – Open from 8 am to 5 pm. It is necessary to hire licensed guides in Mineiros or Chapadão do Céu. Price: R$ 3,00. Contact Ibama before visiting the Park.
Address – Chapadão do Céu, GO, 75828-000. Phones: (62) 224-2441 and 661-4407.
How to get there – There are regular flights from Goiânia and Rio Verde. The Park has an airstrip for small airplanes, which need a permit of Ibama, the government's bureau for environment affairs. By car from Goiânia, take BR-060 until Jataí; then take BR-364 to Mineiros. From Mineiros, take GO-341 to Chapadão do Céu - it is a 85-km drive. It is 27 km from this city to the Park via a dirt road. By bus, take the *Expresso São Luiz* liner – Phone: (62) 661-1475 – from Cuiabá and Goiânia; Viação Gontijo liner – Phone: (62) 661-1863 – from Cuiabá; or *Viação* Andorinha liner – Phone: (11) 220-4212 – from São Paulo to Mineiros.
Infra-structure – The Park has 400 km of dirt roads, airstrip, headquarters with Visitors' Centre, lodging for researchers, policemen and firefighters, a place for the visitors' meals and rest rooms.

TIPS

❍ The bio-luminous phenomenon of the termite moulds occurs mainly in October, at the beginning of the rainy season. During this season, the fields have more flowers, the weather is more humid and pleasant.
❍ Take care with *micuins* - tiny little ticks - which attack mainly in the Jacuba woods region. Use talcum powder and tuck your pants into your socks.If you end up taking a few with you, a bath with sulphur soap helps to remove them.
❍ If you are in Chapadão do Céu and want to go to Jacuba Gate or vice-versa, you should go around the Park, going 50 km on a dirt road plus 30 km on a paved road. It is not permitted to cut through the Park.
❍ For visitors, the open road stretches can be travelled by bicycle.Thus it is possible to see many animals and other birds of the Park.

To know more
ANTAS, P.T.Z. e CAVALCANTI, R.B.
Aves comuns do Planalto Central.
Brasília: Editora UnB, 1988.
FROTA, L.C. **Frutas nativas do Cerrado**. Brasília: Embrapa,1994.
www.chapadadoceu.go.gov.br
www.emas.org.br

SERVICES

Mineiros, GO
🌐 62
✉ 75830-000

Useful Addresses
City Hall. Pça. Coronel Carijó, 1.
Phone: 661-1551. E-mail:
trefmineiro@cultura.com.br.
Bus station. Av. Antônio Carlos
Paniag, s/n°. Phone: 661-1762.
Telephone Station. Segunda Avenida,
s/n°, Centro. Phone: 661-1919.
Post Office. Quarta Avenida, 62,
Centro. Phone: 661-1253.
Hospital. Rua Elias Carrijo
Machado, qd. 2, lote 1.
Phone: 661-1762.
Fax: 661-4000.
Banks. Do Brasil, HSBC, Bradesco,
do Estado de Goiás, Mercantil do
Brasil, Caixa Econômica Federal.

Support for the Visitor
Tourist Bureau. Pça. Coronel Carijó, 1,
Centro. Phone: 661-5678.
Mineiros tour guides association.
Pça. Marcelino Roque, 12.
Phone: 661-7153. E-mail:
ednaldo.marelo@bol.com.br.

Lodging
Dallas. Quinta Avenida, 223.
Phone: 661-1534. 64 rooms, air
conditioning, minibar. Ⓢ Ⓢ
Ema's. Rua Oito, 111, Vila Machado.
Phone: 661-3505. 7 rooms. Ⓢ
Líder. Rua Elias Carijó Machado, 18.
Phone: 661-1149. 19 rooms.
Restaurant. Ⓢ
Mineiros. Rua Onze, 9.
Phone: 661-1040. 8 rooms. Ⓢ
Pilões Palace. Pça. Dep. José
Alves de Assis, s/n°. Phone: 661-1547.
Fax: 661-3580. 54 rooms, tv, air
conditioning, minibar.
Restaurant, bar. Ⓢ Ⓢ Ⓢ
Pinheiros. Rua Oito, 90.
Phone: 661-1942. 20 rooms, tv. Bar. Ⓢ

Dining
Churrascaria Centro-Oeste.
Oitava Avenida, s/n°.
Phone: 661-1192. Barbecued meat. Ⓢ
Líder. Rua Elias Carijó Machado, 18.
Phone: 661-1149. Varied Menu. Ⓢ (Kg).
Pastelaria Dom Felipe.
Av. José Joaquim de Rezende, qd. 32,
lote 6. Phone: 661-2139. Tarts
(A type of Samosa). Ⓢ

Rene Rotisseria. Av. Jardim, qd.
G, lote 11. Centro.
Phone: 661-1004. Varied Menu. Ⓢ

Chapadão do Céu, GO
🌐 62
✉ 75828-000

Useful Addresses
City Hall. Av. Ema, qd. 51.
Phone: 634-1228. Internet:
www.chapadaodoceu.go.gov.br.
Hospital. Av. Orium, qd. 43.
Phone: 634-1261.
Bank. Banco do Brasil.
Bus station. Phone: 632-1644
and 631-1614.
Post Office. Av. Marte, qd. 28,
lote 16. Phone: 634-1313.

Support for the Visitor
Tourist Attending Centre.
Av. Ema, qd. 5, Centro.
Phone: 634-1228.
**Society of Environmental
and Ecotourism.** Av. Ema, qd.
51, Centro. Phone: 634-1228.
Tourist Bureau. Av. Ema, qd.
51. Centro. Phone: 634-1253.
**Licensed Guides of Chapadão
do Céu.** Phone: 634-1228 (Mr.
Rubens) and 634-1309 (Elaine).

Lodging
Pousada das Emas. Rua Ipê, qd.
17, lote 1. Phone: 634-1382. 19
rooms, tv, bathroom. Snack bar. Ⓢ
Raphael. Av. Indaia, qd. 19, lote
11, 709. Phone: 634-1247. 13
rooms, tv. Restaurant. Ⓢ
Thesari. Av. Indaia, 616. Phone:
634-1227. 11 rooms, tv, minibar.
Restaurant. Ⓢ
**Camping Fazenda Santa
Amélia.** Rod. GO-302, km 65.
Phone: 634-1380.
Fax: 634-1136. 4 chalets,
8 rooms. Bathroom,
camping ground with tap,
steam sauna, bar. Horses,
playground, fish and pay,
boat ride. Ⓢ (camping).
Ⓢ Ⓢ Ⓢ (chalets and rooms).

Dining
Churrascaria Thesari. Av.
Indaia, 616. Phone: 634-1227.
Barbecued meat. Ⓢ
Lanchonete Tutti-Fratelli.
Av. Netuno, 887.
Phone: 634-1407. Meat. Ⓢ

Pantanal Mato-grossens

The Pantanal was a high region 60 million years ago. It suffered disruptions which originated the Pantanal depression and later on, the depression was heaped up with hundreds of meters of debris from the neighbouring mountains.

On the border of Mato Grosso do Sul and Bolivia, the Park skirts the Amolar Mountains and has 95% of its lands in flooded areas. Today, the Cará-Cará Hill is the only part which is out of the water. The main feature of the Pantanal Plateau is that it is subject to periodical floods. Seasons are very defined: floods between November and April which are drained from May to October. The flood cycle repeats itself year after year. There is another cycle, which happens less regularly but even so also affects the region: the great floods cycle. The Pantanal Matogrossense National Park was totally flooded during one of those floods. It is believed that a dryer period has now begun. The incredible mixture of ecosystems in the Pantanal allows for different landscapes to show up: fields, flooded areas and forests. The floods and droughts regime are the engine which moves and regulates the region's life. During the flood, bays, lagoons and corixos - outlets of a lake or marsh - show up, bringing a green colour to the region. In the drought, the nourishment brought by the water lays on the soil enriching it, offering food for the region's fauna. The diversity of the fauna and flora is huge. Caymans, Snipes, Jaguars, Giant Otters, Hawks, Deer, Rufescent Tiger-Herons, Snake-Birds, Monkeys and a countless number of insects populate the rivers, forests and lagoons. In the Park's collective nests, Egrets, Roseate Spoonbills and Snipes colour the ecosystem. The rivers are home to more than 260 fish species. Pintados, Dourados, Corumbatás, Piranhas and Pacus are only a few of them.

HISTORY

Human occupation in the Pantanal region started 8.000 years ago, when hunters and gatherers inhabited the areas such as the Amolar mountain range and

Foundation: September 1981
Area: 1.350 km²
Porto Jofre: 4 hours by boat.
From Porto Jofre,
Poconé: 162 km; Cuiabá: 249 km.
⊘
⊕ (65)
☎ 644-1200

Caracará Hill where the floods were less intense. The first Spanish expedition which sailed the Paraguay River upstream, in 1541, met several Indian tribes scattered on the plateau - mainly the Xaray and Orejone -, who were rapidly exterminated. Then, other tribes - like the Guatós - came from the North and settled in the region.

In the 17th and 18th centuries, bandeirantes (explorers who entered the backwoods hunting for Indians to enslave or searching for precious metals and stones) from São Paulo began to explore the region in search of gold via the rivers Tietê, Paraná and Paraguay. After the Paraguay War (1865-1870), with a decline in the production of the gold mines, the settlers slowly moved westwards, occupying the Pantanal region for the first time.

At the end of the 19th century, cattle ranching was already the main economic activity. Today, the cattle herd in the Pantanal is estimated in 3 million animals. Because problems caused by deforestation, uncontrolled hunting and fishing, environmental groups, allied with Indians struggling for land rights, started the task of creating protected natural areas in the region. Until the 1970's the area of confluence of the Paraguay and Cuiabá Rivers was a cattle ranch, but at a time when the region was practically submersed by floods, it was transformed into the Cará-Cará Biological Reservation.

In 1981, it became the Pantanal Matogrossense National Park.

In 1995, the Ecotrópica Foundation bought three neighbouring farms and transformed them into permanently protected areas. In July 2000, the part of the Pantanal between the states of Mato Grosso and Mato Grosso do Sul was declared Natural Patrimony of Humankind by Unesco.

SURROUNDINGS . . . .

Sesc-Pantanal Ecological Stock Farm

⊖ 45 km from Poconé ⊕ Six hours.
Phone: (65) 682-1520
This 920 km² private reservation, which was formed with the acquisition of 11 farms, is located between the São Lourenço and Cuiabá Rivers. In the zone reserved for visitors it is possible to go on photographic safaris. In this area, it is common to see Egrets, Snipes, Blue Macaws, Caymans, Capybaras and other species of the local fauna. The access is via MT-370 until Porto Cercado.

Ecotrópica Foundation

The Foundation for the Support of Life in the Tropics acts mainly in the region of the Pantanal developing environmental education projects, public environmental policies, biological diversity research and conservation. One of its actions was the acquisition of lands around the Pantanal

Matogrossense National Park and their transformation into a Private Natural Patrimony Reserve. The Acurizal, Penha and Dorochê reservations correspond to something like 6.000 km² of protected area. Internet: www.ecotropica.org.br.

Acurizal and Penha Private Reservations

⊖ Thirty minutes by boat from the Park
⊕ One day. Phone: (65) 627-6619
Despite not having a regular ecotourism service (which should be established soon) it is possible to visit the Acurizal and Penha farms. Created in 1995 in the area where the farms of the same names used to be, the reservations are located in a transition zone between flooded and mountain environments with a rich landscape in terms of flora and fauna.

Transpantaneira Road

Originally planned in 1971 to link the cities of Corumbá and Poconé, the road's construction was interrupted four years

Egrets are abundant birds in the Park

more difficult to drive in the rainy season - from October to April. Look out for Caymans, which show up along the extension of the road, and for Deer, Tapirs and Jaguar which occasionally appear. Snipes and Neotropic Cormorants are easily seen early in the morning. Your chances of watching animals increase if you drive slowly - less than 60 km per hour.

TO VISIT

Access – The Park is not open for visitors yet.
Mail address – Av. Historiador Rubens de Mendonça, s/nº, Cuiabá, MT, 78055-500. Phone/fax: (65) 644-1200.
Infra-structure – There is no infra-structure for visitors.

To know more
MAGALHÃES, N.W. de. **Conheça o Pantanal.** São Paulo: Terragraph, 1992. **Philips Guides Pantanal and Bonito.** São Paulo: Horizonte Geográfico, 2000.
www.ecotropica.org.br
www.members.tripod.com/pocone

later in Porto Jofre, at the border of the state of Mato Grosso do Sul. Instead of the original 397 km, the road ended up with 149 km. It is a thrill to cross one of its 125 wooden bridges. Make sure that your tank is filled up as the farms along the road only supply fuel in the case of an emergency. The farm resorts and the lodges are around the 62nd km. It is

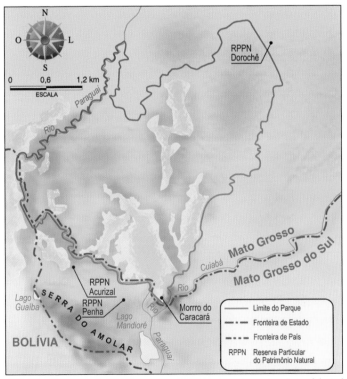

◄◄◄ Wood ibis: the symbol-bird (above); the Paraguay River sets the southern limits of the Park
◄◄ Lakes that are formed in the Pantaneira Plain during the flood season

Serra da Bodoquena

When the Portuguese and Spanish explorers first arrived in this region, the mountains were domain of the Guaicuru Indians, who had been mixing with other tribes such as the Guaná, Guachi, Terena and Kadiwéu for generations. Today the Kadiwéus are the main Indian group in the mountains. After the Portuguese occupation, the region's population has remained more or less stable, despite immigrants coming from the North. The main economic activity was cattle ranching, but, because of the rocky soil and hilly terrain covered with woods, the Bodoquena Mountain Range has remained, to a certain degree, free of this activity. In the last decades, however, deforestation has increased and cattle have begun to take over the area, causing problems such as erosion and the silting up of rivers. At the beginning of the 1980's, the Radambrasil project indicated for the first time that it was necessary to take measures in order to protect the area. Campaigns for the creation of a conservation unit in this region clashed with the interests of local farmers, who claimed that the creation of a park would impair the activities of cattle breeding and agriculture. Instead of the park they suggested the creation of an Environmental Protection Area, whose features and rules are much less restrictive than those of a park. With the construction

Foundation: September 2000
Area: 764 km²
Bonito: 30 km; Campo Grande: 307 km; Corumbá: 356 km; Cuiabá: 1.004 km.

⊘
🌐 (67)
☎ 382-2966

of a gas pipeline, Bolivia-Brazil, compensation was paid to the states through which the pipeline passes. Despite campaigns against the park, and with the help of a TV news report which denounced illegal deforestation in the region, the Serra da Bodoquena National Park was created after ten years of discussions over the area's destiny.

HISTORY

The region where the Bodoquena Mountain Range is located was formed 550 million years ago through the laying of calcareous particles on the bottom of an ancient ocean. Tectonic movements shaped it as steep terrain which looks like a mountain range as seen from the Pantanal. There are underground passages in this huge calcareous formation which allow water to infiltrate and to reappear on the plateau below, where it forms transparent springs and water courses. These are the main touristic attraction of this region. The characteristics of the calcareous formations allow caves to be carved out by the water, for the rock is easily dissolved. The area corresponds to one of Brazil's five cave provinces. The park is split in two - from north to south - by the Salobra and Perdido Rivers. It rains more from November to February while the winter, from June to September, is dry. The landscape is marked by the meeting of three different ecosystems: the Coastal Rain Forest, the *Pantanal* and the *Cerrado*. The forest corresponds to the last remnants of the Coastal Rain Forest of Brazil's central-west region and to the country's largest area of deciduous forest; the kind of vegetation whose leaves fall during a period of the year. In the *Cerrado* twisted trees, grasses and Buriti palms occur on the lowland.

The Betione River flows has more than 40 rapids

Among the plant species, Imbuya, Phoebe, the Ipe tree, Cedar, pink Peroba, *Angico* (a tree of the Mimosa family, genus Piptadenia) and Rosemary stand out. Of the animal species, the most common are the Ant eater, the Coati, the Capuchin monkey and even Jaguars. The birds are most commonly represented by Toco Toucans, Curassows, American Ostriches, blue Macaws and Harpy Eagles - the last two, being threatened species. Besides these, the mountain range is home to a parrot species which is endemic to the region. The wealth of water fauna is easily seen: the transparency of the waters allows visitors to watch schools of *Curimbatás, Dourados, Pacus, Piraputangas* and other colourful fish as if they were in a gigantic aquarium.

SURROUNDINGS · · · · · · · · ·

Baía Bonita Natural Aquarium
⊖ 7 km from Bonito ⊕ Three hours
From R$ 54,00 to 64,00 (includes diving gear). Access by BR-267 towards Jardim. From 7h30 am to 3 pm. Phone: 255-1193

Caves are common througout the region

The resurgence creates a crystal clear lake, with shades going from blues to silver. The water transparency is the main attraction for diving. You can see schools of *Piraputanga* and *Dourado*, besides several species of water plants. A boat follows the group, backing them up and also as an option for those who do not want to go diving.

Aquidaban Waterfall
⊖ 54 km from Bonito ⊕ Six hours
R$ 20,00. Access by the road to Campos dos Índios
It takes two hours to walk a trail of moderate difficulty to the Aquidaban waterfall. The 120-m fall is the highest in the region. It is possible to visit the Terena Indians reservation. It takes three hours to walk to the home of Ms. Almerinda and Mr. Zé Morais, Terena Indians who speak Portuguese. If they are available they might lead the visitors to the reservation, which lies some hours away.

Lago Azul Grotto
⊖ 20 km from Bonito ⊕ Two hours
Price: R$ 10,00
In 1978 the Institute of National Historical and Artistic Patrimony declared the grotto a national patrimony, thus allowing its preservation. It is one of the few grottos with facilities for the visitor. Recently, it has been transformed into the Bonito Grotto Natural Monument together with the Nossa Senhora Aparecida grotto. After going down 100 m, you find the blue water lake. From December 16 to January 15, from 8 to 9 am, sun beams fall directly in the cave illuminating its interior.

Sucuri River
⊖ 18 km from Bonito ⊕ Three to four hours. Price: R$ 40,00 to R$ 47,00.

◄   Dourados (above): the Perdido River is in the south part of the Park

From 8 am to 4 pm. It is permitted to remain in the place until 6 pm
Phone: 255-1736
After walking a trail which goes through a riverine forest, to the east of the Bodoquena Mountain Range, the river source appears. Then you might enjoy a 45-minute boat or buoy ride down the river's transparent waters. Besides the fish, birds also follow the vessel: Toco Toucans, Curassows, Egrets and Parrots.

TO VISIT

Landscape in the lower part of the Park

Access – The park is not open for visitors yet.
Mail address – Rua Treze de Maio, 2967, Campo Grande, MS, 79002-351. Phone: (67) 382-2966. Fax: 325-8987.
How to get there – There are regular flights to Campo Grande from the rest of the country. By car from Campo Grande: go via BR-060,

218 km to the town Guia Lopes da Laguna. Then, take MS-382 and drive 49 km to Bonito.
Infra structure – There is none.

To know more
Philips Guides Pantanal and Bonito.
São Paulo: Horizonte Geográfico, 2000.
www.riosvivos.org.br
www.ecotur-ms.com.br

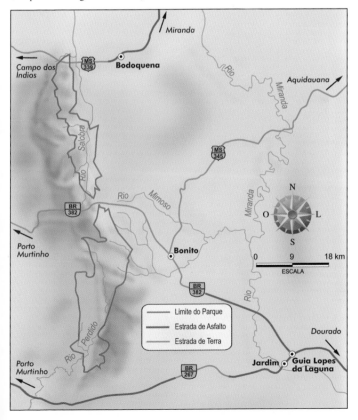

Miranda

Campo dos Indios

MS 339   Bodoquena

Rio Miranda

Aquidauana

Rio Salobra

MS 345

Rio Mimoso

Miranda

BR 382

N
O   L
S

Porto Murtinho

Bonito

0   9   18 km
ESCALA

BR 382

Rio

Limite do Parque
Estrada de Asfalto
Estrada de Terra

Rio Perdido

Dourado

Porto Murtinho

Rio

BR 267

Jardim   Guia Lopes da Laguna

NORTHEAST

NORTHEAST REGION

The Northeast Region has the biggest number of National Parks in Brazil and is the region which preserves the biggest environmental diversity, which ranges from sea islands to the *Caatinga*. The Abrolhos Park is one of the richest places in terms of coral reef in the Brazilian coast. From July to November, the archipelago is visited by Humpback Whales, which mate in its warm waters. The Fernando de Noronha Park is the best diving spot in Brazil and has great beaches. Formed by 21 islands, it is mainly the habitat of the Rotador Dolphin and sea turtles. It also has ruins of forts and allows hikes in the forest and on the beaches. The state of Bahia has four other National Parks besides Abrolhos. The Chapada Diamantina Park allows the visitor to go hiking in a beautiful landscape to waterfalls, grottos and rivers. A highlight is the Fumaça Waterfall, one of the highest in Brazil. The Descobrimento and the Pau-Brasil Parks were founded in 2000 in order to preserve important remains of the Atlantic Forest. They are still not open for visitors. The Monte Pascoal Park is in the same region; its main rock formation is the Monte Pascoal, with 535 m in height; the hill is famous because it was the first piece of land seen by Pedro Álvares Cabral's fleet when it arrived in Brazil, back in 1500. In the state of Piauí there are four National Parks which protect some of the most important archaeologic vestiges in the country. The Serra da Capivara has the biggest concentration of prehistoric sites in the Americas. It has been found vestiges that were up to 50 thousand years old, and the Museum of the American Man Foundation offers an excellent opportunity to understand the discoveries at the place. The Serra das Confusões Park, the biggest *Caatinga* reservation in Brazil, also harbours archaeological sites that can only be visited accompanied by Ibama staff. The Sete Cidades is an important region of river sources and it is known for its peculiar rock formations, which gave the Park its name. There are many rock paintings made by the people who lived there, around six thousand years ago. The Ubajara Park, the smallest National Park in Brazil, is in western Ceará. It is famous for the Ubajara Grotto, a calcareous cave with an area of 1.120 m², of which 420 m² are artificially illuminated and open for visitors, with access by cable car. The state of Maranhão harbours the Lençóis Maranhenses Park. Although it still does not have infra-structure for visitors, its dunes - intermingled with lagoons which look like "sheets spread in the sun to dry" - can be visited by boat or foot.

Carutapera

PARÁ

Santa L

Açailândia

João Lisboa

Imperatriz

Ba Co

BR 010

TOCANTINS

Rio

Balsas

Amaro Leite

Ro Ve

Mount Pascoal: The first piece of land seen from Pedro Álvares Cabral's Fleet

LENÇÓIS
MARANHENSES

JERICOACOARA *

Oceano
Atlântico

São Luís
Morros
Barreirinhas
Tutóia
Parnaíba

BR
135

SETE
CIDADES

Sobral

BR
222

Fortaleza

Piripiri

UBAJARA

BR
316

FERNANDO
DE NORONHA

RANHÃO

Teresina

Crateús

BR
020

CEARÁ

Mossoró

RIO GRANDE
DO NORTE

Fernando
de Noronha

BR
304

Natal

Novo
Oriente

PIAUÍ

Tauá

Iguatu

BR
427

Floriano

Juazeiro
do Norte

Cajazeiras

João
Pessoa

SERRA DAS
CONFUSÕES

BR
324

PARAÍBA

BR
230

Campina
Grande

Canto
do Buriti

SERRA DA
CAPIVARA

Araripina

BR
316

Olinda

Recife

astino
stro

São João
do Piauí

PERNAMBUCO

Floresta

BR
232

Caruaru

São
Raimundo
Nohato

BR
407

Petrolândia

Bonito

Caracol

Petrolina

BR
116

ALAGOAS

Arapiraca

Maceió

ente

SERGIPE

stalândia
Piauí

N. S. do
Socorro

rmosa do
Preto

BAHIA

Aracaju

Estância

eiras

BR
242

Feira de
Santana

Palmeiras
Lençóis
Argoim

BR
324

CHAPADA
DIAMANTINA

Andaraí

BR
101

Salvador

rrentina

orandi
cos

Oceano
Atlântico

Vitória da
Conquista

Itabuna
Ilhéus

| 0 | 112 | 224 km |

ESCALA

NAS GERAIS

DESCOBRIMENTO

Eunápolis

Porto
Seguro

MONTE
PASCOAL

Caraíva
Ponta do Corumbau

Itamaraju

Cumuruxatiba

PAU-BRASIL

Prado

ABROLHOS

Caravelas

ESPÍRITO SANTO

	Rio
	Capital de Estado
	Cidades
·—·—·	Fronteira de País
·—·—·	Fronteira de Estado
——	Estrada de Asfalto
——	Estrada de Terra

* Park founded in 2002. Do not
appear in the itineraries of the Guide.

Chapada Diamantina

The region's geological history is very ancient dating back to 1,8 billion years ago when the area was sea. Many layers of sediment accumulated one upon the other. Then time and pressure began to act and 800 million years ago tectonic movements shook the terrain forming the mountains of the plateau. Then wind and water eroded them forming steep cliffs, rocky walls, canyons and valleys: the Chapada's colourful monuments are of sandstone, limestone and quartzite. With altitudes which range from 400 m in the valleys to peaks of 1.200 m, the plateau which is like a natural border between the São Francisco River valley and the coast of Bahia has more than 100 caves, 70 waterfalls, cliffs and rocky cliffs. The Park is on the plateau's eastern edge, cut from north to south by the Sincorá Mountain Range. The green colour appears in the backwoods. The high cliffs block the clouds and the rain falls all year round, but mainly from November to January. The Park has a wide range of vegetation types, such as the rupestrian fields - which grow on rocky terrain -, Caatinga - a type of stunted spare

Foundation: September 1985
Area: 1.520 km²
Salvador: 427 km; Feira de Santana: 297 km; Ibotirama: 286 km; Brasília: 1.133 km

◯
⊕ (75)
☎ 332-2229

forest found in the drought areas of northeastern Brazil -, riverine forest and forest groves. In the rupestrian fields there are countless species of orchids, bromeliads, and Strawflower flowering in the landscape throughout the year. In the more humid areas there are rain forest species, taller trees and ferns. There are many cacti, such as the Peru Ceres; Uricury, Syagrus Palms and Hog Plums are also common in the Caatinga.

The Park's fauna has species such as the Mocó - a kind of Guinea Pig, typical of the Caatinga -, the Capybara, the Agouti, the Coati - a tropical carnivore related to the raccoon -, the Little Anteater and the Tapir. Big cats such as Jaguars and Mountain Lions sometimes appear. However, the easiest animals to come across within the Park are snakes - Rattle snakes, for instance -, and birds like Parakeets, Finches and Yellow-headed Parakeets.

There are several fish species in the rivers like Piabas and the curious blind catfish, which lives in the limestone caves of the region.

The Lapa Doce grotto is more than 800 m long

HISTORY

The rock paintings found in the caves on the Diamantina Plateau tell us that pre-historic peoples inhabited the region much before the arrival of the first settlers. There are reports which state that the road Cami-nho Geral do Sertão, which linked the state of Minas Gerais to the region of Recôncavo Baiano passing through the Chapada Diamantina, had been blazed before the discovery of gold mines. In the 17th cen-tury, bandeirantes - a Brazilian colonial character who could be described as a mix of explorer, soldier, prospector and slave trader - from Minas Gerais and São Paulo found gold in the region of the plateau, or Chapada. The gold rush changed the landscape and for 200 years the local wealth painted with gold Bahia and the Portuguese Crown. When the gold began to become scarce, the German naturalists Von Spix and Von Martius visited the region and informed about the existence of diamonds, thus provoking another rush to the Chapada. The peak of the mining was during the 19th century, when thousands of men arrived in the *Chapada* invading the land of the local barons and living in tents made of sheets; these camps of sheet-tents gave the name to the main city of the region. Lençóis, the Portuguese word for sheets, was founded in 1844 and today has a population of around 3.000 people. During the mining times the population reached 20.000 people. The town was so rich that France had a precious stones trading house. The building is still in the city, but is not a kind of "consulate" any more. Many other cities were born and flowered during the Gold cycle and their old colonial houses can still be seen today: Rio de Contas, Andaraí, Mucugê and the tiny village of Xique-Xique do Igatu. African slaves were brought to the *Chapada* to work in the mines - as a matter

◄   Puma (above); Pai Inácio Hill, one of the best views of the Park

Pinheirinho-roxo: typical of the fields

of fact, they did all the hard labour - and left important contributions to the local history and culture. You can get to know some of the history in Remanso, a village which was formerly a *quilombo* - a hide-out for slaves, sometimes as big as a village - on the banks of the Roncador River. During the second half of the 20th century as the mineral became more rare machines began to be used in the mining. Riverbeds were detoured and the bottoms dragged, thus destroying the water ways and the forests. Huge craters and the damage caused by this irresponsible activity along the rivers can still be seen today. Mining still exists in the region, but of a more harmless, primitive kind. Along the River Lençóis, you can see some of the sieves and pans used to wash the gold or diamonds. In the 1970's, groups began to fight for the defense of the Diamantina Plateau aiming at preserving its natural patrimony. Their effort was rewarded and in 1985 the Park was established.

The cliffs at the Chapada range from 400 to 1.200 m in height

HIGHLIGHTS

🔟💧♨ Andorinha Waterfall Trail

On the outskirts of the city of Mucugê; the trail is 4 km long and has many waterfalls and potholes that are good for a bath on the way. You can go via one pathway and return via the other, a 10-km walk.

🔟💧♨ Fumaça Waterfall

The water falls 340 m off a cliff and disperses in the heights, thus forming a smoke-like curtain; the waterfall's name in Portuguese actually means 'smoke'. The waterfall disappears in the dry season. It is possible to reach it via a pathway from Lençóis, in the valley, or via a trail from Capão, which goes up the mountain: a two-hour walk. The hiking via Lençóis is one of the most traditional in the *Chapada*. It takes three days and it is necessary to hire an experienced guide. You can either go across the Veneno Mountain Range and take the Capivara River - around 20 km - or follow this river up to the foot of the waterfall - around 25 km. The trek is a difficult one and is suggested for hikers in good shape who enjoy camping.

🔟🔟 Buracão Waterfall

The water drops 120 m off a cliff into the canyon. The waterfall is in the south of the Park at the city of Ibicoara. The water from many streams and rivers converge in this "big hole" (*buracão*) forming the waterfall with the highest volume of water in the region.

🔟💧♨ Capivari Waterfall

The water drops off the colourful cliffs of green, red, pink and white pebbles into a dark pool. Good for a dip. The hike to the waterfall is a bit difficult and in order to best enjoy the trip, you should take more than one day for the visit.

🔟💧♨ Ramalho Waterfall

The 110-m drop into the River Paraíba forms a large pool which is good for a bath. The trail to the waterfall is 7 km long and takes two and a half hours just to go. The trail goes through a less visited part of the Park on slippery terrain and part is along a riverbed. The access to the trail is via BA-014, from Andaraí.

🔟♨ Sossego Waterfall

The dark waters of the Ribeirão River drop 15 m onto sandstone and sedimentary step-like rocks. The trail along a riverbed to the waterfall is 7 km long and takes two and a half hours just to go. On the way back, you can go to the Meio Stream and to the Escorrega Waterfall.

🔟 Bom Jardim, Roncadeira, Herculano and Encantada Waterfalls

The sequence of waterfalls is near Colônia, an agricultural community in the city of Itaetê. The waterfalls, whose heights range around 100 m, are still little known. The way is difficult when it rains a lot, but adventure is guaranteed. Herculano waterfall has three falls into one big pool.

Morrão

Or Mount Tabor. It is isolated in the middle of a field, which highlights its 1.418 m in height. It can be reached via the Lençóis – Capão trail or via Campina, an alternative lifestyle community near the road which links Palmeiras to Capão.

Paty Valley

The valley can be crossed on a trek which may take up to five days (40 km) going from the village of Caeté-Açu to Andaraí. See the Castelo or Lapinha – in quartzite – grottos on the second day. The Gerais do Vieira open up for trekkers into wide fields. There are many rivers and waterfalls - like Funis, Altina and Cachoeirão - with a 150-m fall - which are good for bathing. The Branco Hill - 1.580 m high - is also in the Paty Valley. The trek can be divided into many parts according to your program. It must be undertaken with an experienced guide.

SURROUNDINGS

💧♨🔟 Serrano Way, Salão de Areias Coloridas and Waterfalls

🕐 Two hours

A short hike from Lençóis along the Lençóis River, which goes past the Salão de Areias Coloridas up to the Paraíso Pothole. It has many places which are good for bathing.
On this tour you can also visit the Cachoeirinha and the

N
O — L
S

0   14   28 km
ESCALA

Limite do Parque
Trilhas
Estrada de Asfalto
Estrada de Terra

Gruta
Pratinha
Gruta
Azul
Gruta Lapa
Doce
Barreiras
BR 242
Rio Santo Antônio
Morro do
Pai Inácio
Rio Mucugezinho
Caminho
do Serrano
BR 849
Morrão ou
Monte Tabor
Gruta do
Lapão
BR 242
Salvador
Palmeiras
Rio Lençóis
Salão Areias
Coloridas
Lençóis
Ribeirão
do Meio
Cachoeira
da Fumaça
Rio São José
Cachoeira
do Sossego
Caeté-Açú
Cachoeira
do Capivari
Marimbus
Lençóis
Serra
Veneno
Marimbus
Andaraí
SERRA DA GABAPA OU RONCADOR
Vale do Paty
Cachoeira do
Ramalho
Andaraí
Rio Preto
Xique-Xique
do Igatu
Rio Paraguaçu
SERRA
Poço
Azul
Poço
Encantado
Capãozinho
Mucugê
Cachoeira
Andorinha
Cachoeira
Bom Jardim
Cachoeira
Herculano
Cachoeira
Roncadeira
DO SINCORA
Rio Mucugê
Cachoeira
Encantada
Rio Paraguaçu
Cachoeira
do Buracão
Barra
da Estiva

Most rivers have black waters, usually with waterfalls and potholes for a bath

Primavera waterfalls and the Halley pothole, all on the Grizante River.

🦇 Lapa Doce, Sol and Torrinha Caves
⊖ 70 km from Lençóis ⊕ Five hours
The Lapa Doce cave has halls of more than 30 m. From there to Gruta do Sol it is only a few minutes walk. Attractions are the pre-historic rock paintings. The Torrinha Cave has many speleothemes - natural formations inside the cave. The shade of the Hog Plum at the bar near the caves invites a rest from the heat.

🦇 Lapão Cave
⊖ 4,5 km from Lençóis
⊕ Three hours
The hike on dry and rocky terrain (take drinking water) leads to one of Brazil's biggest quartzite caves with a 20-m high mouth. It can be crossed from one side to the other.

🦇 🐢 Pratinha and Azul Caves
⊖ 75 km from Lençóis
⊕ Three hours
In the Pratinha Cave you can dive with a torch in the lake to see the calcareous formation on the walls. Look for turtles and fish, which live both in the cave and in the lake outside.

Marimbus
⊖ 18 km from Lençóis
⊕ Three hours
A generic name for the flooded areas of the region. Also known as *pantanal,* or swamp, because of the great amount of water. The Marimbus de Lençóis is along the Santo Antônio River and has greatly diversified fauna and flora. It is in the Marimbus Environment Protection Area - Iraquara with an area of 1.254 km². The Marimbus de Andaraí has facilities for the visitors.

Pai Inácio Hill
⊖ 28 km from Lençóis
⊕ Two hours
Located in a private property in the Sincorá Mountains, it can be reached via an old 18-km trail which was used back in the times of mining. If you are going by car take BR-242 towards Seabra. From the top of the hill you have one of the best views of the *Chapada.* Legend has it that Pai Inácio was a slave who ran away with his master's lover.

🐢 Diabo Pothole
⊖ 20 km from Lençóis
⊕ From one to two hours
It is located in the Mucugezinho River and it takes 20 minutes to walk there. The dark water pool is good for a dip.

⬤ ◉ Encantado and Azul Potholes
◌ 150 km from Lençóis

For you to go to the pools it is better stay in the cities of Andaraí, Mucugê or Xique-Xique de Igatu. Located in the city of Itaetê, the Encantado pothole has crystal clear water which changes its colour according to the direction of light. Between April and September a beam of light falls straight onto the water illuminating the pool in a special way.

The Azul Pool - 40 km from Encantado - is in another cave of the region, in the town of Nova Redenção. It also has transparent water and it is possible to take a bath in order to quench the heat of the backwoods.

⬤ ◉ ⓜ Meio Creek
◌ 3 km from Lençóis ⊕ Two hours

One of Lençóis nearest attractions; here the river forms the Escorrega waterfall, which allows you to slide on the smooth rocks that lead to a pool below.

Xique-Xique de Igatu village
◌ 114 km de Lençóis

The village's official name is Igatu de Andaraí. One of the regional capitals of the age of mining, it was abandoned due to the exhaustion of its reserves at the end of the second half of the 19th century. Everything in the village is made out of stone: houses, gardens, sidewalks, and fences. Located on the top of a hill, the village overlooks a beautiful landscape with many cacti growing amid the rocks, as the name of the city states.

The light incidence makes the water of the Poço Encantado blue

TO VISIT

Access – Always hire a local guide: Lençóis Visitors' Guides Association and Ecotourism Guides Association also in Lençóis. In Andaraí and Palmeiras, look for the visitors' guides associations.

Address – Rua Barão do Rio Branco, 25, Palmeiras, BA, 46930-000. Phone: (75) 332-2229. Fax: 332-2116.

How to get there – By plane: there are regular flights to Lençóis. The airport is 25 km from Lençóis; there is a shuttle to the city from the airport which costs R$ 20,00. By car from Brasília: take BR-242 to the city of Lençóis. From Salvador: take BR-324 up to Feira de Santana; then take BR-116 up to Argoin. After that, go via BR-242. By coach: there are several couches to Lençóis: from Salvador, from São Paulo, Volta Redonda and Uberaba, from Feira de Santana, Aracaju, Maceió, Recife and Palmas.

Infra-structure – Only at the headquarters in Palmeiras.

TIPS

⭕ The Chapada Diamantina can be visited at any time of the year. In summer, from December to March, the rain is more intense and the waterfalls are fuller. However, it is from April to September that the light beams fall inside the Encantado Pool, one of the greatest local attractions.

⭕ Always hire a local guide. It is always advisable to go hiking on the trails with a guide. They know the short cuts and show the best lookouts to overlook the region.

⭕ Rain showers often occur in the *Chapada* and they may cause the rivers to brim and spoil your hike. The guides know how to avoid such situations.

⭕ Despite being located in the middle of the backwoods, the transparent rivers of the *Chapada* allow excellent dives. Take mask and snorkel with you.

To know more

SANTOS, M. **Estradas reais: Introdução ao estudo dos caminhos do ouro e do diamante no Brasil.** Belo Horizonte: Estrada Real, 2001.
www.secturdelencois.cjb.net/
www.festivaldelencois.com.br/
www.bahiatursa.ba.gov.br/
chapada.html

SERVICES

Lençóis, BA
🌐 75
✉ 46960-000

Useful Addresses
City Hall. Pça. Otaviano Alves, 1. Phone/fax: 334-1121. E-mail: pml@sendnet.com.br.
Bus station. Av. Senhor dos Passos, s/nº. Phones: 334-1112 and 331-1044.
Airport. Rod. BR-242, km 209. Phone: 625-8100.
Hospital. Av. Senhor dos Passos, 78. Phone: 334-1267.
Telephone station. Rua Miguel Calmon, s/nº, Centro. Phone: 334-1109.
Post Office. Pça. Cel. Horácio Matos, 18, Centro. Phone: 334-1122. Fax: 334-1149.
Banks. Do Brasil.

Support for the Visitor
Tourist Bureau. Av. Senhor dos Passos, s/nº, Centro. Phone: 334-1622. Fax: 334-1358.

Lodging
Canto das Águas. Av. Senhor do Passos, s/nº, Beira-rio. Phone/fax: 334-1154. E-mail: cantodasaguas@gd.com.br. 43 rooms, air conditioning, minibar, tv, tel. Swimming pool, restaurant, bar, parking lot. $ $ $ $
Colonial. Pça. Otaviano Alves, 750, Centro. Phone/fax: 334-1114. 8 rooms, fan. Bar, parking lot. $ $
Hotel de Lençóis. Rua Altina Alves, 747. Phone: 334-1102. Fax: 334-1201. Internet: www.svn.com.br/lencois. 48 rooms, air conditioning, minibar, tel., tv, safe. Swimming pool, restaurant, bar, laundry, play ground, billiard room, parking lot. $ $ $
Hotel Fazenda Guaxo. Estrada da Granja, s/nº, Rod. BA 850. Phone: 334-1356. 22 rooms, fan, tv. Swimming pool, river, lake, forest and 45 ha of green area. $ $
Portal Lençóis. Rua Chácara Grota, s/nº, continuation of rua Altina Alves. Phone/fax: 334-1233. E-mail: portal@svn.com.br. 69 rooms,15 chalets (up to five persons), air conditioning, minibar, tv, tel., safe. Swimming pool, restaurant, bar, sauna, massage, billiard room, leisure area. $ $ $ $

Andaraí, BA
🌐 75
✉ 46830-000

Useful Addresses
City Hall. Rua da Glória, 48. Phone: 335-2118.
Bus station. Viação Águia Branca. Phone: 335-2160. Viação Novo Horizonte. Phone: 335-2146.
Post Office. Rua da Glória, s/nº. Phone: 335-2156.
Ambulatory. Av. Paraguaçu, s/nº. Phone: 335-2129.
Bank. Do Nordeste.
Car rental. Lukdan. Av. Alto da Bela Vista, s/nº. Phone: 335-2178.

Support for the Visitor
Tourist Bureau. Rua da Glória, 48 . Phones: 335-2056/2118.
Tourist Information Service. Associação de Guias Andaraí. Rua Dr. José Gonçalves Sincorá, s/nº, Centro. Phones: 335-2126/2255. E-mail: acvandarai@bol.com.br.

Lodging
Paraguassu. Estrada Andaraí-Mucugê, km 2,5, Beira-Rio. Phone/fax: 335-2073. 32 rooms, air conditioning, minibar, tv, tel. Swimming pool, restaurant, bar, parking lot. $ $ $ $
Pousada Andaraí. Av. Paraguaçu, 550, Centro. Phone/fax: 335-2008. 15 rooms, fan, tv, air conditioning, minibar. Swimming pool, restaurant, parking lot. $ $

Mucugê, BA
🌐 75
✉ 46750-000

Useful Addresses
City Hall. Rua Dr. Rodrigues Lima, 10, Centro. Phone: 338-2143. E-mail: pmmadm@uol.com.br.
Bus station. Pça. Coronel Propécio, s/nº, Centro. Phone: 338-2162.
Hospital. Rua Augusta de Medrado Matos, s/nº. Centro. Phone: 338-2112.
Post Office. Pça Coronel Propécio, 84, Centro. Phone: 338-2224.
Bank. Do Brasil.
Car rental. Osório Motos. Phone: 338-2193.

Support for the Visitor
Tourist Bureau. Rod. BA-142. Phone: 338-2156. Internet: www.vovosmilenio.pro.br/diario.

Descobrimento

The region's plain and homogeneous topography is marked by a hot and moist tropical climate. The vegetation described in the letter of the fleet's scribe, Pero Vaz the Caminha, to the king of Portugal reporting the newly found land, dominated 12% of the Brazilian territory. Today, little is left of the original forest but the Descobrimento National Park preserves the biggest strip of Coastal Rain Forest in southern Bahia. This forest is rich in species, with high trees, grasses and bushes covered by moss, lichen, orchids, bromeliads and vines.

Among the most common species there are Bulletwoods, Bahia Rosewoods, Souari Nut trees, Sapucaia Nut trees, Red Quebrachos, Jundibas, Juaranas, Imbiriçus, and other species intensely exploited by the timber industry.
The small creeks whose sources are in the Park form the Imbassuaba, Japara and Caí Rivers which flow to the Corumbau Sea Exploitation Reservation. Bird species like Parrots - mainly the species locally known as Chauá -, Tyrant Hawks and Harpy Eagles can be easily seen here.
Among the mammals there are Tapirs, Little Anteaters, Brockets,

Foundation: April 1999
Area: 220 km²
Itamaraju: 17 km; Prado: 30 km;
Porto Seguro: 192 km; Teixeira de
Freitas: 85 km
⊘
⊕ (73)
☎ 298-1145

Black Sloths and even felines such as the Mountain Lion and the Jaguar. There are still illegal predatory activities in the Park, like timber exploitation, hunting and fires. Aiming at educating the communities who live around the Park's area, making them aware of the environmental problems and teaching how to avoid fires, the Park promotes a programme on environmental education every third year.

HISTORY

When Pedro Álvares Cabral's fleet arrived at the Brazilian coast, a small boat was sent ashore. Nobody really knows where this rowing boat stopped but it was probably on the Caí River's mouth, which flows through the Prado, where today lies the Descobrimento National Park. The Tupiniquim Indians lived in the Vera Cruz Land, one of Brazil's early names. They belonged to the Tupi-Guarani ethnic group and their territory was all the way from the south of today's state of Bahia to the Doce River's mouth, in the state of Espirito Santo. The coastal exploitation begun with the Brazil wood tree's cycle.

Later, the Jesuits founded missions to convert the Indians. This work continued until the 18th century and then the region remained almost unexplored in the following centuries.

Isolated due to the difficult access, the area has preserved many of the original historical, cultural and biological features. However, the scenery begun to change with the 20th century's fast populational and economical growth and with the setting up of wood and coal industries.

The imbiriçu is typical of the river banks

The area of the Descobrimento National Park, as well as the Pau-Brasil Park's, used to belong to a wood company which had been exploiting the land since 1971. As the company used the selective extraction method, the vegetation is relatively well preserved and has important samples of the Coastal Rain Forest.

HIGHLIGHTS

Main Gate
It is 28 km of dirt road which can be only endured by 4 wheel drive vehicles. The starting point is the Park's entrance at BA-489. It goes through lakes and rivers, such as the Imbassuaba and the Estiva.

Só Não Vou Lake
The lake's name means "I'm not going alone" and it is due to something that happened to this employee of the Brasil-Holanda company. He had been chased by a Jaguar and whenever someone invited him to come along to the lake he would answer: "I'm not going alone". At the lake, it is possible to watch drakes.

Bird Watching
All species of Bahia's Parrots can be found in the Park. The most common are the ones locally called Chauã and Mutum.

● Imbassuaba River
Animals usually come down to the river to drink water. Look for footprints of Tapirs and White-collared Peccaries.

Talhões
Old forest blocks, separated one from the other by 1-km trails which allowed the timber company employees to walk about the area cataloguing the trees that would fall. There are crystal clear rivers,

big sized trees, bromeliads and birds, such as the Rei-da-Mata.

SURROUNDINGS

Barra do Caí
⊖ 13 km from Cumuruxatiba
🕐 Two hours
Barra do Caí lies northwards from Cumuruxatiba. The chapel is one of place's attractions. It is made of stones withdrawn from the bottom of the sea.

Cumuruxatiba
⊖ 32 km from Prado
🕐 One to three days
The beach and its sea cliffs are a must. This fishermen village turned into a balneary that has good infra structure.

Corumbau Sea Exploitation Reservation
⊖ 7 km from Cumuruxatiba
🕐 Two hours
Located between Corumbau and Cumuruxatiba, it is important for the

Rivers with clear water are common

◄ Great Anteater (above); here lies the biggest area of Atlantic Forest in southern Bahia

ecosystem maintenance because it manages the fishing resources, such as shrimps, shell fish and snooks.

To Visit

Access – The Park is still not open for visitors. *Ibama* is about to finish a study and a management plan for the Park and depending on the conclusions facilities will be set up for visitation.
Mail Address – Rua 4, quadra c, 31, Novo Prado, Prado, BA, 45980-000. Phone: (73) 298-1145. E-mail: pdescobrimento@uol.com.br
How to get there – By car from Porto Seguro: take BA-367 and drive for 62 km up to Eunápolis. Then take BR-101, towards Vitória, up to km 803. In Itamaraju, go for 42 km via BA-489 to Prado, until the Park's gate.
Infra-structure – At the moment, there is none.

High trees bear vines and climbing plants

To know more:
BUENO, E. **Náufragos, traficantes e degredados: As primeiras expedições ao Brasil, 1500-1531.** Rio de Janeiro: Objetiva, 1998.
CAMINHA, P.V. de. **A carta de Pero Vaz de Caminha.**

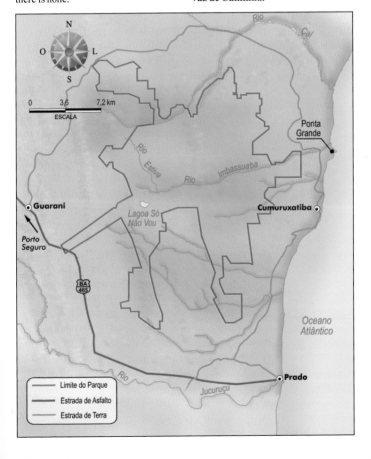

Lençóis Maranhenses

The Lençóis Maranhenses were formed by the constant action of the wind, the tide and the sea streams. The dunes begun to be formed 10.000 years ago, when the Preguiças and the Parnaíba Rivers started to grind quartz from their beds. Dumped into the sea, the waves return the sand to the continent. Then, the wind builds and destroys the dunes, which may reach up to 40 m in height.

The sand stretch spreads 90 km and enters 50 km into the continent and keeps advancing in a continuous, formative process. Flying over the Park, the lagoon in the middle of the sand look like sheets spread out in the sun to dry. The name of the place comes from this view, as *lençol* is Portuguese for sheet. The protected area stretches from the Preguiças River bar to the mouth of the Parnaíba. There are two well defined seasons: the

Foundation: June 1981
Area: 1.550 km²
São Luís: 351 km; Urbano Santos: 140 km; Tutóia: 90 km; Barreirinhas: 50 km

○
⊕ (98)
☎ 349-1155

rainy season, which usually begins between November and January and ends in June; and the dry season, between July and November. The rain fall is 1.600 mm per year and the temperature reaches more than 40ºC during the day.

The lagoons among the dunes have different colours: blue, transparent, black or brown, depending on the kind of soil and vegetation. Vegetation is rare but diversified on the banks of the Preguiças, Fome, Novo, Negro, Grande and Piriá Rivers, which water the region. Palms like the Buriti and the Açaí are common and attract several bird species. Mangroves grow where there is salty water. In the northeastern part of the Park the "flooded area" is mainly formed by three tree species: red mangrove - which reaches 12 m in height -, white mangrove and siriúba mangrove.

On the beaches and dunes the vegetation is represented by Panic grass, Sedge, Starbur, Cocklebur and Pepper. On the areas away from the sea, on flat terrain subject to the sea wind, we find the Restinga - salt marsh - vegetation with plant species such as Cipó-de-leite - a climbing plant of the spurge family -, Sensitive Plants, Sumarés-da-areia - a kind of sand orchid -, Araticuns - a tree of the genus Annona -, Restinga orchids, Frangipanis, Restinga Onions and Mangabeiras - a red wooded tree whose latex produces an inferior grade of rubber. There are many species of fish, crab and mollusks in the mangroves. They are a source of food for birds and Paraguay Caymans. A species of green turtle, locally known as Aruanã is another tenant of Lençóis. It comes to the beaches at night in order to lay its eggs. Among birds, there are some migratory species, which stop in Lençóis for a rest. The Ruddy Turnstone, the Tern, the Blue-winged Teal, for instance, come from the United States and visit the Park during February and April.

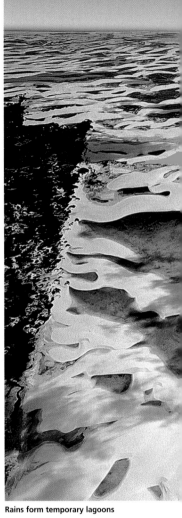

Rains form temporary lagoons

HISTORY

The region of Lencóis is isolated in the state of Maranhão and for this reason it was set apart in the state's history, a theater of conflict among Dutch, French and Portuguese settlers. Before them, the Caetés Indians used to live in the area. They were a nomadic people, settling during the dry season in the river beds in their mud huts, thatched with Buriti leaves, and roamed about on the sand during the rainy season. Very skilled fishermen, the Caetés also cultivated the Buriti Palm and the Carnauba.

Preguiças lighthouse: nice lookout

◄ Long-billed Tern (above); some dunes are fixed because of the vegetation

As the sand dunes of Lençóis are shifting dunes and where the wind sometimes reaches the speed of 70 km per hour (mainly in September and October), there are stories - some of them true and some of them legends - about people, animals and even villages that were swallowed by the moving sand. The village of Caeté, for instance, would have disappeared 150 years ago. People live today as they have been living for centuries: during the rainy season, when lagoons are formed, the population migrates to the dunes and fishing is, then, the main activity; during the rainy season, they move to the river banks and live from agriculture. The dunes, known by the natives as *morraria*, which would translate as something like "set of hills", keep revealing the power of nature. In 1979 the dunes covered the airstrip of Tutóia, a city near the Park. In the 1980's a petrol prospecting base camp also ended up covered in sand. Due to this characteristic, the region drew the attention of the Radambrasil Project researchers who recognized the importance of preserving the region's ecosystem. As a result, in 1981 the Lençóis Maranhenses National Park was created.

HIGHLIGHTS

It is possible to enter the Park from many points as there are no roads, only sand. The most common passages are through Barreirinhas – by ferry –; Atins, in the West corner; Sucuriju and by Santo Amaro, also in the West.

Baixa Grande
Small village where some families live isolated from other centres.

Lagoa Azul
Near the Park's limits; you must walk 30 minutes to get to the lake of transparent water. Some parts of the lake reach 3 m in depth.

Boa Esperança Lagoon
It is only full in the rainy season. It is at the Park's edge, near the source of the Negro River. You can go swimming or canoeing.

Bonita Lagoon
It is one of the perennial lagoons in Lençóis. Here, the dunes go around a natural swimming pool. It is located at the Park's border and you can get there via a pathway blazed back in the 1970's.

Santo Amaro Lagoon
The Park's biggest. It is another perennial lake.

Sucuriju Village
Another tiny little village within the Park. You can only get there with a 4-wheel-drive vehicle.

Queimada do Brito
Four hours by Jeep from Sucuriju, it is an oasis in a sea of dunes, through which the Negro River flows. The houses of the villagers are thatched with Buriti leaves.

⬤ Negro River
The Boa Esperança Lagoon is its source. It is a shallow river which does not permit the sailing of boats.

Park's Crossing
Estimated at a 24-hour walk, so it is necessary to stay in the house of one of the natives' house overnight. It is also necessary to go with a guide and to be in good shape. You will cut through the Park from East to West. On the way there are lagoons inviting you for a dip. Hiking is done from April to July and begins at 3 am. It takes 12 hours to get to the first stop, Baixa Grande. On the second day, the hiking goes through dunes and lagoons up to Queimada dos Britos, another small village in the Lençóis area, and then to Santo Amaro. From Santo Amaro you can go to São Luís by river boat.

SURROUNDINGS

Caburé
⊖ 8 km from Atins ⏲ Two hours
The fishermen's village is on a sand stretch which forms a bar between river and sea. If you walk 200 yards, you will get to the Atlantic. It is possible to go canoeing. There are simple huts thatched with Carnauba leaves.

Parnaíba's Mouth
⊖ Seven hours by boat from Tutóia
⏲ Two days
The mouth of the Parnaiba is the natural border between the states of Maranhão and Piauí. There are more than 80 islands among rivers and creeks; included are mangroves, Carnauba groves, dunes and primary forests. You can also see rich local fauna, such as Egrets, Scarlet Ibis and Caymans.

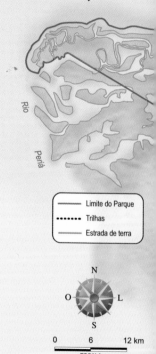

——	Limite do Parque
······	Trilhas
——	Estrada de terra

```
        N
   O  ✦  L
        S
```

0   6   12 km
ESCALA

Mandacaru village: around a hundred houses nearby the meeting of the ocean and the river

Mandacaru
⊖ 7 km from Atins ⊕ Two hours

The origin of this one-hundred-house village is the Preguiça lighthouse. From the top of it - 160 steps, as high as a 14-storey building - you have a nice all around view of the region: dunes, river and sea.

☼ Preguiças River Boat Tour
⊕ Four hours

Departing from Barreirinhas, the waters keep flowing towards the sea for 150 km more. It is the best view of Lençóis. Observe, at the beginning of the tour, the tropical vegetation: palm trees and mangroves.

Pequenos Lençóis
⊖ 50 km from Barreirinhas ⊕ One day

We get there via the Preguiças River. It is a protected environment area where you can hike to the Boi Hill, Espadarte, Vassouras and Alazão. It is on the way to Tutóia for those who come from the mouth of the Parnaíba.

São Luís
⊖ 351 km from Barreirinhas
⊕ Two days

The city, with one of the biggest architectonic complexes of European origin in Brazil, is on the route for those who go to Lençóis. Also, the city is the third centre of African origin in Brazil, thus an excellent place to observe Afro-Brazilian traditions, such as the Divino and Bumba-Meu-Boi festivals. Pay attention to the tiles covering the house's façades in the historic centre.

TO VISIT

Access – The best places to stay overnight in the Park are the villages of Queimada dos Britos and Sucuriju. However, you must hire guides and tranportation in the neighbouring towns. Contact Ibama before visiting the Park. The entrance fee is not charged yet.

Address – Av. Joaquim Soeiro de Carvalho, 746, Centro, Barreirinhas, MA, 65590-000. Phone: (98) 349-1155.

How to get there – By plane: there are regular flights from Barreirinhas to São Luís. There is an airport in Barreirinhas for single-motor planes. The ticket from São Luís is R$ 120,00 and it takes one hour. Information at Aeroclube de São Luís (São Luís Airclub). Phone: 245-5733. By car from São Luís: take BR-135 to Rosário, and then take the road to Morros. It is 84 km from here to Urbano Santos and 90 km more to Barreirinhas. The trip takes ten hours and the last 150 km are bad dirt road and much sand. By couch: there are two daily couches from São Luís to Barreirinhas. From Barreirinhas the only way to go is by boat. The boat trip to the village of Atins on the Preguiças River takes four hours. By launch, the trip takes one hour. It takes two hours to go to Mandacaru village; migratory birds are seen on the way

Infra-structure – There is none. You can get some information at Ibama's office in Barreirinhas

TIPS

➲ The best time to visit the Park is from April to June, when the lagoons are high and there is no wind. The rain stops falling in July; then the lagoons begin to dry and the temperature rises greatly.
➲ Dark glasses are essential to hike on the sand dunes.
➲ For those who go camping, it is possible to take a hammock instead of a tent and, in the villages, negotiate a roof with the natives.
➲ In Barreirinhas, there is much buriti-straw handicraft, such as baskets, purses and hats with better prices than those of São Luís.

To know more
www.visiteomaranhao.com.br

SERVICES

Barreirinhas, MA
🌐 98
✉ 65590-000

Useful Addresses
City Hall. Av. Joaquim Soeiro Carvalho, 759, Centro. Phone: 349-1144.
Bus station. Rua Inácio Lins, s/nº. Phone: 349-1146.
Airport. Pista de Pouso de Barreirinhas – only for small planes of up to six people in capacity. Phones: 244-1511/245-1268.
Hospital. Av. Carvalho, 360. Phone: 349-1182.
Barreirinhas Port. Av. Beira-Rio, s/nº, Centro.
Telephone station. Phone: 349-1110.
Post Office. Av. Brasília, s/nº. Phone: 349-1175.
Bank. Do Brasil.

Support for the Visitor
Tourist Bureau. Praça da Matriz, s/n. Centro. Phones: 9975-1240/349-1631.

Lodging
Chalés do Caburé. Caburé Village– one hour by launch from Barreirinhas. Phone: 9984-0026. Reservation: 9984-0040. 10 chalets. Bar, restaurant. 💲💲
Pousada do Buriti. Rua Inácio Lins, s/nº. Phone/fax: 349-1053. 30 rooms (up to four people each). Air conditioning, minibar, tv, tel. Swimming pool, bar, restaurant, playground, parking lot. 💲💲
Pousada Filhos do Vento. Atins Village. Phone: 9966-7100. Reservation: 349-1420. E-mail: filhosdovento@yahoo.com.br. 10 chalets (up to 3 persons). Restaurant, bar, launch. 💲💲
Pousada Giltur. Av. Brasília, 259. Phone: 349-1177. Reservation. Phone: 232-6041. 15 rooms, air conditioning, launch. 💲
Pousada Lins. Av. Joaquim Soeiro de Carvalho, 550. Phone: 349-1203. 9 rooms, air conditioning, tv. Restaurant, launch, parking lot. 💲

Dining
Lins. Av. Joaquim Soeiro de Carvalho, 550. Phone: 349-1203. Varied menu. 💲

Located outside the Park, the Azul lagoon has some places as deep as three metres

Fernando de Noronha

Fernando de Noronha's volcanic rocks, surrounded by clear sand stretches and white foam, stand out in the huge turquoise sea. Its 21 islands were formed 12 million years ago by underwater volcanoes which correspond to the top of a submerged mountain range whose base is 4.000 m deep. The Mount Peak (323 m in height) is its highest point. On the side of the island called Mar de Dentro (Inside Sea) - which faces the northeast - the sun sets behind the ocean, a phenomenon which occurs in only a few beaches on the Brazilian coast. On the side that faces the ocean, the platform is shallower and

the surf stronger due to winds which blow from southeast. Located at latitude 3º54' south of the Equator, the archipelago is hot all year round, with a dry season - from August to December. The rainy season is from February to July.

As on all island ecosystems, it is ideal for the appearance of new species and has a high rate of endemic species, occurring in only a few places.

There are neither terrestrial mammals nor amphibians, only those brought by man: *Mocós* - a kind of Guinea Pig -, rats, mice, dogs, goats, etc. Noronha's environment has many birds and

Foundation: September 1988
Area: 112,7 km², 85% in the sea
Natal: 360 km;
Recife: 545 km

(81)
3619-1128

endemic species such as the *Manbuia* lizard, the Two-headed Snake, and the birds *Sebito* and *Cucuruta.*

The much exploited forest has endemic tree species such as the *Gameleira* - a kind of Fig tree - and the *Mulungu.* Other species of the flora that stand out are the *Burra-leiteira,* a tree whose sap burns the skin; and the *Jitirana* vine, today a plague which infests the archipelago's vegetation.

The sea fauna is very rich composed in part by many fish and coral species. Here, the endangered sea-turtles have found a perfect shelter to feed and lay their eggs. Another sea animal which comes to the waters of Fernando de Noronha to rest and mate is a Dolphin from a species called *Rotador.* Some animals which were introduced by man deserve attention, such as the *Teju* lizard, taken to the island back in the 1970's to prey on the rats that had arrived with vessels to the archipelago. Instead of hunting rats, the *Teju* fed on the eggs of the birds which build their nests on the ground causing serious harm to the native bird population. Species introduced without a thorough study may be a great threat to the islands, as they compete with native species and may become predators, thus unbalancing the local ecosystem.

HISTORY

Human occupation on Fernando de Noronha is almost as old as that on the continent: in 1502 the archipelago appears in Cantino's map with the name of *Quaresma* (Lent). Amerigo Vespucci sailed along it on the Portuguese's second exploratory voyage to Brazil; it was then called São Lourenço island. In 1504, the area was given to Fernando de Noronha who had financed the expedition; the Island became the first Brazilian *Capitânia* - a colonial jurisdictional division corresponding to a province. Then, the island was abandoned for 200 years. In the 17th century it was occupied by Dutchmen - who called it *Pavônia* - and in the 18th century it was taken over by Frenchmen, who called it *Delphine* Island. As the island was considered vulnerable to invasion, the Portuguese Crown decided to build a defense system of ten forts - the largest in Brazil during the 18th century. Among them there is the Nossa Senhora dos Remédios, which has been declared a Monument of the National Patrimony since 1961. In the 18th century the island became a prison and the prisoners were used to build the houses, the roads and the fort. The prison's rules were cruel and the solitary cells so tiny that the prisoner

could hardly move. In order to prevent prisoners from hiding in the jungle while attempting to escape on rafts to reach the continent, the native forest was cut. For this reason, the original vegetation today has survived in only a few places, such as on Mount Pico, the Sapata point, on the Leão beach and at the Sancho and Golfinhos lookouts. Notorious visitors, such as the English naturalist Charles Darwin, have visited the archipelago doing research on its biology and geology. The local biological diversity drew attention of the author of the theory of evolution while on his journey aboard the HMS Beagle, in 1832. In 1938, the archipelago was given to the government for the establishment of a political prison. In 1942, with World War ll, the Federal Military Territory was created. At the same time, an American military base was established on the main island. More

Dolphins: somersaults and acrobacy

◄   Coney (above); sea cliff in Sancho beach

Conceição beach and its natural anchorage place

than 3.000 soldiers overpopulated the archipelago. The island was managed by the Army, Navy and Air Force until 1988. In that year, the archipelago became part of the state of Pernambuco's territory, as state district and in the same year the National Sea Park was created.

Rotador Dolphin Project

Created in 1990, it studies the dolphins' activities by means of photographs and video-identification, and also includes environmental education programs for both local residents and visitors. In Noronha, dolphins have an appropriate environment to live and at the Dolphins harbour you may see groups from five to 1.200 individuals. In the calm and protected waters of the harbour, the dolphins have found an oasis to rest, mate, look after their offspring and shelter from sharks, their natural enemies. Noronha is one of the few places where this happens; the other is Hawaii. The animals get to the harbor at dawn and may be observed from the lookout jumping out of the water and falling head over heels. The somersaults are actually part of a complex system of communication which they use among them; this system uses body language and sound codes. In the evening, they head offshore and spend the night in search of food.

In the afternoon, you can get a boat and sail around the islands to see dolphins in the waters that envelope the archipelago. Hours of the boat tours are controlled in order not to scare or impair the animals. Phone: 3619-1295.

HIGHLIGHTS

Golfinhos Harbour
The cliff which overlooks the harbour is the best place to watch the *Rotador* Dolphin from land. Dawn is the best time. It is not permitted to enter the water.

Porcos Bay
The small bay in front of the Dois Irmãos Hill has pools and a nice view from the top of the rocks, where you will also see traces of the Fort São João Baptista dos Dois Irmãos.

Sueste Bay
Calm beach; good for skin diving and sea-turtle watching. There is a small mangrove - the only on South Atlantic ocean islands. The ruins of the Fort São Joaquim do Sueste are also here. The shallower parts are indicated with buoys in order to prevent ships from crashing against the reefs.

Buraco da Raquel
A big pool with outcrops of rocks on the surface. There is a lookout with a nice view of the place from the cliffs above the pool. From the lookout you can watch sea-turtles as they rise in the water in order to breath. Here, it is not permitted to go diving.

Diving
Great visibility, which reaches up to 40 m and high temperatures around 26°C, require that you wear diving mask, snorkel and flippers all the time. If you have never gone diving, you can try it here. Some diving agencies hold diving courses in the archipelago.

Boat tours
These go through Mar de Dentro up to Portão harbour and Cape Sapata for Dolphin watching. This tour takes four hours; another tour sails round other islands, such as Rasa, Sela Gineta, do Meio and Rata. It sails from Santo Antônio Wharf.

Caracas Cape
Here, rocks and pools appear during the ebbing tide. It is forbidden to go down onto the reefs, but the view from the high ground rewards the visit.

Sapata Cape
The Cape is formed by rocky cliffs; it is in the south of the island, in a region with preserved forests and trails. If you go by boat, you will be able to see the Sapata's Gate, a crack in the rock which, depending on the angle that you look at it, seems like a map of Brazil. There is an under-water cave in the sea with a "eels' garden" at its entrance. Good for skin diving.

Atalaia Beach
It has a huge pool for skin diving - better during the ebbing tide. It is in front of the Frade Hill. Visits are scheduled with Ibama at Sueste beach by order of arrival and with a limited number of visitors per day. Phone: 3619-1128.

Caieira Beach
Surrounded by reefs which flush the water during the high tide. A good place to go for watching sea birds such as the White-bellied Booby.

Leão Beach
This is the favorite beach for *Aruanã* turtles to lay their eggs. The reefs along it spray water high up, as if flushing up during the high tide. Visits are restricted to controlled hours during the mating season - from December to July. Information with Projeto Tamar/ Ibama.

Morro Dois Irm

Baía dos Po

Sancho

Baía dos Golfinhos

Oceano Atlântico

Ponta da Sapata

Ilha da Viúva

Phone: 3619-1171. In this region you can find traces of the Fort Bom Jesus do Leão.

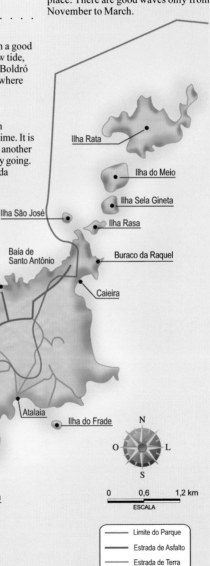 Sancho Beach

You get here via stairs carved out of a crack in the cliff or by boat. The trail starts at Cacimba do Padre beach. One of the islands most beautiful beaches; good for a dip and skin diving.

SURROUNDINGS

Boldró Beach

Its strong waves make the beach a good place for surfing. During the low tide, reefs appear. The São Pedro do Boldró Fort is on the top of a hill from where you can enjoy the sunset.

Conceição Beach

Strong waves crash here between November and March - surfing time. It is one of the island's longest and is another beach where local residents enjoy going. The ruins of the Nossa Senhora da Conceição Fort are here.

Quixabinha and Cacimba do Padre

It is only possible to go to Quixabinha during the low tide. The Cacimba do Padre is next to the Dois Irmãos island and is surrounded by hills and native vegetation. It is one of the best Brazilian beaches to go surfing and where world surf tournaments take place. There are good waves only from November to March.

Ilha Rata

Ilha do Meio

Ilha Sela Gineta

Ilha São José

Ilha Rasa

Cacimba do Padre

Baía de Santo Antônio

Buraco da Raquel

Morro do Pico

Cachorro

Quixabinha

Conceição

Bode

Caieira

Boldró

Americano

BR 363

Atalaia

Ilha do Frade

N

O — L

S

Sueste

a do Leão

Ilha Cabeluda

a da Caieira

Ilha Chapéu do Sudeste

0   0,6   1,2 km

ESCALA

—— Limite do Parque

—— Estrada de Asfalto

—— Estrada de Terra

TO VISIT

Access – Open every day from 8 am to 6 pm.
Address – Al. do Boldró s/nº, Fernando de Noronha, PE, 53990-000. Phones: (81) 3619-1128/1176. Fax: (81) 3619-1210. E-mail: parnamar@ig.com.br.
How to get there – There are regular flights from Natal (1:10 hour), Recife (1:40 hour) and Fortaleza (1:30 hour). The trip by boat takes from one to two days, depending on the kind of boat and on the wind, that is if it happens to be a sailing boat. There are no regular sea cruisers. However, some boats use to make the trip with passengers from Recife and Natal.
Infra-structure – In the archipelago's Eixo Ambiental there are the visitors' centres and the Museu Aberto da Tartaruga Marinha (Sea-turtle Open Museum), with auditorium for 100 people, panels, information and services. There are 10 km of trails for hiking and lookout towers.

TIPS

➲ You can go to Fernando de Noronha at any time because all months are good to visit the archipelago. From August to December it rains less and the water is clearer to go diving. During the high season - from January to March - it rains more and the waves are good for surfing.
➲ It is vital to take a diving mask, snorkel and flippers. The clear water is always inviting for a dive.
➲ Comfortable velcro sandals, good for walking, are obligatory items.
➲ Walking on the beach is always a good sport; at Porcos bay, for instance, it is possible to see the Dois Irmãos rock.

To know more
BUENO, E. **Náufragos, traficantes e degredados: As primeiras expedições ao Brasil, 1500-1531.** Rio de Janeiro: Objetiva, 1998.
HETZEL, B.; LODI, L. e NEGREIROS, S. **Fernando de Noronha.** São Paulo: Prêmio, 1995.
LINS e SILVA, M. B. **Fernando de Noronha: Lendas e Fatos Pitorescos.** Recife, Inojosa, 1999.
www.noronha.pe.gov.br
www.wwf.org.br/wwfpr15.htm
www.fernandodenoronha.tur.br

SERVICES
Fernando de Noronha
🌐 81
✉ 53990-000

Useful Addresses
City Hall. Palácio São Miguel, s/nº, Vila dos Remédios.
Phones: 3619-1378/1352.
Fax: 3619-1229. Internet: fernandodenoronha.pe.gov.br.
Airport. Vila do DPV, Aeroporto, Km 3. Phone: 3619-1182.
Santo Antônio Port. Vila do Porto, s/nº.
Telephone station. Vila dos Remédios. Phone: 3619-1118.
Post Office. Vila dos Remédios. Phone: 3619-1135.
Hospital. Vila dos Remédios. Phone: 3619-1377.
Bank. ABN/Real.
Car rental. Noronha Taxi. Bugies and taxis. Phone: 3619-1142; Olho de Gato. Phone: 3619-1105; Tartarugão. Phone: 3619-1331;Tropical. Phone: 3619-1205.

Support for the Visitor
Tourist Bureau. Palácio São Miguel, s/nº, Ed. Prefeitura, Vila dos Remédios.
Phones: 3619-1378/1352.
Fax: 3619-1229. Internet: fernandodenoronha.pe.gov.br.
Tourist Information Service. Visitors' Centre. Al. do Boldró. Phone: 3619-1171.
Tour Agencies. Águas Claras. Boldró. Phone/fax: 3619-1225. Internet: www.aguasclaras-fn.com.br. Apnéia Turismo. Porto de Santo Antônio. Phone: 3619-1247. Atlantis. Phone: 3619-1371. Centro de Turismo Científico Golfinho Rotador. Phone/fax: 3619-1295. E-mail: rotador@elogica.com.br. Noronha Drivers. Praia do Cachorro. Phone/fax: 3619-1112. E-mail: noronhadivers@uol.com.br.

Lodging
Hotel Esmeralda do Atlântico. Al. do Boldró, s/nº. Phones: 3619-1255/ 3619-1355. Fax: 3619-1277. 40 rooms, 2 chalets (up to 4 people), air conditioning, minibar, tel. Restaurant. 💲💲💲💲
Pousada Atalaia. Rua D. Juquinha, 126, Vila do Trinta.
Phone/fax: 3619-1300. E-mail: atalaias@elogica.com.br. 5 rooms, air conditioning, tv, minibar. 💲💲💲
Pousada Brisa Mar. Av. Major Costa, 4, Vila do Trinta.
Phone/fax: 3619-1139. 2 rooms, air conditioning, minibar. 💲💲💲
Pousada da Mana. Rua Pinto Branco, 214, casa 3, Vila do Trinta.
Phone: 3619-1240.
Fax: 3619-1133. 3 rooms, air conditioning, minibar, tv. 💲💲💲
Pousada da Morena.
Rua Nice Cordeiro, 2600, Floresta Nova. Phone: 3619-1142.
Fax: 3619-1414. E-mail: morena@noronha.com.br. 5 rooms, air conditioning, tv, minibar, tel. Restaurant, bar, courts. 💲💲💲
Pousada dos Corais. Conj. Residencial Floresta Nova, Quadra D, Casa 7. Phone/fax: 3619-1147.
Internet: www.corais.com.br .
6 rooms, air conditioning, tv, minibar, tel. 💲💲💲
Pousada Monsieur Rocha. Rua Dom Juquinha, 139, Vila do Trinta. Phone: 3619-1252.
Fax: 3619-1138. 14 rooms, air conditioning, fan, minibar. Bar. 💲💲💲
Pousada Nativa. Rua Amaro Preto, 125, Floresta Velha.
Phone/fax: 3619-1250. 5 rooms, air conditioning, minibar, tv. Horse riding. 💲💲💲
Pousada Solar dos Ventos. Estrada do Sueste. Phone: 3619-1347.
Fax: 3619-1253. 4 chalets (up to 4 people), air conditioning, minibar, tv, tel. 💲💲💲
Pousada Tia Zete. Rua Nice Cordeiro, 8, Floresta Velha.
Phone: 3619-1242.
Fax: 3619-1459. 10 rooms, air conditioning, minibar, tv. 💲💲💲

Dining
Ecologiku's. Estrada do Sueste. Phone: 3619-1404. Sea food. 💲💲
Nascimento. Rua Major Costa, 115, Vila do Trinta. Phone: 3619-1546. Sea food. 💲💲
Tartarugão. Al. do Boldró, s/nº, Praia do Cachorro. Phone: 3619-1331.
Meats and snacks. 💲💲
Trattoria da Morena. Rua Nice Cordeiro, 2600, Floresta Nova. Phone: 3619-1542.
Pasta and pizza. 💲💲
Tubalhau. Av. Joaquim Ferreira Gomes, 40, Vila do Porto. Phone: 3619-1365. Varied menu and snacks. 💲

Marinho dos Abrolhos

The islands of Abrolhos began their formation between 42 and 52 million years ago, with submarine volcanic eruptions. Coral, calcareous algae and other organisms developed its base, thus forming the reefs of the region. Sixteen thousand years ago, the sea level was 130 m below today's level, but it is believed that part of Abrolhos had remained submersed, thus allowing the coral to survive. The region was a kind of a "reserve" of the world's coral which would have spread to other places when the water level rose again. The islands are coastal for they are located on the continental platform. The vegetation is not much more than a few species of trailing plants and

Foundation: April 1983
Area: 913 km² - 110 km² in the Timbebas Reef
From Caravelas, Alcobaça: 36 km; Prado: 57 km; Salvador: 886 km

(73)
297-1111

palm species brought by man. The terrestrial fauna is represented by lizards and other species introduced by man, such as rats and bird spiders which arrived to the islands on the first vessels; they ended up becoming adapted to the region. There are many species of sea birds which are attracted to the archipelago because of the abundant food. Among them there are Yellow-fronted Woodpecker, Brown-bellied Boobies, Grazinas, Frigates, and Pilotos - the Park's most common bird; it makes its nest on the ground. Migratory birds, such as the Vira-pedra, also use the islands to rest and feed. Under-water algae and Gorgônias form the "submarine meadows". The coral reefs shelter a countless number of fish species: small, big, striped, flat and colourful which turn the waters of Abrolhos

into a giant aquarium. Palometas, Groupers, schools of Pipefish, Blue Parrotfish, crabs and other creatures dance against a background of sponges and coral, performing a life and death spectacle in the transparent waters of Abrolhos. A species of turtle called Cabeçuda, or bigheaded, also lives in the region's hot sea; they lay their eggs during the summer.

It is prohibited to go ashore on the islands because of the nests made on the floor by the sea birds

HISTORY

On the early voyages to Brazil, back in the 16th century, the advise "abra os olhos" (open the eyes) was passed on to all sailors who approached the reefs of the small archipelago in southern Bahia. The advise soon became the name of the Abrolhos Archipelago (Abrolhos is the contraction of abra os olhos), the first South American National Sea Park. The region's

White-bellied booby: habitat preserved

◀   The gentle Butterfly Fish (above); lighthouse on Santa Bárbara island

Chapeirões, gigantic mushrooms from the bottom of the sea

The greatest formation of coral reefs in the South Atlantic is in the region of Abrolhos and the Chapeirões are among its main

The brain coral only exists in Bahia

attractions. They are 30-m-high columns which rise from the bottom and open near the surface, reaching up to 50 m in diameter, as if they were huge mushrooms. The warm waters envelope these sea 'creatures' of common domain. The Chapeirões are formed mainly by a species called Cérebro (brain) which only exists in Bahia, but there are 15 other species of coral that form the reefs of Abrolhos. The reefs near the coast get so close to one another that they unite and form platforms.

diversity, which had already impressed English naturalist Charles Darwin in 1832, drew the attention of ecologists at the beginning of the 1970's. Up to that time the region had been suffering several types of aggression against the environment: predatory fishing, limestone exploitation in coastal waters and the cutting of forests along the coast, which caused more debris to be in the water, thus impairing life in

the coral reefs. Only one out of the five islands that form the archipelago - Santa Bárbara - does not belong to the Park but to the Navy, because of a light house established in 1861. Until some decades ago, the lighthouse was fueled with kerosene. Today it is electric and has a range of 29 km. Besides the islands, the Park includes two blocks of coral reefs: the Abrolhos and Timbetas reefs.

Project Humpback Whale

From July to November Humpback Whales visit the Archipelago; the Jubarte whales, as they are known in Brazil, leave the Antartic Circle during the winter, in search of warmer waters in which to mate. The Humpback Whale Project has existed since 1988 and it aims at protecting and studying these whales. One of its main tasks is to identify individuals by means of photographs of the tail fins; these are really like "fingerprints" which allow the individual to be recognized and catalogued. Until 1999, 802 individuals had been catalogued in Abrolhos. Seventy six of them have returned to the archipelago many times. Biologists estimate that the Humpback Whale population in Abrolhos is around 2.000 individuals. The project also carries out projects of environmental education with the coast communities.

The tail allows the identification of the animal

The Humpback whale is 16 m in length and may weigh up to 40 tons. Despite its size, it feeds on Krill and on small fish, and it is friendly and enjoys showing off: they jump, show their tail fin and "sing". These sounds and showing off are actually part of the mating dance performed by the bulls in order to attract the females during the mating season. In November, when their offspring is well nourished, they begin their journey back to the freezing Antartic waters. Internet: www.cria-ativa.com.br/jubarte.

The archipelago is a paradise for divers

HIGHLIGHTS

Siriba Cave
The cavities in the Siriba island walls attract many fish which look for shelter. You can see Caramurus – or Green Moray eel -, Angelfish, Trunk fish and the colourful Royal Angelfish.

🐚 Santa Bárbara Island Harbour
Here you can see Groupers and Blue Parrotfish which are so used to human presence that they calmly approach divers without fear.

🐚 Guarita Island
It is the Park's smallest and full of round stones which appear to be painted white. In fact, the colour is due to the feces of the many birds which live here.

🐚 Redonda Island
The highest of the Park's islands - smaller than Santa Bárbara, which does not belong to the Park. On its steep cliffs, Frigates make their nests. During the summer, Cabeçuda turtles visit the island to lay their eggs.

🐚 Siriba Island
The only island in the Park which is open for visitation. A 1.660-m trail goes around the island; on the way there is a small beach covered in shells; there are also many ponds with colourful fish and snails. Many Piloto birds make their nests on the Siriba island.

🐚 Sueste Island
The best preserved island of the archipelago due to the difficult access. There are birds' nests all over the place.

🐚 🐚 Rosalina Shipwreck
The stern of the ship is 20 m deep in the water but the prow protrudes from the surface with the ebbing tide. The ship, loaded with cement and Scandinavian beer, sank in 1939. Today it is home for several sea creatures and offers a very good opportunity to go skin or scuba diving. Take care with the sea streams which are usually strong here.

Siriba - Redonda "Meadow"
The area between the Siriba and Redonda Islands is shallow, sandy and with plenty of coral formation. Here there are huge Groupers and schools of Surgeonfish swim here.

🐚 Timbebas Reef
Far from the Archipelago. It is possible to see the reef during the ebbing tide and it is a nice place to go skin diving.

Observe the large fan-like coral formations of a species called Fire coral.

SURROUNDINGS · · · · · · · · ·

🐠 Caravelas River Bar
⊖ 10 km from Caravelas ⊕ One day
The small village has several long beaches at the mouth of the river. Good for walking. Another good option is to go on a boat tour on the river and its mangrove. The visitor's centre of the Park is between Caravelas and the Barra, or sand bar, and it is a good place for a stop before sailing to the archipelago.

Caravelas
Founded in 1503 by Amerigo Vespucci - the Italian traveller to whom America owes its name - the village became important during the mining cycle when it was the final station of the Bahia-Minas railway. The historic centre still has landmarks from the colonial period and houses from the 18th century.

🐠🐚🐌 Cassumba Island
⊖ One hour by boat from Nova Viçosa ⊕ Four hours
Its 100 km² including mangroves and an area of Coastal Rain Forest. It is possible to visit many sea and river beaches and to go on a boat tour in the mangrove. Barra Nova, a sea beach with clear sand and dark water, is one hour by boat from the wharf at Ponte Grande. Observe the trunks of dead trees craved by the wind and the sea. Barra Velha is nearer: 40 minutes by boat from the wharf at Ponte Grande.

🐚🐠 Paredes Reef
⊖ Around two hours by boat from Caravelas - half way to Abrolhos ⊕ Six to eight hours
Good for diving - both skin and scuba -; the reefs outcrop on the surface during the ebbing tide, painting the blue sea brown.

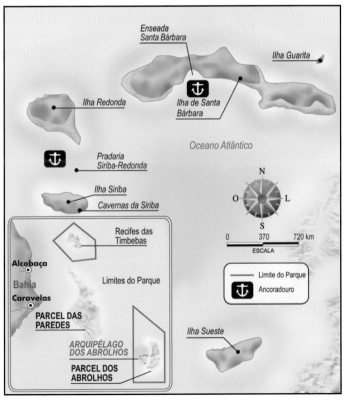

TO VISIT

Access – Open daily. Boats depart at 7 am and return at 5 pm. Admission fee: R$ 10,00 (included in the price of the agencies' package tours).
Address – Praia do Kitongo s/nº, Caravelas, BA, 45900-000.
Phone/fax: (73) 297-1111.
E-mail: parna-abrolhos@tdf.com.br.
How to get there – The trip to Abrolhos takes from 1:30 to 6 hours, depending on the kind of boat. There are around 30 licensed boats: of which two depart from Nova Viçosa and the others from Caravelas. In Caravelas there is an airport with non regular flights to the rest of the country. By car from BR-101 road: take BA-290 in the city of Teixeira de Freitas towards Alcobaça; then turn right towards Caravelas (the road is paved). There are regular coaches from Teixeira de Freitas to Alcobaça and Caravelas.
Infra-structure – The Park's headquarter in Caravelas, at Kitongo beach.

TIPS

◐ The best time to go diving in the Park is from December to February when the sea water is clearer. The Humpback Whales pass by the Park on their migratory route from July to November when it is another good season to visit Abrolhos.
◐ When getting to Abrolhos, a Park's employee supplies information about the Park's rules. Nobody can take a dip before listening to him.
It is not permitted to stay overnight on the islands and those who want to stay more than one day in the Park must sleep on the boat.
◐ It is only possible to go ashore on Siriba Island and only together with one of the Park's employees.
◐ A diving mask and snorkel are essential.

To know more

CASTRO, C.B. e LEÃO, Z.M. **Corais do sul da Bahia.** Rio de Janeiro: Nova Fronteira, 1994.
SECCHIN, C. e LEÃO, Z.M. **Abrolhos: Parque Nacional Marinho.** Rio de Janeiro: Cor/Ação, 1986.
www.abrolhos.com.br

SERVICES

Caravelas, BA
🌐 73
✉ 45900-000

Useful Addresses
City Hall. Rua Barão do Rio Branco, 65. Phones: 297-1113/1064.
Bus station. Pça. Teófilo Otoni, s/nº. Phone: 297-1151.
Airport. BR-418, km 14. Phone: 297-1183.
Hospital. Rua da Liberdade, 238. Phone: 297-1035.
Telephone Station. Rua Firmino Pereira, s/nº. Phone: 229-7159.
Post Office. Rua Ernesto Caetano, s/nº. Phone: 297-1077.

Support for the Visitor
Tourist Bureau. Rua Br. do Rio Branco, 65. Phone: 297-1113.
Tour Agencies. Abrolhos Embarcações. Av. Adalício Nogueira, 1294. Phone/fax: 297-1172. Internet: www.abrolhosembarcacoes.com.br.
Abrolhos Turismo. Pça. Dr. Embassay, 8. Phones: 297-1149/1332. Fax: 297-1109. Internet: www.abrolhosturismo.com.br. Coral de Fogo. Pça. Dr. Embassay, 8. Phone: 297-1332. Gemini. Rua Marechal Deodoro, 44. Phone/fax: 297-1381. Parcel Paradise. Rua das Palmeiras, 58. Phones: 297-1433/297-1433. Internet: www.abrolhos.com.br/caravelas/paradise. Princesa de Abrolhos. Rua Getúlio Vargas, 10. Phone: 297-1375. Internet: www.abrolhos.com.br/caravelas/princesa.

Lodging
Camping Ubaitá. Av. Adalício Nogueira, s/nº. Phone: 297-1350. Fax: 297-1089. Bathrooms, laundry, security, parking lot. $
Farol Abrolhos Hotel Iate Clube. Praia de Quitongo, km 3. Phone: 297-1002. Fax: 297-1173. 15 chalets, tv, air conditioning, minibar, tel. Swimming pool, restaurant. $$
Marina Porto Abrolhos. Praia do Graučá, s/nº, Barra de Caravelas. Phone/fax: 674-1064. 34 rooms, tv, air conditioning, tel. Swimming pool, restaurant, bar, sauna. $$
Pousada Canto do Atobá. Rua das Palmeiras, 45, exit to Alcobaça. Phone/fax: 297-1009. 12 rooms. Swimming pool, bar. $$
Pousada Caravelense. Rua Teófilo Otoni, 1. Phone/fax: 297-1182. 36 rooms. $$
Pousada da Juquitá. Praia do Graučá, s/nº, Barra de Caravelas. Phone: 674-1038. 14 rooms, tv. $$
Pousada dos Navegantes. Rua das Palmeiras, 45, exit to Alcobaça. Phone: 297-1366. Fax: 297-1230. 15 rooms, minibar, tel. $$
Pousada das Sereias. Praia do Graučá, s/nº, Barra de Caravelas. Phone: 647-1033. 20 rooms. Swimming pool, parking lot. $$
Pousada Shangrilá. Rua Sete de Setembro, 219. Phone: 297-1059. 6 rooms, tv, minibar. $
Pousada e Spa da Ilha. Ilha da Cassumba (10 minutes by boat). Phone/fax: 297-1109. 2 rooms. Restaurant (vegetarian food), bar, massage. $$
Pousada da Torre. Av. Adalício Nogueira, 115. Phone/fax: 297-1766/297-1570. 12 rooms, air conditioning, tv. Swimming pool, gym, courts, sauna, lookout, parking lot. $$

Dining
Carenagem. Rua das Palmeiras, 210. Phone: 297-1280. Varied menu. $
Casa Nova. Pça. Quinze de Novembro, 39. Phones: 297-1745/1457. Varied menu. $$
Encontro dos Amigos. Rua das Palmeiras, 370. Phone: 297-1600. Sea food. $$
Museu da Baleia. Praia do Graučá, s/nº, Barra de Caravelas. Phones: 674-1000/1055. Sea food. $$
Tio Berlindo. Praia do Graučá, s/nº, Barra de Caravelas. Phone: 674-1075. Varied menu. $$

Alcobaça, BA
🌐 73
✉ 45990-000

Useful Addresses
City Hall. Pça. São Bernardo, 130. Phones: 293-2010/2110.
Bus station. Av. Sete de setembro, 567. Phone: 293-2212.
Boats for Abrolhos. Cais Santo Antonio, 60. Phone: 293-2259.
Hospital. Rua Nova Viçosa, 1083. Phone: 293-2272.

Support for the Visitor
Tourist Bureau. Pça. São Bernardo, 130. Phone: 293-2010.

Monte Pascoal

The 536 m of Mount Pascoal dominate the landscape. The Park's lands have no uniform distinctive age; the metamorphic rocks of the mountain itself - gnaisses - are the most ancient. Near the sea, the sedimentary lands are more recent. The vegetation benefits from the humid tropical climate: much rain all year round, mainly from April to September. The Park is one of the main Coastal Rain Forests in southern Bahia. In 1999 the Park was declared Human Kind Patrimony by Unesco. In the areas near by the sea, there is extensive mangrove and riverine vegetation. The Rain Forest, of broad leaved plants, is among the richest of ecosystems in terms of biological diversity. The Park's forests represent an important area of conservation of biological diversity in the Brazilian northeast. This wealth is due to the presence of endemic species, restricted to the Park's environment, as well as plants and animals that are typical of the Atlantic ecosystem. Among the trees there are some rare or threatened species, such as the Rue, the Bahia Jacaranda (Rosewood), the red *Juerana*, the *Arapati* and the *Aparaju*. There are also Nitta Trees, Fig trees locally known as *Figueira-brava*, *Araribás*, a gender *Sassafrás* called cinnamon, *Jequitibás*, *Maçarandubas* and Brazilwood. In the dry terrains there are Piassava palms, whose fibers are used to make brooms and ropes for ships. In the moist areas there are Hearts of Palm and several species of Orchid. Among the most common animals there are several kinds of monkey - such as Capuchins and Howling Monkeys - Marmosets, Little Anteaters, *Caxinguelês* - a kind of Chipmunk -, Agoutis, Tapirs, *Surucucu*

Foundation: November 1961
Area: 225 km²
Porto Seguro: 156 km;
Salvador: 910 km; Prado: 68 km;
Itamaraju: 26 km.

(73)
294-1110

snakes, Tyrant Hawks, *Maracanã* - a type of Macaw - and the rare Harpy Eagle. The trees are not so tall in the riverine forest, which develops on sandy stretches near the sea. In this forest, there are countless species of bromeliads, including the just discove-red *Neoregelia pascoalina*.

HISTORY

In the 15th century, a small Iberian country aimed at discovering a closer route to India. In order to achieve its aim, Portugal performed a real technological revolution in the art of sailing. In 1494, with the blessing of the Pope, Portugal and Spain signed the Tordesilhas Treaty, which divided the world between the two countries; Following this treaty, in 1498, Vasco da Gama finally circumnavigated Africa and reached India with a few, battered, ships and went back to Portugal to report that the Indian Rajas would have no business with such an unimportant people. So as to show Portugal's power to the unimpressed Rajas, the King armed a mighty fleet and gave its command to Pedro Álvares Cabral whose mission was to consolidate their relation with the land of spices. On the way, they would take over the unknown land to the west which belonged to the Crown. Cabral's fleet had seen such signs of land as algae and sea birds and on

April 22, 1500 they saw the summit of a mountain which they called Mounte Pascoal, because it was Easter (Páscoa is Portuguese for Easter). The first stretch of land reached by Europeans only begun to be occupied in 1945, when intense cutting of the forest started. It is estimated that less than 0.5% of the original Coastal Rain Forest remains today. The idea of creating a preserved area for the local patrimony is also old: it dates back to the 1930's. In 1943, the region was made into a reserve by the state of Bahia, and later, in 1961, it became a National Park. But the Park's administration still faces conflicts with the Indian population as well as problems such as fires and illegal timber extraction. Today the conservation unit is administered by the Ibama - Brazilian Institute of Environment and Renewable Natural Resources - and with the support of the Indians.

HIGHLIGHTS

🌑 Visitor's Centre
There is a small exhibit
with information about
the Park's fauna and flora.
It is possible to purchase
Pataxó' handicrafts.

Mount Pascoal
The highest point in the
region with 536 m.
The 1.5-km trail to the
top is a difficult one.
It is not advisable for
people out of condition
or with heart problems.
After a 30-minute walk
you get to the first lookout.
The last 15 minutes are
the most difficult, as the
ground gets steeper and rocky.
The view from the summit
is awesome: to the east,
the sea of southern Bahia; to
the west, long stretches of
forest cut across by the
Caraíva and Corumbau Rivers.
On the way down you will
need to be careful for it is
slippery. There is no water on
the way, so take your own
bottle with water enough.

Crossing to Corumbau
A nice trek which
goes across the Park
from east to west. It goes
from the Visitors' Centre
westwards, to Ponta do
Corumbau. It takes
12 hours and you can
choose to go horse riding.

🍃 Fonte Trail
Going down from the
Visitors' Centre, there is a
1-km pathway to a small
creek which flows from a
spring. It is considered to
be a sacred place by the
Indians. It is a 400-m walk.

🍃 Trail to the
Visitors' Centre
This 1-km trail is easy
and has informative signs.
The largest tree on the
trail is a 250-year-old
Souari Nut tree. Take a
look at its gigantic roots.

SURROUNDINGS

🌑 Barra Velha Village
⊖ 10 km from Corumbau ⊕ Two hours
The biggest Pataxó village
in the region. It is interesting
for those who want to know a
bit more about these Indians.
Try the typical Pataxó food
and *cauim*, an alcoholic
beverage made out of manioc.

Pataxó Village
⊖ 13 km from the Park, near BR-101
⊕ Two hours
Here the Indians guide visitors through
the areas where their families work in
the Park. You can go via BR-101 or
walk a 13-km trail which cuts
through the forest.

▼ Maracanã parrot (above); The Pascoal hill takes over the landscape

Caraíva

⊖ 42 km from Trancoso
🕐 One to two days
Internet: www.caraiva.com.br
The main highlights of
this tiny village to the
Park's northern border
are the beaches. You can
get there via road from
Trancoso or by boat from
Porto Seguro. It is always
possible to go by bus from
Eunápolis, Trancoso or
Arraial da Ajuda.
To the south of Caraíva -
a 6-km walk - you can
get to another Pataxó village.

🌀 🐬 🦀 Ponta do Corumbau

⊖ 81 km from the Park
🕐 One day
It takes two hours to drive to
Corumbau on a badly conserved
dirt road. White sands of the beach
and blue sea are in front of the
small fishing village. At the ebbing
tide, a 1-km stretch of sand goes
into the sea. The well preserved
mangrove is part of a Sea
Exploitation Reservation. Another
way to get to Corumbau is by boat.
There is a boat tour which departs
from Cumuruxatiba and stops
along the way for skin diving.

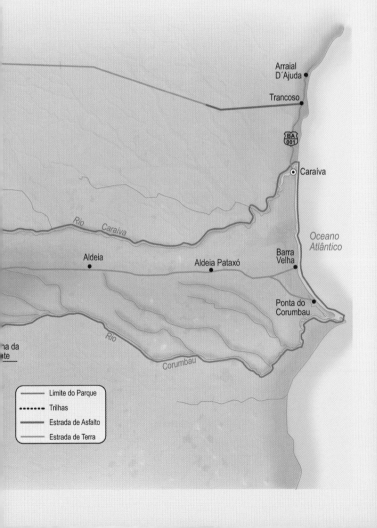

Pataxós: the first inhabitants

Ritual painting is part of the tradition

The population of the Pataxó Indians who live in the area around the Park is approximately 4.000 people spread in eight villages. The Pataxó Indians have probably inhabited the region since the arrival of the Portuguese discoverers. However, they were only described by travellers in the Mount Pascoal area at the beginning of the 19th century. It is believed that in colonial times these Indians from the Tupi nation were the major ethnic group on the southern coast of Bahia and shared the territory with the Maxakalis, Botocudos and Tupiniquins. They lived on hunting, fishing and hunting for crabs along the coast.

Cape Corumbau: access via a badly conserved dirt road or by boat

◀ Pataxó Indians live 13 km away from the Park in the villages near the BR-101

TO VISIT

Access – Open from 7 am to 6 pm. Admission fee: R$ 3,00.

Mail address – Rua Marechal Deodoro, 294, Porto Seguro, BA, 45810-000. Phone: (73) 288-3178.

How to get there – By car from Porto Seguro: take BA-367 and drive for 62 km until Eunápolis. Then, take BR-101 towards Vitória up to km 789, where there is an informative sign indicating the Park. It is 14 km further to the Park's entrance. By coach: there are several companies which depart from Porto Seguro to Itamaraju. From Itamarajú there is no regular transportation but you can take a taxi.

Infra-structure – Visitors' Centre without rest rooms. It is possible to camp in the area.

TIPS

❏ The best season to visit the Park is in summer, from December to February, when it rains less and the water is clearer. The months with most rain are from April to July.

❏ If you want to take a picture of the natives it is advisable to ask permission before using the camera. Pataxó Indians do not usually decline or mind, but they may expect something in exchange; mainly the Indian children.

❏ In the winter, many hostels, restaurants and kiosks of the coastal towns close and it may be difficult to find even coconut water. So, if you are going to a beach far away, remember to take food and drink in your backpack.

❏ If the idea is to go skin diving at the Itacolomi reefs, do not forget the diving mask. Do not wear swimming flippers for they may cause great damage to the reef.

❏ When buying the Pataxó handicraft, try not to purchase big sized pieces - such as vases - made out of the Coastal Rain Forest woods. Give preference to necklaces and other ornaments made from seeds and hay.

To know more

BUENO, E. **A viagem do descobrimento: A verdadeira história da expedição de Cabral.** Rio de Janeiro: Objetiva, 1998.

PINHO, R. C. (coordenação.). **Museu aberto do descobrimento: O Brasil renasce onde nasce.** São Paulo: Fundação Quadrilátero do Descobrimento, 1994.

RICARDO, C.A. (edit.) **Povos indígenas do Brasil, 1996-2000.** São Paulo: Instituto Socioambiental, 2000.

www.socioambiental.org/website/epi/tupiniq/tupiniq.htm

SERVICES

Caraíva, BA
🌐 73
✉ 45824-000

Useful Addresses
Wharf. Access via Praia de Caraíva, s/n°. Phone. 288-2516. Crossing to Porto Seguro in canoes.
City Hall. 288-1599

Support for the Visitor
Tourist Information Services. Casa Barra Velha. Phone: 9985-0241. Internet: www.caraiva.com.br.

Lodging
Pousada Casinhas da Bahia. Praia de Caraíva, s/n°. Phone: 9985-6826. E-mail: ouricos@caraiva.com.br. 6 rooms. Restaurant, bar, caiaks, launchs. 🅢 🅢
Pousada Lagoa. Praia de Caraíva, s/n°. Phone: 9985-6862. Internet: www.tuta.com/caraiva. 4 rooms, 3 chalets. Restaurant, bar, launch, volleyball court, boats, parking lot. 🅢 🅢
Pousada do Neném. Praia de Caraíva, s/n°. Near the border of the Pataxó Reservation. Phone: 9985-4232. Fax: 288-4395. 2 rooms, 1 chalet (up to 5 people). 🅢 🅢 🅢
Pousada Outeiro das Brisas. Cond. Outeiro das Brisas, km 21. Phone: 868-1137. Fax: 9985-5434. Reservation: (11) 866-5152. Internet: www.outeiro.com.br. 12 rooms, minibar. Bar, parking lot. 🅢 🅢 🅢 🅢
Pousada Porto Espelho. Access to Cond. Outeiro das Brisas, km 21. Phone: 868-1142. Fax: 9985-4482. 11 rooms. Restaurant, bar, parking lot. 🅢 🅢 🅢 🅢
Pousada da Praia. Praia de Caraíva, s/n°. Phone: 9985-4249. 11 rooms 🅢 🅢 🅢
Pousada da Terra. Praia de Caraíva, s/n°. Phone/fax: 9985-4417. Reservation. Phone: (31) 3227-6428. E-mail: terra@caraiva.com.br. 7 rooms. Bar. 🅢
Pousada Vindobona. Cond. Outeiro das Brisas, km 21. Phone: 9103-7019. Fax: 9985-5434. 7 rooms, minibar. Bar, parking lot. 🅢 🅢 🅢 🅢

Dining
Beira Mar. Rua do Cruzeiro, s/n°, Centro. Phone: 9985-1180. Fish, varied menu. 🅢 🅢
Brilho do Mar. Phone: 9985-2851. Fish, typical local food. 🅢 🅢

Itamaraju, BA
🌐 73
✉ 45836-000

Useful Addresses
City Hall. Pça. Internacional, 92, Novo Prado. Phone: 294-3322. Fax: 294-1434. Internet: www.itamaraju.ba.gov.br.
Bus station. Pça Castelo Branco, s/n°, Centro. Phones: 294-3666/294-3355.
Hospital. Phones: 294-1242/1192.
Telephone station. Rua Presidente Kennedy, 72. Phone: 294-7133.
Post Office. Pça. Nações Unidas, 28, Centro. Phone: 294-3177. Fax: 294-3582.
Banks. Do Brasil, do Nordeste, Baneb, Bradesco, Santander.
Car rental. Yes Brasil. Av. Presidente Getúlio Vargas, 3336, loja 2. Phone/fax: 291-5585.

Support for the Visitor
Tourist Bureal. Pça. Internacional, 92, Novo Prado. Phone: 294-3170. Fax: 294-1434. Internet: www.itamaraju.ba.gov.br.

Lodging
Barcaça. Pça. da Independência, 268, Cidade Baixa. Phone/fax: 294-3010/294-3262. 20 rooms, tv, air conditioning, minibar. Bar, parking lot. 🅢
Maracaia. Rua José de Anchieta, 65, Cidade Alta. Phone/fax: 294-3114/294-3154. 26 rooms, air conditioning, fan, minibar, tv, tel. Restaurant, bar, parking lot. 🅢
Monte Pascoal. Rod. BR-101, km 808, Sto. Antônio do Monte. Phone/fax: 294-1194/294-3334. 40 rooms, air conditioning, minibar, tel., tv. Restaurant, bar, billiard room, playground, kennel, parking lot. 🅢 🅢 🅢
Pousada Matos. Av. Antônio Carlos Magalhães, 223, Cidade Alta. Phone/fax: 294-1841. 20 rooms, fan, minibar, tv. Restaurant, parking lot. 🅢

Dining
Bom Baiano. Av. Brasil, 822, Centro. Phone: 294-1615. Varied menu. 🅢
Churrascaria Bem-Te-Vi. Rod. BR-101, s/n°, km 814. Phone: 294-1008. Barbecued meat. 🅢
Da Mara. Av. Brasil, 926, Centro. Phone: 294-4004. Fish, varied menu. 🅢 🅢

Pau-Brasil

Located in a region of flat topography, it is cut by medium depth valleys locally known as *boqueirões*. The Rivers Jacuba, Trancoso, Barra and Norte flow through the Coastal Rain Forest on their way to the Atlantic Ocean. Trees such as Bulletwood, Jequitibá, Massaranduba and the Nitta tree are prominent; the two trees, Massaranduba and Nitta, are typical of the Amazon region, indicating that the southern Bahia's forest would have been linked to the Amazonian ecosystem by a vegetation corridor.

The hot, moist, tropical climate favors the development of thick forest vegetation, with trees like Sassafrás, Porcupine Podtrees, Black Rosewoods, Souari Nut trees and California Pepper trees. There are still some Brazil wood trees in the Park but in areas of thick forest which are of difficult access. Today, they are seldom taller than 15 m, half the height they would have reached in the past. In the more humid areas, there are Hearts of Palms, Ferns and several species of orchids. Among the animals there are

Foundation: April 1999
Area: 115,3 km²
Porto Seguro: 40 km; Arraial da Ajuda: 25 km; Eunápolis: 46 km; Salvador: 740 km.

⊘
⊕ (71)
☎ 240-7913

Caxinguelês - a kind of Chipmunk -, Alouatta howling monkeys, Tapirs, White-collared and White-lipped Peccaries, which live near the rivers and leave their tracks everywhere.
There are Little Anteaters, Agoutis, Tapirs, Jaguars and Mountain Lions. Two endemic species that can be easily seen are the Black Porcupine and the Black Sloth. Among birds the Park shelters Harpy Eagles and Tyrant Hawks, both big prey birds on the top of the food chain. The region is famous for the great amount of snakes such as the Bushmaster and the Jararacuçu - both highly dangerous viperine snakes; the Bushmaster, locally called by its Indian name, Surucucu, is the largest Brazilian poisonous snake.

HISTORY

After the discovery of this country, the Portuguese soon lost interest in Brazil for they found neither precious minerals nor spices. Amerigo Vespucci, the Italian traveller to whom America owes its name, wrote: "We have not seen anything valuable, but there are many Brazil wood trees on this coast".
As a matter of fact, this tree was the most valuable product of the newly discovered land. The exploitation of Brazil wood was marked by trade with the Indians who chopped the trees and transported the wood in exchange for axes, knives, beads and other utensils. The extraction was predatory: during one hundred years, around two million trees were cut. The south coast of the state of Bahia remained practically untouched due to the difficulty of reaching it by land, but other cycles followed. In 1970 the road BR-101 was built and the scenery was dramatically changed: Papaya and Coffee plantations were introduced, wood extraction companies begun to operate in the region, and uncontrolled growth of the population and of tourists resulted in the deforestation of a large area.

The controversies about the name of Brazil

The tree which is the symbol of the country

There are two theories that attempt to explain the name of Brazil. One of these theories connects the name of the country to the name of the wood, which is still known by its Indian names in some places: Muirapiranga, Ibirapitanga or Orabutã. The other theory states that the name comes from a mythical land known in the Medieval maps as 'Island of Brasil' or 'Hy Brazil', that would have been discovered by Saint Brendan.

So, Brazil has its origin in the Celtic word bress, root of the English verb 'to bless'. Thus Brazil means 'Blessed Land'. Cited for the first time in the Map by Angel Dalorto (1325), it was to the west of Ireland's South Coast. During the Middle Ages many reports about this mythical island, mysterious land of bliss, appear indicating it in different parts of the Atlantic Ocean.

With the approach of the 500th anniversary of Brazil's discovery, the need for conserving the land first visited by Cabral's fleet became evident. Thus, two new National Parks were created on this stretch of the coast: The Pau-Brasil, which means Brazil wood, and the Descobrimento Park. Both help to preserve what remains of the original coastal rainforest in the region.

HIGHLIGHTS

ⓜ 🌳 Jacuba River Waterfall
The access is via a 1-km trail. The entrance of the trail is marked by a beautiful tree, a Juerana.

⬤ Barra River
Flows through the Park forming pools and cascades.

⬤ Buranhém River
Its banks are covered with vegetation of thick forest.

⬤ Trancoso River
Flows through the park forming deep valleys and reaches the ocean near the village of Trancoso.

SURROUNDINGS

Arraial d'Ajuda
◒ 25 km from the Park
◷ Four hours. Access via BA-001
The village atop a hill has hostels and restaurants. Among the most famous beaches we should mention Mucugê, Pitinga and Taípe.

Vera Cruz Station
◒ 15 km from the Park   ◷ Two hours
Open on Tuesdays and Thursdays from 8 am to 4 pm. Free.
Phone: (73) 281-8025
The Brazil wood is still found here and in the Park. The station has thematic trails and an exhibit of prey birds.

Porto Seguro
◒ 40 km from the Park
◷ From one to two days
The city's historical centre, in the uptown area, has monuments that date back to the colonial time. Visit the beaches, surrounded by reefs. The city has the best facilities for visitors to the region.

Jaqueira's Ecological Reservation
◒ 45 km from Porto Seguro
◷ Three hours

◀ Paca (above); the rivers of the Park flow through the Atlantic Forest towards the ocean

It is managed by the Pataxó Indians. Visit Santa Cruz de Cabrália, where the First Mass in Brazil was celebrated.

Trancoso
⊖ 50 km from the Park ☼ One day
The village was founded is 1586 by Jesuits.The façades of the houses are from the 17th century. Long beaches invite walks by the sea.

Vale Verde
⊖ 5 km from the Park ☼ One hour
This small historical village was declared National Patrimony by Instituto do Patrimônio Histórico e Artístico Nacional (Iphan); it has examples of Brazil wood. Try typical products from the region, such as the cocada, a coconut sweet.

TO VISIT · · · · · · · · · · ·

Access- The Park is not open for visitation.
Mail Address – Caixa Postal 070, Eunápolis, BA, 45820-000. E-mail: pnpaubrasil@bol.com.br. Phone: (71) 345.7322/240.7913.
How to get there – By car from Porto Se-

Orchids are common in the canopy of the forest

guro: take BR-367 towards Eunápolis and at km 53 take the exit to Trancoso.
Infra-structure – None.

To know more
BUENO, E. **Capitães do Brasil: A saga dos primeiros colonizadores.** Rio de Janeiro: Objetiva, 1999.
www.socioambiental.org/website/povind/povos/index.html.

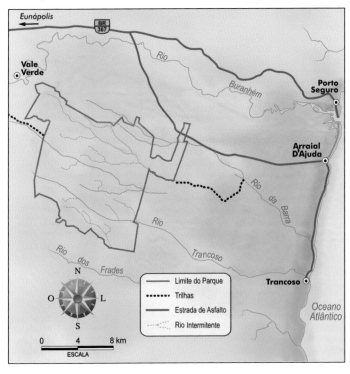

Serra da Capivara

With an impressive landscape, full of canyons, cliffs and rock formations carved out in sandstone, the Serra da Capivara shelters a huge open air museum with the largest concentration of archaeologic sites in the Americas, of which 107 can be visited.

The Park's wide range of topography includes plains, plateaus and canyons - locally called boqueirões. The climate is hot and semi-arid, with six very dry months - from May to October. Around 60.000 years ago, a humid forest covered the state of Piauí. With the raising of the temperature 10.000 years ago some species vanished and others only survived in the more humid areas. Today, there are no perennial rivers in the Park; the natural water reservoirs are the caldeirões - potholes, or holes dug in the rocks by erosion. The Caatinga - a type of stunted spare forest found in the drought areas of northeastern Brazil - has different forms depending on the kind of soil, mainly the one locally called Carrasco (hangman), with more trees and bushes; the vegetation of the boqueirões - forests with high trees whose leaves do not fall in autumn -; the mountainside vegetation - where the Angico tree grows -; and the table mountain vegetation where trees like Hog Plums and Jujubes grow in the areas cultivated near the homes of the natives. Trees stand out among the bushes,

which are woven together with a thick web of vines. There are many thorny plant species, such as cacti, in the Park. Among them the Peru Cereus, the Violet Melon cactus, the Facheiro (a cactus of genera Cereus) and the Xique-xique are the most common ones.

Of the fauna there are endemic species such as the Mocó - a kind of Guinea Pig-; the Large-tailed Bug; and the Mountain-Wall Lizard which have only been found in the Park. The Cavy, the Rattle Snake, a lizard species called Preguiça, toads and Chilean Eagles are common in the Park. In the boqueirões the moist forest shelters Macaws and Guariba monkeys. Other important animals in the Capivara Mountains are the Armadillos and the Little Anteater which play the role of "guardians of the historic patrimony" because they feed on ants and termites, insects which cause damage to the archaeologic sites.

HISTORY

In pre-historic times, southeastern Piauí was inhabited by primitive hunters and gatherers called pimenteiras (Pepper plant). From the middle of the 17th to the beginning of the 19th century the Indians were catechized; at the same time they lost their land and were annihilated. The country was then used for cattle

Foundation: June 1979
Area: 1.291 km²
Teresina: 530 km, Petrolina: 311 km,
São Raimundo Nonato: 20 km

(89)
582-2085 e 582-2031

ranching and for growing small crops. Cattle ranching had been the main economic activity until the middle of the 19th century, when the exploitation of Maniçoba - a tree from the Caatinga whose latex is used to make rubber - became the main economic activity, to the extent of exhausting the species. Archaeologic research in the region began back in 1970 with a French-Brazilian joint team followed by the first scientific expedition to the area in 1973. Today, there are more than 500 archaeologic sites catalogued. Human skeletons, polished stone tools, ceramics, around 40.000 rock paintings, the remains of fires and fossilized animals have been found at the sites. Long ago, species now extinct, such as the Saber-toothed Tiger, the Llama, the Armadillo and the Giant Sloth, roamed the region. Around 380 archaeologic sites have rock paintings with scenes of dancing human figures and animals. As a rock painting can not be directly dated, the archaeologists can only calculate their age by means of analysing the styles. The styles' age itself is estimated on the basis of the remains, such as coal and bones, found in the shelters near the paintings. It is common to see, side by side on the same wall, a graphic pattern painted thousands of years after the one which is painted next to it. There are three main styles in the state of Piauí: Serra da Capivara whose figures are

painted in action performing dynamic movements; Serra Talhada with images enacting dramatic scenes; and the Serra Branca, the most recent and elaborated one, with static, colourfully adorned figures, painted some 3.000 years ago. In 1978, the archaeologist Nième Guidon found human vestiges in Boqueirão da Pedra Furada which dated back to 50.000 years. If the evidence is true and accepted by the scientific community, that they are really human, then it will be the most ancient indication of the presence of Man in the Americas. This would change the traditional theory of the occupation of the American continent.

The Park was created in 1979 and in 1991 was included in Unesco's list of the Human Kind's Cultural Patrimony. Three years later a joint-management agreement for the Park was signed between Ibama - the government's bureau for environmental affairs - and Fundação do Homem Americano (American Man Foundation).

HIGHLIGHTS

Baixão das Andorinhas
A high cliff from which you can watch the swifts, or andorinhas in Portuguese, returning to a cave in the afternoon.

Baixão das Mulheres
A 25-km trail which goes through a 60-m canyon with three archaeologic sites.

Boqueirão da Pedra Furada
The most ancient vestige of the human presence in the Americas was found here: fires built 60.000 years ago. There are also rock paintings in the three styles. The Pedra Furada, which is covered with Mandacarus, stands out in the Caatinga.

Serrinha's Circuit
The circuit leads to the Toca da Roça, Rosa and the Serrinha archaeologic sites, all with rock paintings.

Caldeirão do Boi Circuit
A 8-km trail. The underground lake is one of the few places with permanent water in the Park. It has endemic fish and offers a good view of the Plain. Take a look at the Caatinga's trees and at the ferns in the rainy season.

Caldeirão dos Rodrigues Circuit
You can get here by a 4-wheel-drive vehicle from the support centre or walk via the Baixão da Pedra Furada. It includes several archaeological sites with rock paintings: the grottos do Caldeirão dos Rodrigues I and II, Açoita Cavalo, Bilro, Papagaio, Pedras Chiadeiras, Baixa das Europas, Baixa do Ovídio, Baixão do Nenen and Grotão da Esperança. It is permitted to camp in the circuit.

Pedra Furada, Canoas and Caldeirão do Rodrigues Circuits
A one-day hiking for those who enjoy long walks. It starts at the Boqueirão da Pedra Furada and goes past the geologic formation of the same name. Next you will see the Fumaça, Arame, Sansão and the Pedra Furada pits. The descent in the mountains, amongst rocks and beautiful views, is not a difficult one. You will then get to the Canoas circuit - with six archaeologic sites - taking 40 minutes to go from one circuit to the other. Most figures portray men, Capybaras and American Ostriches. In the second pit there are more recent paintings and the figures are more geometrical and detailed. On the Caldeirão dos Rodrigues circuit you will have to face going up and downstairs on an iron stairway set in the rock. If you feel like going further, you can reach the Grotão da Esperança with a view to the mountains. There are more archaeologic sites on the way, like the Toca do Paraguaio. Visit the old graveyard at the village of Zabelê, which has been renewed.

Pedra Furada, Canoas and Caldeirão do Rodrigues Circuits
A one-day hiking for those who enjoy long walks. It starts at the Boqueirão da Pedra Furada and goes past the

Teresina

SERRA BOM JESUS DO GURGUÉIA

Toca do Ba do Perna
Toca do F

Baixão Andori

Portaria
Terra Vermelha

BR 324

São Raimundo Nonato

Petroli

geologic formation of the same name. Next you will see the Fumaça, Arame, Sansão and the Pedra Furada pits. The descent in the mountains, amongst rocks and beautiful views, is not a difficult one. You will then get to the Canoas circuit - with six archaeologic sites - taking 40 minutes to go from one circuit to the other. Most figures portray men, Capybaras and American Ostriches. In the second pit there are more recent paintings and the figures are more geometrical and detailed.

On the Caldeirão dos Rodrigues circuit you will have to face going up and downstairs on an iron stairway set in the rock. If you feel like going further, you can reach the Grotão da Esperança with a view to the mountains. There are more archaeologic sites on the way, like the Toca do Paraguaio. Visit the old graveyard at the village of Zabelê, which has been renewed.

☞ Perigoso Circuit

Archaeologic sites with rock paintings on the edge of a high cliff. It leads to Quincas Pit. Starting point for the Caldeirão do Boi Circuit.

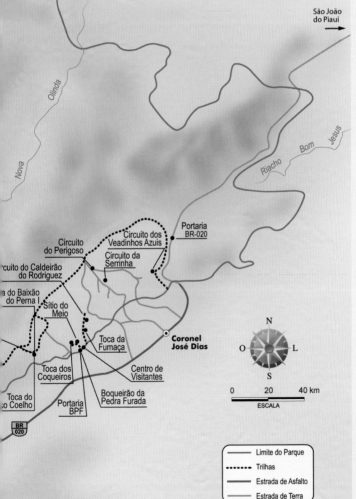

São João
do Piauí
→

Olinda

Nova

Jesus

Riacho Bom

Portaria
BR-020

Circuito dos
Veadinhos Azuis
Circuito
do Perigoso
Circuito da
Serrinha

rcuito do Caldeirão
do Rodriguez

a do Baixão
do Perna I

Sítio do
Meio

Toca da
Fumaça

Coronel
José Dias

Toca dos
Coqueiros

Centro de
Visitantes

Toca do
o Coelho

Portaria
BPF

Boqueirão da
Pedra Furada

BR
020

N
O — L
S

0   20   40 km
ESCALA

Limite do Parque
······· Trilhas
━━━━ Estrada de Asfalto
━━━━ Estrada de Terra

Pathways between the archaeologic sites

🐾 Veadinhos Azuis Circuit
Four archaeologic sites with rock paintings in blue - the first ones found in the world. It is an easy two-hour walk to visit the site.

Capivara's Ravine
A 43-km canyon-like narrow dirt road which goes between high cliffs. The access is via BR-020.

🐾 Meio Site
Rock paintings in the Serra da Capivara and Serra Talhada styles. A narrative panel representing a scene with deer and men. Here, the most ancient ceramics of the Americas - 8.960 years old - was found, also the first American tool made out of polished stone - a 9.200-year-old hand axe.

🐾 Fumaça Pit
It was used as shelter by the natives until recently; the smoke from the kitchen covered many paintings such as the one of a big deer, upon which white American Ostriches were painted.

🐾 Baixão do Perna (I) Pit
Many paintings have vanished because of the crumbling of the rock. Take a look at the panel on the bottom section of the wall. Excavations found stone tools, remains of red paintings and bones of animals which had been roasted and eaten; the findings date back to 3.000 to 10.000 years ago.

🐾 Baixão do Perna (II) Pit or Forno Pit
This archaeological site has paintings from two distinct ages. Some figures, where there is passing among them a small human figure or round object, perform actions which may tell a kind of myth or legend.

Rock paintings: narrative panels

The pre-historic man from Piauí

In the museum, there are human skeletons found in funerary urns

There is evidence of the human presence in the Capivara mountains that dates back to 50.000 years. It is still not known how the first human beings arrived in America nor how the occupation of the continent occurred. What is known is that between 50.000 and 12.000 years ago human groups lived in the São Raimundo Nonato region. The dates calculated are not accepted by the scientific community but they have cast new light on the traditional theories about the occupation of the Americas. These theories state that

Digging is part of the daily life

Man would have entered the continent between 10.000 and 20.000 years ago through the Bering Strait that connected Asia and North America during the glacial ages. Despite being polemic, the discoveries helped to support theories which state that Man also arrived in America by the sea coming from Polynesia and the region of the Pacific Ocean. The first inhabitants of the Capivara mountains brought innovations to the region making cutting tools as well as wooden and stone utensils. The rocky shelters which had potholes were used as hunting bases and the more spacious ones were used as homes. Between 12.000 and 5.000 years ago the climate changed to semi-arid and a new cultural period developed. Utensils began to be made using different technics and ceramics appear for the first time. Many of the rock paintings which had been made for millenniums portraying the inhabitants' daily life, their ritual and animals, disappeared from the region. Around 3.500 years ago the region was assumed by a people who knew of agriculture, made ceramics items and buried their dead in the ground or in funerary urns. These people stayed in the region until the arrival of the Europeans, when they were annihilated.

◉ Chico Coelho Pit
Paintings representing deer and human beings performing rituals and making group sex. There is also a large human figure which witnesses an occupation from another age.

◉ Coqueiros Pit
Here archaeologists found stone tools and a 9.870-year-old human skeleton. It also has rock paintings.

SURROUNDINGS

◉ Petrônio Portela Dam
⊖ 25 km from the Park ⊕ Two hours
If you want to take a refreshing bath after hiking through the Caatinga, the dam's lake is the only option available in this neighbourhood. There is a small snack bar here.

American Man's Museum
⊖ 30 km from the Park ⊕ Six hours
Phone: (86) 582-1612. Hours: from Tuesday to Thursday from 9 am to 6 pm; Fridays from 9 am to 9 pm; Saturdays and Sundays, from 9 am to 6 pm. Admission ticket selling stops one hour before the closing of the museum. Price: R$ 3,00 to R$ 6,00. E-mail: fumdham@terra.com.br
Inaugurated in 1998, it shows panels of the local pre-history. It is divided into three sections: geological history of the region; information about the mountains' animals and plants (with pre-historic fossilized animals); and archaeology, whose exhibition includes America's most ancient stone artifacts and replicas of human skeletons.

The Fundação Museu do Homem Americano (Fumdham - Foundation of the American Man's Museum) was created in 1986 in order to back up the archaeologic works at the Serra da Capivara National Park. Apart from archaeology, the foundation also supports the local community while preserving the Caatinga and its' archaeologic sites; the search for non-destructive economic activities is among Fumdham's main priorities. So far, in the area around the Park, the foundation has developed projects for the community, such as beekeeping and pottery, and has set up four schools which give free education to more than 600 students. The main income of the local population comes from their work as tour guides while helping to preserve the Park.

São João do Piauí
⊖ 98 km from the Park
🕐 Three hours
In the state of Piauí, São João is a typical backwoods village. Here, on June 24 they commemorate the day of São João (Saint John) with a traditional festival: folk music and dance, also plenty of regional food and drinks.

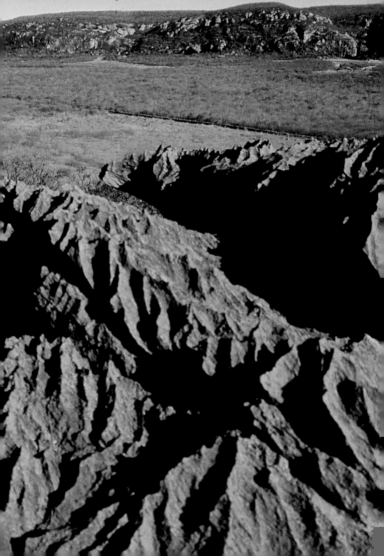

TO VISIT

Access – There are four roads; the most used ones are the Boqueirão da Pedra Furada and the Serra Vermelha. Admission fee: R$ 3,00. Visitors must be accompanied by guides (R$ 25,00 per group of up to 10 people).

Address – Praça do Rotary s/n°, Caixa Postal 21, São Raimundo Nonato, PI, 64770-000. Phones: (86) 582-2031 and 582-1612 (Visitors' Centre).

How to get there – There is an airstrip in Raimundo Nonato. By car from Petrolina: take BA-235: 311 paved km up to São Raimundo Nonato. From Teresina: take BR-343 to Floriano; then take PI-140 and after BR-324 to São Raimundo Nonato. By coach: there are daily departures from Teresina and Petrolina.

Infra-structure – The Visitors' Centre has VCR room, snack bar, shop and rest rooms. There is also a camping ground, hostel for visitors and telephone station. At sites such as the Boqueirão da Pedra Furada, there are pathways to see rock paintings

TIPS

✪ The best time to visit the Park is from March to June at the end of the rainy season when the vegetation is greener and the weather more mild for hiking. July is also a good month to go; the weather is cooler but the vegetation is drier. The hottest months are from September to January.

✪ The best time to go hiking is early in the morning, because the temperature is milder.

✪ At Baixão das Andorinhas the evening is the nicest part of the day, when birds come back to the gorge.

To know more
MONTEIRO, S. e KAZ, L (coordenação.).
Caatinga – sertão sertanejos. Rio de Janeiro: Allumbramento / Livroarte, 1994-95.
www.iadb.org/exr/IDB/stories/1997/eng/xpat2e.htm
www.biodiversitas.org/caatinga/
www.minc.gov.br

◀ Sandstone rocks contrast with the vegetation of the *Caatinga*

Plains and rocky formations compose the landscape of the region

SERVICES

São Raimundo Nonato, PI
⊕ 89
✉ 64770-000

Useful Addresses
City Hall. Rua José Leandro, 288, Centro. Phones: 582-1411 and 582-1412.
Bus station. Pça. José Ferreira, 476, Centro. Itapemirim. Phone: 582-1266; Transpiauí. Phone: 582-1268; Princesa do Sul and Gontijo. Phone: 582-1372.
Hospital. Rua Cel. Rubens de Macedo, 135, B. Aldeia. Phones: 582-1413 and 582-1322.
Post Office. Rua Capitão Newton Rubem, 1051, Centro. Phone: 582-1435.
Banks. Do Brasil, do Nordeste, Caixa Econômica Federal.

Support for the Visitor
Tourist Bureau. Rua José Leandro, 288, Centro. Phones: 582-1411/ 582-1412.
Tourist Information Service. Fundação Museu do Homem Americano (Fumdham). Rua Projetada, s/nº, Campestre. Phone/fax: 582-1612. E-mail: fumdham@terra.com.br.

Tour Agency. Trilhas da Capivara. Av. Professor João Menezes, 472, Centro. Phone: 582-1798.

Lodging
Real. Largo Manoel Agostinho de Castro, 704, Centro. Phone/fax: 582-1495. 18 rooms, fan, air conditioning, tv, minibar, tel. Bar, restaurant. $ $
Serra da Capivara. Rod. PI-140, km 0, Santa Luzia. Phone: 582-1760. Fax: 582-1389. 18 rooms, tv, air conditioning, minibar. Swimming pool, bar, restaurant, parking lot. $ $
Camping da Pedra Furada. Av. Nestor Paes Landim, km 28, Sítio do Mocó. Cel. José Dias. Phone: 582-1100. Camping ground and 4 chalets (up to 6 people). Bar, fridge. $

Dining
Fresamary. Rua Major Gerônimo Belo, s/nº. Variada. $
Mãe Sinhá. Av. Prof. João Menezes, 581. Phone: 582-1004. Typical local food. $
Soares. R. Bartolomeu Ribeiro de Castro, 175, Phone: 582-1347. Typical local food. $ $

Serra das Confusões

The Serra das Confusões National Park is the largest in the Northeast region. Located between a crystalline mountain - the Serra Grande formation - and a sedimentary basin - Piauí-Maranhão plateau - its topography is divided into two with altitudes ranging from 650 to 700 m: the Gerais Plateau and the mountains – Confusões, Semi-Tumba, Guaribas, Perdidas, Macacos, Peneira and Pitombas.

The region divides the basins of the São Francisco and Parnaíba Rivers. Several river sources flow through the Park forming the Itaueria and Piauí Rivers which are important for the arid state of Piauí.

This region is the largest unexplored *Caatinga* reserve in Brazil. The *Caatinga* is a type of stunted, sparse forest found in the drought areas of northeastern Brazil. The

Foundation: October 1998
Area: 5.024 km²
Teresina: 640 km; Caracol: 20 km;
São Raimundo Nonato: 114 km;
Petrolina: 454 km;

⊘
🌐 (89)
☎ 589-1208 e 589-1209

Park is also considered an extremely important area in biological terms because it is located in a zone where the *Cerrado* and the *Caatinga* encounter.

The *Caatinga* has many forms, with open zones and others with more trees - the *Carrascos*. The research that was carried out for the Park's creation, identified 87 plant species. The most common ones are the Courbaril tree, the *Feijão-Bravo* (many tropical shrubs and trees of the pea family), the *Camaçari*, the Funnelvine, the Mungo Bean, the *Cangalheira*, the California Pepper tree, the Cinnamon-bark tree, the Jack-in-the-pulpit, the Jack Bean, the Acacia, the Jujube, the Quince, the Hog Plum, the *Piquiá*, the *Angico* (a tree of the mimosa family, whose hard wood is much used in Brazil for heavy construction) and the Trumpet Bush. There are also cacti such as the Peru cereus, the Violet Melon cactus, the *Facheiro* (a cactus of genera Cereus) and the *Xique-xique*.

With regards to the fauna, the research found 14 amphibian species, 32 species of reptiles and 46 of mammals. Among them, the Great Anteater, the Armadillo, the Pampas Deer, the Jaguar, the Capuchin and the Guariba monkey stand out. Among the birds we should mention the Zabele Red-Footed Tinamou, the Guan and the Yellow-Headed Parokeet.

HISTORY

The state of Piauí was covered with a moist rain forest 60.000 years ago. However, in the last 10.000 years a period of drought has changed the Serra das Confusões landscape. Some species vanished and some survived in more humid places. The history of the region's occupation is similar to the Capivara Mountains, 100 km away. At the beginning it was inhabited by pre-historic peoples who hunted and gathered, making wooden, stone and ceramics tools. They recorded their daily life in rock paintings. It is known that there are many archaeologic sites in the Park which have been catalogued by the Iphan - National Historical and Artistic Patrimony

Sandstone mountains with needle-like formations are common in the Park

Riacho dos Bois Grotto

In the last 3.500 years, new peoples appeared with new agricultural technics and stayed until the coming of the Jesuits, in the 17th century. Following the Jesuits, white settlers came and the Indians were fought and vanished from the region. The land was then used for cattle ranching and cultivation. However, because of the difficult access, Confusões remained with a low occupation rate: it was just a passage way to the cities of Caracol, Cristino Castro and Santa Luz. It takes days to walk the trails carved in stone at the beginning of the 20th century. Just a few people, such as the Priests who celebrated Mass in the different villages, walked the trail. Today these trails are still the region's main access.

The area was transformed into a Park in 1998, because of the archaeologic sites and the preserved ecosystems.

HIGHLIGHTS

Riacho dos Bois Grotto
The 3-km grotto under rock formations was carved out by the Bois Creek. Some parts are 50 m high. The access is

◄ The agile capuchin monkey (above); cliff walls have rock inscriptions difficult because there are no roads to the grotto. It is necessary to go via trails blazed in the *Caatinga*.

Guardião Rock

A sandstone rock formation that can be seen from a lookout which overlooks the Andorinha Mountains.

Gerais Mountains

It is away from the villages, in the Park's less explored region. The access is difficult and the vegetation is thicker in this area.

Pinga do Velho Pit

Archaeological site with rock paintings.

Andorinhas Mountains

A region of sandstone mountains, with big rock formations and many grottos with rock paintings. The vegetation here is more open, which makes walking easy.

SURROUNDINGS

Serra da Capivara National Park

⊖ 114 km from the Park

⊙ Two to five days

The Park, older than Confusões and with good facilities for the visitor, allows you to get to know the *Caatinga*, apart from having many archaeologic sites with rock paintings.

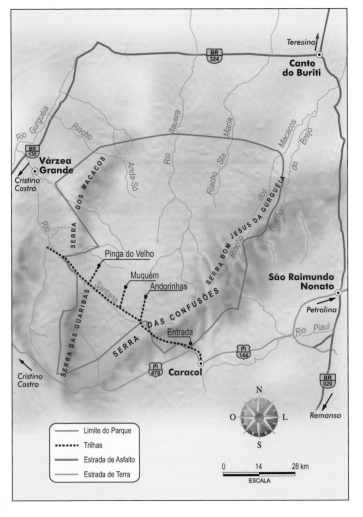

TO VISIT

Access – The Park is not open for visitors yet.

Mail address – Rua Luiz Ribeiro, s/n°, Caracol, PI, 64795-000. Phones: (86) 589-1208 and 589-1209.

How to get there – By car from Petrolina (Piauí): take BA-235 for 340 km until São Raimundo Nonato. From Teresina (Piauí), take BR-343 until Floriano. Then take PI-140 until Canto do Buriti. There you will take BR-324 up to São Raimundo Nonato. From São Raimundo Nonato to Caracol you must take PI-144 and drive 94 km on a dirt road. From Caracol to the Park it is 20 km. By coach to Caracol: there are two daily departures from São Raimundo Nonato and one weekly departure from Teresina.

Infra-structure – There is none.

TIPS

❍ From March to June, at the end of the rainy season, the vegetation is greener and the weather milder. The strongest heat is from September to January, when it is difficult to go hiking. The average temperature is 28°C but the nights in the mountains are cold and the temperature may go down to 10°C.

To know more
MONTEIRO, S. e KAZ, L (coordenação). **Caatinga – sertão sertanejos.** Rio de Janeiro: Allumbramento / Livroarte, 1994-1995. www.biodiversitas.org/caatinga/

Rock paintings portray the daily life of ancient civilizations

SERVICES

Caracol

🌐 89
✉ 64795-000

Useful Addresses
City Hall. Pça. Padre Francisco, 63, Centro. Phones: 589-1220 and 589-1181.
Telephone station. Rua João Dias, 125, Centro. Phone: 589-1120.
Post Office. Rua Luis Ribeiro, s/nº, Centro. Phone: 589-1144.
Ambulatory. Rua João Dias, 221. Phone: 589-1175.

Support for the Visitor
City Hall. Pça. Padre Francisco, 63, Centro. Phones: 589-1220/ 589-1181.

Lodging
São Bento. Rua Padre Francisco, 77, Centro. Phone: 589-1219. 6 rooms, colective bathroom. Bar, restaurant, parking lot. $

Dining
Novo Horizonte. Rod. Caracol - Campo Alegre de Lourdes, BA, km 1, Morro do Ouro Branco. Typical local food and meats. $
Alto do Cruzeiro. Rod. Caracol - Serra das Confusões, km 0. Typical local food. $

São Raimundo Nonato

🌐 89
✉ 64770-000

Useful Addresses
City Hall. Rua José Leandro, 288, Centro. Phones: 582-1411/1412.
Bus station. Pça. José Ferreira, 476, Centro. Itapemirim. Phone: 582-1266; Transpiauí. Phone: 582-1268; Princesa do Sul and Gontijo. Phone: 582-1372.
Hospital. Rua Cel. Rubens de Macedo, 135, B. Aldeia. Phones: 582-1413/1322.
Post Office. Rua Capitão Newton Rubem, 1051, Centro. Phone: 582-1435.
Banks. Do Brasil, Nordeste, Caixa Econômica Federal.

Support for the Visitor
Tourist Bureau. Rua José Leandro, 288, Centro. Phones: 582-1411/1412.
Tourist Information Service. Fundação Museu do Homem Americano (Fumdham). Rua Projetada, s/nº, B. Campestre. Phone/fax: 582-1612. E-mail: fumdham@terra.com.br.
Tour Agency. Trilhas da Capivara. Av. Professor João Menezes, 472, Centro. Phone: 582-1798.

Lodging
Real. Largo Manoel Agostinho de Castro, 704, Centro. Phone/fax: 582-1495. 18 rooms, fan, air conditioning, tv, minibar, tel., bar, restaurant. $$
Serra da Capivara. Rod. PI-140, km 0, B. Santa Luzia. Phone: 582-1760. Fax: 582-1389. 18 rooms, tv, air conditioning, minibar. Swimming pool, bar, restaurant, parking lot. $$
Camping da Pedra Furada. Av. Nestor Paes Landim, km 28, Sítio do Mocó, Cel. José Dias, PI, Parque Serra da Capivara. Phone: 582-1100. Camping area and 4 chalets (up to 6 people). Bar, fridge. $

Dining
Fresamary. Rua Major Gerônimo Belo, s/nº. Varied menu. $
Mãe Sinhá. Av. Prof. João Menezes, 581. Phone: 582-1004. Typical local food. $
Real. Largo Manoel Agostinho de Castro, 704. Phone: 582-1495. Typical local food. $

Cidades

Sete Cidades

The Park lies on Paraiba's sedimentary basin, which was formed 400 million years ago. At that time, the area was very moist and the rocks started to be moulded by wind, rain and heat. The region's climate had been hot and moist until 18.000 years ago, when the landscape became bare. The many rock formations, with different colours and sizes, look like the ruins of towers and walls, which made some believe they were made by men.

The gentle topography of the sandstone rock is dominant in the area. Eroded over the centuries, they show table and conic forms. The region is located in a transition zone between the plateau and the costal plain, with a semi arid climate whose seasons are very well defined. It is hot all year round, with rains from January to March. The Park is also important because it protects many river sources located in its area. There are 22 springs which water the state of Piauí's North region. The vegetation is typical of dry climates, mainly the *Cerrado*

(bushland), with some spots of *Caatinga* - a type of stunted, spare forest found in the drought areas of northeastern Brazil -, some open grassland that sometimes floods and riverine forests. Most plant species are typical of the *Cerrado*, such as the *Murici*, the *Cascudo*, the Bacury, the Souari Nut Tree and the *Pau-Terra*. In the *Caatinga* there are Jujubes, Acacias, California Pepper

Foundation: June 1961
Area: 77 km²
Piripiri: 22 km; Teresina: 190 km;
Parnaíba: 182 km; Sobral: 208 km;
Fortaleza: 458 km

○
⊕ (86)
☎ 343-1342 e 233-3369

Trees and cacti such as the *Xique-Xique* (Rattlebox). In the riverine forest, species such as the Trumpet bush and the Trumpet Tree are present. Water lilies adorn ponds and lakes, adding a special colour to the landscape. In the Park there are also palm trees such as the Buriti, the Carnauba and the *Tucum*. They have survived exploitation by the local population, which did not happen with the *Babaçu*; much prized for its many products, it is thought to have once existed in the region. In the flooded fields different grasses and the Sundew, an insectivorous herb, stand out. The most common mammals are Brockets, Tapirs, Little Anteaters, Agoutis, Wild Dogs and *Mocós*, a kind of Guinea Pig. Among the birds there are Parrots - whose noisy flocks announce the dawn - the Crested Seriema and the Tinamou. The Jamacai Oriole and the Yellow and Red-rumped Cacique are particularly colourful and beautiful.

HISTORY

The Sete Cidades National Park's area was inhabited in pre-historic times by peoples who marked their presence with rock paintings. The inscriptions show geometrical figures in red paint - probably of mineral origin, as there is much iron oxide in the region -, black and yellow. They were painted on smooth sandstone walls, natural shelters or around small cracks in the rocks. Although not precise, it is estimated that the paintings are 6.000 years old, indicating that they were made by peoples with nomadic habits who abandoned the dry areas and moved into the moist Amazonian parts of where today the state of Maranhão is. Other sources state that the paintings would be much more recent, from the 17th century or even later. If this is so, they would have been painted by the Tapuia Indians, who used to live in the region around the Ibiapaba mountains. Later, the Tabajara Indians took over the region. Jesuit priests tried to pacify the Indians but failed. With the white men occupation of Piauí these Indians were exterminated and today only a few remain who barely manage to preserve their culture. From the 18th century on, the region was

The Tartaruga Rock is in the sixth city; it looks like a huge carapace

◄   The parrot uses the cliffs to shelter (above); eroded rocks with uncommon forms

The Biblioteca Rock, in the second city, looks like a bookshelf

shared by many cattle ranches and small agricultural areas, which altered the environment.

The first reference to the "Rock Cities" appears in the notes of a Brazilian Historical and Geographical Institute meeting, in 1886. In 1928, stopping in Brazil on a trip, the Austrian Ludwig Schwennhagen declared the Sete Cidades as the ruins of an ancient Phoenician city. The origin of the place is also considered to be connected to the Vikings and even to ETs. However, geological studies show that the Seven Cities are natural formations, carved by wind and rain.

Nowadays, the region's main economic activity is cattle ranching. The Park, founded in 1961, aims at protecting the area's archaeologic and environmental patrimony.

The nery melon: a cactus typical of the *Caatinga*

HIGHLIGHTS

First City

Visit the Canhões, formed by iron sandstone, more resistant to erosion. Other attractions in this city are the Rock Forest, the 2-km Sambaíba Trail, the Piscina dos Milagres and the river's waterfall.

Second City

From the Arco do Triunfo - an 18-m-high rock formation - you will be in the area of the Park where most of the Park rock paintings are. The red colour is probably a mixture of iron oxide, plant oil and animal blood. The hand impressions suggest that they may have been painted by the Tabajara Indians. The most famous painting is one at Mão dos Seis Dedos site. There is a 80-m-high lookout which allows you to overlook the Park. At the Sítio Pequeno and the Americano Rock there are rock paintings too. Among the rock formations are the Castelo Rock and the Biblioteca (Library) – which resembles a pile of books on a shelf. Visit the Paredão das Bromélias and the Sítio do Camaleão.

Third City

Look for the Dedo de Deus (God's Finger), the Três Reis Magos (Three Magi), the Curral de Pedras (Rock Corral), the Pedra do Beijo (Kiss Rock) and the Furo Solsticial (Solstice Hole) - where the sun beams beautifully illuminate in the winter solstice. Dom Pedro's Head is another rock formation eroded by rain.

The wild-dog is seldom seen

Fourth City

The Cidadela (Citatel), the Grande Muralha (Great Wall), the Archete, the Portal (Gate), the Beijo dos Lagartos (Lizard's Kiss) and the Mapa do Brasil (Map of Brazil) are some of the rock formations you will find here. The access to the Passagem do Índio (Indian's Passage), another rock formation, is a bit difficult for it is on steep terrain.

Fifth City

Here, the most interesting natural monuments are the Pedra do Gorila (Gorilla's Rock), the Furna do Índio (Indian's Cave), the Pedra do Camelo (Camel's Rock), the Pedra do Último dos Moicanos (Last Mohican Rock) and the Pedra do Imperador (Emperor's Rock). From the top of this city you oversee the Park. Visit the Catirina Grotto. It is said that a hermit used to live in the grotto, where he buried his son, whose grave can be visited. Among the rock paintings, the best known is one which portrays a hunting ritual. The fifth city's trail is 1,2 km.

Sixth City

The Pedra da Tartaruga (Turtle's Rock), the Pedra do Elefante (Elephant's Rock) and the Pedra do Cachorro (Dog's Rock) are here. The first of them was thus named because it looks like a huge turtle's carapace formed by pentagons, which pose a difficult question to geologists. Some theories have them as a heritage from glacial eras.

Seventh City

Here are the Park's best preserved rock paintings - most of them in red. The Pedra do Leque (Fan's Rock), the Gruta do Pajé (Witchdoctor's Grotto) and the Casario (Houses' row) are also here.

⑩ Riachão Waterfall

Here you will find two falls which form a pond: one is 7-m high and the other, 16-m. The 200-m way down to the fall is, on slippery ground.

❷ Milagres Spring

Near the rock formations of the first city, this small river source is a good place for a refreshing dip.

Sete Cidades Trail

The 12-km trail goes through all cities and takes a whole day to walk. You can also go in phases on different days. It is possible to go by bicycle.

SURROUNDINGS

Pedro II City

50 km from the Park ⊕ Two hours

It is the only place in Latin America where there are opal - a precious stone - mines. Part of the production is used in jewellery and sold in the city itself. It is possible to visit some mines near the city's centre, such as the Boi Morto and the Roça. It is worth buying a hammock made in the city's primitive looms.

Parnaíba

182 km from the Park ⊕ Two days

A good base for a visit to the Parnaíba River's Mouth, in the state of Piauí. It is where the river forks in five arms to reach for the sea, forming countless islands, mangroves and dunes.

There is a tour which takes you to the Cajú Island: 25 km of virgin beaches, dunes, streams and lagoons formed by the rain.

Cachoeira do Urubu Ecological Park

65 km from Piripiri ⊕ Three hours

Access via Batalha, through Esperantina, on a paved road

Between the cities of Batalha and Esperantina, the main highlight is the Urubu Waterfall, formed by the Longa River waters. There are many hotels and hostels in the region, where you can try typical dishes from Piauí, such as the tasty sun-dried meat and the *paçoca* (a dish made of bits of sundried meat mixed with manioc meal).

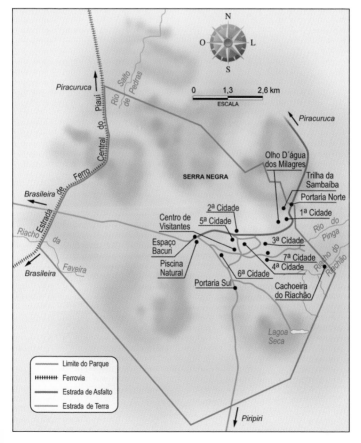

TO VISIT

Access – The Park is open daily from 8 am to 5 pm. Admission fee: R$ 3,00. It is obligatory to have a guide.

Mail address – Caixa Postal 35, Rod. Min. Vicente Fialho, Piripiri, PI, 64260-000. Phones: (86) 343-1342 and 233-3369 (Ibama in Teresina).

How to get there – By car from Teresina: take BR-343 towards Parbaíba until the Park. From Fortaleza, go via BR-222 until Piripiri and then take BR-343 for 23 km more. By coach: there are couches departing from Teresina and Piripiri.

Infra-structure – The Park has well marked trails whose access is easy. There is a visitors' centre with exhibitions and rest rooms, hotel, restaurant, souvenir shop and a natural swimming pool.

TIPS

❍ The best time to visit the Park is from January to July, when the ponds and waterfalls are fuller and the weather is milder.

❍ Do not miss the rock paintings, many of them concentrated mainly in the Second City.

❍ As you have come as far as here, do not fail in visiting the Ubajara National Park, 120 km away. The access is via BR-222, towards Fortaleza.

To know more
COUTINHO, R. **Enigmas de Sete Cidades.** Piripiri: Ideal, 1997.
FORTES, F. **Geologia de Sete Cidades.** Teresina: Fundação Cultural Monsenhor Chaves, 1996.
SCHWENNHAGEN, L. **História antiga do Brasil: de 1100 a.C. a 1500 d.C.** Teresina: Imprensa Oficial, 1928.
www.piauihp.com.br

Services

Piripiri, PI
🌐 86
✉ 64260-000

Useful addresses
City Hall. Av. 4 de Julho, 280, Centro. Phone: 276-1703.
Bus station. Av. Estado de Pernambuco, s/nº. Phone: 276-1638.
Post Office. Rua Severiano Medeiros, 323, Centro. Phone: 276-1136. Fax: 276-2211.
Hospital. Av. Dr. Pádua Mendes, 300. Phone: 276-1325.
Banks. Do Brasil.

Support for the Visitor
Secretaria de Turismo (Tourist Bureau). Pça. da Bandeira, 148. Phone: 276-3315.

Lodging
Califórnia. Rua Dr. Antenor Freitas, 546. Phone: 276-1645. 16 rooms, 4 bedrooms, air conditioning, minibar, tv. Parking lot. 💲💲
Fazenda Sete Cidades (near the Park). Access via BR-222, km 63. Phone. Fax: 276-2222. Reservations: 232-3996. 37 rooms, air conditioning, minibar, tv. Swimming pool, bar, restaurant, court, children's playground, bicycles, horse. Parking lot. 💲💲

Dining
Churrascaria Chico Jovem. Av. Aderson Alves Ferreira, s/nº. Barbecued meat. 💲
Restaurante Fazenda Sete Cidades. BR-222, Km 63. Phone/fax: 276-2222/ 989-8035. 💲💲

Eroded sandstone formations lie at Sete Cidades

Ubajara

Located on the border of the state of Piauí, The Ubajara National Park is at a plateau surrounded by green valleys. The steep cliffs and the moisture impress the visitor who goes there through the Caatinga - a type of stunted sparce forest found in the drought areas of northeastern Brazil. There are two versions for the meaning of Ubajara: "Lord of the Canoe" or "Canoe Mother of Water". Anyway, water is in the name highlighting its importance in the place. The region's climate is hot, semi-arid, with seven or eight dry months per year - from May to December. However, the plateau's weather is milder, with yearly average temperatures between 24 and 26°C. The monthly rain fall is 1.436 mm, very high for the Caatinga. The Park's area is considered to be an island in the middle of the backwoods of the state of Ceará. The moist forest and the mild climate caused the flora and fauna to be different from the rest of the region. On the plateaus and in the plains there is a type of Caatinga with more shrubby trees; it is locally known as *Carrasco*. On top of the canyons and cliffs there are moist forests with tall trees, ferns and bromeliads. In the dense vegetation there are trees such as the Ipe tree, the Muskwood, the Copal wood, the Cattley Guava and the Babaçu palm, which reach up to 15 m in height. Below,

Foundation: April 1959
Area: 5,63 km²
Sobral: 110 km; Fortaleza: 333 km; Teresina: 314 km; São Luís: 758 km

⬤ (88)
☎ 634-1388

in the low land, the white forest - Caatinga in the Tupi Indians' language - and its thorny vegetation take over the place; there are trees like Cedars, the Angico (a tree of the mimosa family, whose hard wood is much used in Brazil for heavy construction), Acacias and Jujubes. In order to survive the lack of water, the vegetation adapts itself to the environment. Thus the trees have small leaves, with a smaller evaporative surface in order to loose less water. The transition vegetation between the two formations has species such as the Floss-silk tree and the Coralbean. In the smallest Brazilian National Park, there are animals as Mocós - a rodent very much like the Guinea Pig which is typical in the Caatinga -, Armadillos, Lizards, and Snakes - such as Surucucus, Rattlesnakes and the Boa Constrictor. Some animals, like the Anteater and the Agouti, are more easily

seen at sunset when the temperature is milder. Among the birds, the most common are the Northeast Buff-throated Wood-hewer, the Jay, a species called Cancão - and the Chorozinho-de-bone. In the forests on the plateau, there are two species of Capuchin monkeys which go about in groups, swinging from one tree to another: the species are locally called prego (nail), and estrela (star). There are more than ten species of bats which live in the caves.

Waterfalls in and out of the Park form pools

HISTORY

The Tabajara and the Tapuia Indians were the first inhabitants of the region around the Ibiapaba mountains. In 1607, Jesuits from Pernambuco came to their territory to preach and stayed until 1661, when an uprising expelled priests and soldiers. In the middle of the 18th century there were rumours about silver mines in the region, but the expedition sent to examine the region never found anything. Many things changed from that time on for this mild climate oasis in the middle of the state

of Ceará backwoods. Farmers cultivated coffee, explorers entered the caves and today there are even vineyards on the top of the plateau. The Ubajara grotto has been known since the 18th century. There is an altar carved in the rock with the image of Our Lady of Lourdes at the entrance. For years the cave suffered with visitors who broke stalactites and inscribed the walls with graffiti. A local belief states that the Ubajara grotto's has underground passages which lead to the Sete Cidades National Park, 150 km away in the state of Piauí.

A bear from Ceará

In 1979, a expedition of the Brazilian Society of Cave Exploration was exploring the Park's caves and found a skull of a fossilized animal with two prominent eye teeth. After identification, the 10.000-year old skull turned out to be that of an extinct bear species. Its presence shows that the region's climate was much colder in the past. Bears of a

Fossilized skull of extinct species

similar species still live in the Andes mountains. The cave where the skull was found was called Gruta do Urso Fossil (Fossilized Bear Grotto).

◀ Calango (above); plateaus and valleys contrast with the *sertão*

Where bats dwell

Most caves are formed by dissolution processes of calcareous rock. When water and carbonic gas come into contact within the soil, they react and form carbonic acid. When the carbonic acid goes through cracks in the rocks, it reacts with limestone, forming calcium carbonate which is then washed away by the water. In time, the rock erosion forms galleries, halls and abysses. The walls become unstable and may crumble, enlarging the cave further still. In a third phase, water drips into the cave and the calcium carbonate dissolved in it creates - as if it were an artist - the beautiful decoration which is so typical of caves: the speleothemes. Stalactites hang from the roof of the cave and stalagmites arise from the floor. There are other peculiar formations, whose different colours are due to the presence of minerals such as the iron oxide, responsible for the reddish shades. A cave can be considered a special environment because it has light only at the entrance, constant temperature due to the soil's insulation properties and keeps the relative humidity of the air close to saturation. Even in these extreme condition some species survive, such as crickets, spiders and fungi. Bats also use the caves as shelter during the day and their feces feed several species that live there.

The Ubajara Cave has artificial lights for visitors

HIGHLIGHTS

🌑🌀🌓 Cafundó Waterfall

Near Boa Vista stream, a pool is formed above the highest waterfall on a tributary of the Ubajara River. The view of the Park is beautiful. Access via the Araticum trail, a detour on the Ubajara.

🌑 Pendurado and Morcego Branco Caves, de Cima and Urso Fossil Grottos

They are still closed for visitors. There are pathways of 110, 207, 82 and 130 m. The first one is near the Caboclo Pendurado Rock. The name, which translates as "Hung Hillbilly", is due to a legend which tells of a man who was walking around, slipped, got his hand jammed and was hung forever in the rock by his hand.

🌐 Visitors' Centre

Near the Neblina gate, there is a library and VCR room, as well as an exhibit of pictures and information about the region.

🌑 Ubajara's Grotto

Take the Ubajara-Araticum trail or the cable car down from the plain to the entrance in low lands. Take a look at the speleothemes - the patterns of stalactites and stagmites. The area of the limestone cave is 1.120 m, of which 420 m are artificially lit and open to visitors. The tour begins at the Image Room, goes through the halls called Corridor of Wonders, the Rose, Curtains, Portraits, Breasts, Indians and Nativity scene.

🌓🌑🌀 Minas River

This is the name of a part of the Ubajara River, 500 m away from the Ubajara grotto, at the junction of the Ubajara–Araticum trail. There are some pools for bathing.

🌓🌑🌑 Ubajara – Araticum Trail

The 3.5-km walk takes you to the entrance of the Ubajara grotto. It begins at the Planalto gate and goes by the Cafundó waterfall and the Minas River; good stops for bathing. If you are going from the gate towards the grotto, the pathway begins on the plain and goes all the way down. There are two natural lookouts: one at Cafundó and other near the Mijo da Velha (old woman's pee) spring. Take a look at the calcareous formations on the way: large grey rocks eroded by water.

SURROUNDINGS

🌑🌀🔺🌓 Ipu Spring

⊖ 75 km from Ubajara
🕐 Five hours

The 90-m high waterfall forms many pools in the lower part. It takes 1 hour and 30 minutes to go on steep terrain. At the top, there is a camping ground and a lookout with views of the whole region. Here is a good place for basic level rappellers. Information: Cia. da Aventura. Phones: (85) 9995-4944 and 243-1496.

🌑 Boi Morto Waterfall

⊖ 13 km from Ubajara 🕐 Two hours
Access via the paved Ubajara city road
It is on the Ubajara River, dropping off a 40-m-high cliff.

Valley in the Ibiapaba mountains: besides the uncommon moist forest, it harbours many caves

🔟 Floresta Waterfall
⊖ 25 km from Ubajara 🕑 Two hours
Access via BR-222, to Acarape, then
you take a dirt road to the left
It is in the city of Tianguá, on private
property. There is a snack bar.

🔟 Viçosa do Ceará
⊖ 50 km from Ubajara
🕑 Three hours
This is the oldest city of the Ibiapaba
plain and it will probably be declared a
National Patrimony - thus untouchable -
by Iphan, the National Historic and
Artistic Patrimony Institute. In the
town's centre there are one-hundred-
year-old houses and a church. Among
the most interesting places, you can
visit the handicraft centre and the Céu
Chapel, the hanglider ramp, the Castelo
de Pedras and the Itarumã waterfall.

🔟 Ibiapina
⊖ 15 km from Ubajara 🕑 Five hours
Access via the road to Ibiapina
One of the main attractions of this
mountain town are waterfalls, such as
the Ladeira (steep street). The access is
steep, but the exuberant vegetation and
the view of the plain pay the effort.
There is also the Buraco do Zeza, with
the Galo waterfall, and the Buraco do
Zeca, with the Curimatã waterfall.

🔟 💠 🔟 Frade Waterfall
⊖ 25 km from Ubajara 🕑 Four hours
The Jaburu dam outflow is in the
Jaburu canyon. A 1-km trail goes across
the Carrasco vegetation. Near the
waterfall, there is a steep descent on a
rock cliff which must be climbed down
with the help of ropes and vines. A good
opportunity for rappel beginners.

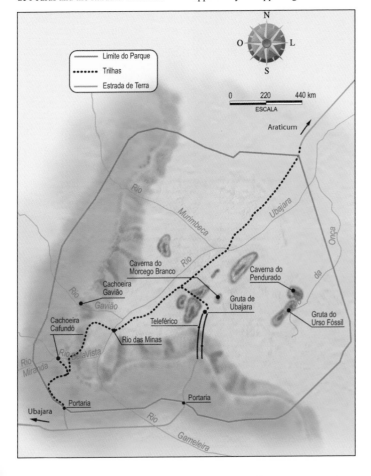

TO VISIT

Access – The Park closes on Mondays, except on holidays when it opens regularly. It is open from 8 am to 5 pm and the cable car from 10 am to 4 pm. Admission fee: R$ 5,00 including the cable car (round ticket).

Address – Rodovia da Confiança (CE-087), Zona Rural, Ubajara, CE, 62350-000. Tel/fax: (88) 634-1388. E-mail pnubajara@bol.com.br.

How to get there – There are daily flights from Fortaleza or Teresina to Sobral, the closest airport to the Park; it is then necessary to take a coach to Ubajara. By car from Fortaleza: the trip takes six hours. Take BR-222 to Tianguá, then take CE-187 and drive for 18 km to the Park's entrance. From Teresina: take BR-343 until Piripiri, then take BR-222 to Tianguá. From the bus station at Fortaleza there are departures for Ubajara; the bus companies are Ipu-Brasília and Brasileiro.

Infra-structure – Two gates (Planalto and Neblina), a visitors' centre with exhibition hall, rest rooms and snack bar. Cable car to Ubajara grotto.

TIPS

◯ The best time to visit the Park is between July and December, summertime for the natives. The winter is the rainy season and some of the Ubajara grotto halls are closed because of the mud.

◯ The baião de dois and the carne de sol (sun dried meat), two of the main dishes of the Brazilian northeastern cookery, can be tried in many restaurants of the region.

◯ The cable car, besides saving the travellers' breath, overlooks all the region of the Park. If you prefer, use it just to come back, taking advantage of the ascent to get to know the other attractions, mainly the cave.

To know more

MONTEIRO, S. e KAZ, L (coords.).
Caatinga – sertão sertanejos. Rio de Janeiro: Allumbramento / Livroarte, 1994-95.
www.guiace.com.br/mrt2-uba.htm
www.parnas.com.br/brasil/parnas/ubajara/ubajara.htm

SERVICES

Ubajara
🌐 88
✉ 62350-000

Useful Addresses
City Hall. Rua Juvêncio Pereira, 514, Centro. Phone/fax: 634-1200. E-mail: prefeituramunicipaldeubajara@bol.com.br.
Bus station. Av. Dr. Joaquim Fontenele, s/nº. Phone: 634-1300.
Ambulatory. Rua Raimundo de Barros, s/nº, Bairro S. Sebastião. Phone: 634-1449.
Telephone post. Rua Agapito Pereira, 163, Centro.
Post Office. Rua 31 de Dezembro, 40. Phone: 634-1135.
Banks. Do Brasil.

Support for the Visitor
Tourist Bureau. Av. Dr. Joaquim Fontenele, s/nº (bus station). Phone/fax: 634-1300, extension 224.

Lodging
Clube Pousada de Inhuçu. Rua Gonçalo de Freitas, 454, S. Benedito. Phone/fax: 626-1173. 16 rooms and 1 chalet (up to 6 people), tv, minibar. Swimming pool, sauna, restaurant, bar, courts, parking lot. 💲 💲
Pousada da Gruta. Estrada do Teleférico (cable car road), km 1, Sítio Amazonas. Phone: 634-1375. 14 rooms.

Restaurant, bar. 💲 💲
Pousada da Neblina. Estrada do Teleférico (cable car road), km 2. Phone/fax: 634-1270. 36 rooms, tv, minibar. Swimming pool, restaurant, bar, lake, parking lot. 💲 💲
Pousada São Benedito. Rod. da Confiança, km 21, S. Benedito. Phone: 626-1592. 10 rooms and 5 chalets (up to 3 people), tv, air conditioning, minibar. Restaurant, courts, parking lot. 💲
Pousada Sítio do Alemão. Estrada do Teleférico (cable car road), km 4, Sítio Santana. Phone: 9961-4645. 4 chalets, parking lot. 💲
Ubajara. Rua Juvêncio Pereira, 370, Centro. Phone: 634-1261. 18 rooms Bar, parking lot. 💲
Marina Camping. Rod. da Confiança, km 4. Phone/fax: 634-1364. 22 rooms, tv. Swimming pool, restaurant, bar, multi-sports court, parking lot, camping. 💲 💲

Dining
Alô Cristina. Av. dos Constituintes, s/nº. Phone: 634-1156. Snacks, pizza and pasta. 💲
Nevoar. Rua Monsenhor Gonçalo Eufrásio, s/nº. Typical local food. 💲
O Macaxeira. Av. dos Constituintes, 296. Typical local food. 💲.
Zé Maria. Estrada do Teleférico, s/nº, Sítio da Gameleira. Typical local food. 💲 💲

Calcareous rocks, eroded by rain, have created this scenery in Ubajara

NORTH

NORTH REGION

The North Region harbours the highest peak in the country, the Neblina Peak, 3.014 m, located within the National Park of the same name, in the state of Amazonas. It is possible to climb to the top of the peak in a 10-day ascent which demands effort and determination. The Ianomami Indians have a great part of their land in the Park, which also harbours the 31 de Março Peak, 2.992 m, the second highest peak in Brazil. The Cabo Orange Park is in the northernmost part of the state of Amapá. A coastal plain near by the Oiapoque River, it is the only place in Brazil which shelters the two species of manatee: the sea and river manatees. The Park is not open for visitors, though. The Jaú is the biggest National Park in the Brazilian territory, with an area equivalent to that of the state of Sergipe. It protects the ecosystems of dry land forest and seasonally flooded forest of the Amazonian Rain Forest and, in the rainy season, river beaches appear on its rivers, tributaries of the Negro River.

The Amazônia National Park, between the states of Amazonas and Pará, on the northern bank of the Tapajós River, also has as landscape the Amazonian Rain Forest of dry land and forests which are seasonally flooded. River beaches appear on the Tapajós River when rain is scarce. The two Parks can be visited with guides.

In the state of Roraima there are three National Parks. The Monte Roraima is known for its rock formations in the shape of tables or tepuis, the most famous one is the Mount Roraima, 2.875 m. The mount can be climbed via the Venezuelan side, through the Canaima National Park. The Mocidade and Viruá Parks, which lie to the south of the state, preserve areas of fields and *Cerrado* and have many rivers.

They are still not open for visitors. The Pacaás Novos, in the state of Rondônia, which preserves samples of Amazonian Rain Forest and *Cerrado*, and the Serra do Divisor Parks, in Acre, are not open for visitors either. The Serra do Divisor is closer to the Pacific than to the Atlantic. The North Region also harbours the Araguaia Park, in the state of Tocantins, which occupies one third of the Bananal Island, the largest river island in the world.

COLÔMBIA

São Gabriel
da Cachoeira

PERU

SERRA DO
DIVISOR

Rio
Moa

Rio
Cruzeiro
do Sul

Rio
Bran

ACRE

Rio
Bra
Xapu

Rio	
◉	Capital de Estado
◉	Cidades
–··–··–	Fronteira de País
–·–·–	Fronteira de Estado
——	Estrada de Asfalto
——	Estrada de Terra

N
O   L
S

0   240   480 km
ESCALA

River beaches in the Negro River, by the Jaú National Park

Amazônia

The third largest Park in the country is on the southern bank of the Tapajós River; most of the Park's area is in the state of Pará, around the city of Itaituba, and a small part in the state of Amazonas, at the city of Maués. The topography is undulating in the more ancient areas, while the sedimentary areas along the rivers are more recent. The climate is typically Amazonian, with a dry season between July and October. The main landscape is composed of dry land Amazonian Forest, but in areas that are seasonally flooded the Park also has Igapó forests: a kind of forest with palms bordering a dark water river which is subject to fluctuations in the water level. For months the trees are partly inundated. The tallest trees reach up to 50 m or more in height and some, like the Brazilnut tree, sometimes reach 60 m. The Brazilnut exploitation has always been one of the region's traditional economic activities. Rubber trees - there are two species in the Park - are typical in the region as well as Acapaus, Cow trees, Rosewood, *Tabebuias*, Amapas, *Cumarus*, *Itaubas*, *Tachi-Bravo-Da-*

Foundation: February 1974
Area: 9.940 km²
Santarém 433 km; Itaituba 53 km; Altamira: 763 km; Jacareacanga: 270 km

○
⊕ (91)
☎ 518-1530

Mata, Cedars, Mahogany, *Pau-Rosa* and *Fava-Arara-Tucupi*. Biologic diversity is high, with an average of 40 tree species per hectare. On the river banks and in the igapó forests there are many palm species, such as *Açaí*, *Patauá* and *Buriti*. Among the species of native fauna which stand out, there are many monkeys, a species of Sloth called *de-Bentinho*, a species of wildcat called *Maracajá*, Jaguars, Pumas, Great Anteaters, Peccary, Giant Armadillo, Bush Dogs, Short-eared Crab-eating Fox, Giant Otters, Manatees, Tucuxi and Pink River Dolphins. Around 250 bird species have already been identified within the Park, some of them, such as the King Vulture and the Harpy Eagle, endangered. The most common fowl are Great Egrets, Cocoi Herons, Roseate Spoonbills, Superciliated Guans, Curassows and many species of Macaws, Parakeets and Parrots. Among the reptiles there are Red-footed Tortoise, Arrau, Paraguay Caymans, Black Caymans, Bushmaster and the Green Boa Constrictor. The largest fish in the region is the *Pirarucu*, but Tucunarés and Tambaquis are also common.

Palms and big-sized trees are common in the forest

HISTORY

The Tapajós River has always been the key factor to human occupation of the region. Before colonization, tribes - including the Tapajós, the Arapiuns, the Maraus and the Andirás - spread along its banks. During the colonial period, the river's green waters were the main access. However, until the first half of the 20th century very little changed in its scenery. From 1964 on, the region's isolation began to end, as the military government aimed at integrating the Amazon with the rest of the country. The military actually brought environmental destruction, as with them mines were established and the local population's means of survival were destroyed. In the National Integration Program of Presidente Médici, who ruled from 1969-74, the construction of 15.000 km of roads was scheduled. This included the Transamazônica and the Cuiabá–Santarém, which would definitely change the region's landscape. A huge number of migrants looking for new forms of economic exploitation led to the development of activities such as cattle ranching, uncontrolled tree cutting and mining. The saga of the Transamazônica road construction with its many tales has one about the Arara Indians, back in 1977. They had been considered an extinct ethnic group. However, while the road works were in their territory, between the cities of Altamira and Itaituba, the Indians captured and beheaded four labourers. Pará was one of the states which suffered most with the environmental destruction. At the height of the gold mining

boom, the airport in the city of Itaituba had the highest number of aeroplanes operating in Brazil. In the 1970's, in order to resolve local social and environmental problems, a 6-million-ha region called Polígono de Altamira was destined for expropriation. The Amazon Operation Group proposed that one-million-ha of the polygon should be reserved for the creation of a National Park. Thus the Amazônia National Park came into being, and has ever since faced conflicts with the Indians because of land invasion.

HIGHLIGHTS

🐚 Beaches

During the dry season, from July to October, white sand beaches appear on the banks of the Tapajós River. The greenish water is a great invitation for quenching the Amazonian heat.

Trails

The network of trails and pathways which cut through the Park is around 70 km in extension and allows hikes in the forest for spotting local fauna and flora.

Transamazônica Road

The road cuts through the conservation unit for 112 km along the Tapajós River, on the Park's southeastern border. It is possible to see rapids and river beaches from the road. Despite facilitating illegal activities within the Park, it is a good access for those who want to travel through the Amazonian Rain Forest by land.

◀ Big-bellied woolly monkey (above); the Tapajós River is one of the main access

SURROUNDINGS

Paraíso Cave

⊖ 87 km from Itaituba ⏱ Three hours

The entrance to the cave is between the Baixa Fria and Jibóia *Igarapés* - a waterway in a forest passable by the natives' canoes. Its halls and galleries amount to 300 m² and are full of speleothemes - a natural cave ornamentation. Access is via the Transamazônica (BR-230) up to km 72. Between Itaituba and Rurópolis, turn left on to the auxiliary road, "Transforlândia", for 15 km more.

Petal of the royal water lily reaches up to 15 cm

Tapajós National Forest

⊖ 120 km from Itaituba ⏱ One day

Its 6.000 km² are covered in Amazonian Rain Forest, with trees taller than 50 m, such as the Brazilnut tree. The main activity in the National Forest is scientific research, but you can walk around spotting Guiana Crabwoods, Freijó-cinzas, Sucupiras and Tabebuias, among other species. Access is via BR-163 (Santarém–Cuiabá road), or via the Tapajós River, from Aveiro. Phone: (93) 552-7032.

Boat tour on the Tapajós River

⊖ 53 km from the Park ⏱ Fifteen hours

Between Santarém and Itaituba, you can watch Pink River Dolphins and Amazonian fowl beside the river beaches and thick forest on the banks of the river. Fishing is one of the traditional activities, with Tucunaré fishing being very common.

São Luiz do Tapajós

⊖ 60 km from Itaituba ⏱ Three hours

With nice beaches and islands along the Tapajós River. Between August and October, the water is very clear due to the rocky riverbed found in this region.

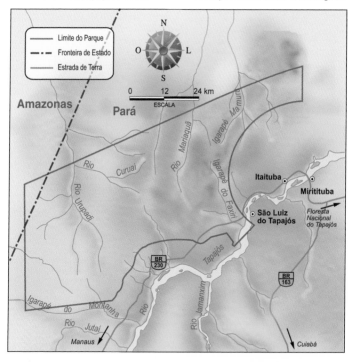

TO VISIT

Access – Hire a guide in
Itaituba to visit the Park.
Prefer one who knows
the local fauna and flora.

Address – Av. Marechal Rondon,
s/nº, Itaituba, PA, 68181-010.
Phone/fax: (93) 518-1530.
How to get there – By plane via Belém,
Manaus and Itaituba – there is an airstrip
in the Park. Via Tapajós River: it is 18
hours from Santarém. By bus: from
Santarém to Itaituba (380 km) and from
here to the Park (53 km), via
Transamazônica (BR-230).
Infra-structure – The Park has a
network of trails and pathways, lodging
for 25 people and rest-rooms. You
should make reservations beforehand.

TIPS

❍ The best time to visit the Park is from
July to August, when it rains less.
However, during the driest time of year
animal watching is impaired as stepping
on dry leaves is noisy and the animals flee.
❍ Sportfishing is one of the
activities which has most
grown, mainly in the
Tapajós River, tributary
of the Amazon.

To know more
MARTINELLI, P. **Amazônia,
o povo das águas.** São Paulo:
Terra Virgem, 2000.
BATES, H.W. **Um naturalista no rio
Amazonas.** Belo Horizonte: Itatiaia/
Edusp, 1979.
www.cdpara.pa.gov.br/turismo/
eco_itai.html
www.ipam.gov.br

SERVICES

Itaituba, PA

☎ 91
✉ 68180-000

Useful Addresses
City Hall. Travessa 15 de Agosto, 169. Phone: 518-1070.
Bus station. Rua João Pessoa, s/nº. Phone: 518-5248.
Post Office. Rua Hugo de Mendonça, s/nº. Phone: 518-2029.
Hospital. Av. Marechal Rondon, Centro. Phone: 518-1659.
Banks. Do Brasil. Bradesco, Banpará.

Lodging
Apiácas. Rua Dr. Hugo de Mendonça, s/nº. Phone: 518-2041. 48 rooms, tv, air conditioning, minibar. Swimming pool, sauna, billiard room, parking lot, restaurant. $$
Central Plaza Hotel – Travessa 13 de maio, 54. Phone: 518-1175. 20 rooms, tv, air conditioning, minibar, parking lot, restaurant. $

Dining
Cantina Italiana. Av. Getúlio Vargas. Phone: 518-2777. Italian food. $
Carioca. Rua Nova Santana, s/nº. Phone: 518-1979. Varied menu. $
Maria Jô. Av. Maranhã, Bela Vista. Phone: 518-2031. Varied menu. $

Cayman with its offspring in one of the *igarapés* which flow through the Park

Araguaia

Araguaia

The extensive sedimentary plain which occupies the northern part of Bananal Island - the largest river island in the world - was formed in the quaternary period and is seasonally flooded by the Araguaia and Javaés Rivers. The weather is hot, with rains more frequent from November to March and higher temperatures from September to October. It is irrigated by many rivers, springs and lakes, which overflow during the rainy season and flood the island. The only part which is not affected is the Torrão area, where the Park's headquarters are. The landscape has features of the *Cerrado* (a type of open forest formed by stunted, twisted trees), *Pantanal* (marshy lowlands in the state of Mato Grosso, with a typical flora and fauna), and Amazonian Rain Forest ecosystems, as well as transition zones among these environments. Fields that can be flooded, or *varjões,* predominate, but there are features of the *cerradão*, riverine forests, dryland forests and *igapó* forests (a kind of temporarily inundated forest). Along the rivers, during the dry season, long white sandy beaches appear. In areas that are flooded, there are Piassava and Buriti palms; in the forests trees that stand out are Cow trees, Canchara Cabraleas,

Foundation: December 1959
Area: 5.623 km²
Lagoa da Confusão: 62 km;
Cristalândia: 117 km; Santa
Teresinha: 10 km; Palmas: 270 km
⊘
⊕ (66)
☎ 558-1138

Tabebuias, *Pau-terra*, Black Sweetwood, and Genipap, which is used by the Karajá Indians in rituals or festivals to paint their skin. In the *Cerrado,* the Souari Nut tree and the *Pau-d'alho* are common, together with many species of grasses.

The fauna is highly diversified with species such as Marsh Deer, Capybara, Herons and Egrets, all of which are linked to flooded environments. Mammals that stand out are the Great Anteater, Maned Wolf, Jaguar, Giant Otter, Armadillo, Deer and Peccary. Common birds are Toco Toucan, Water Turkey, American Ostrich, Quail, Partridge, Fish Hawks and Orinoco Geese. There are also Blue Macaws, typical of the *Pantanal,* Hoatzins, and Musician Wren which are typical of the Amazon. Among reptile species that are prominent there are South America Anacondas, Paraguay Caymans, Black Caymans, and Arraus, which lay their eggs on the beaches of the Javaés River in August and September. In the waters, Pink River and *Tucuxi* Dolphins swim among Piranha, Stingrays,

Poraquês, Pacus, Pirarucus or *Pirosca, Tucunarés, Curimatás* and *Surubins.*

HISTORY

The Karajá Indians, who were probably the original inhabitants of the region, first had contact with Europeans back in 1658 via the Jesuit missionaries from Pará. The next record is of the *bandeirantes* in the middle of the 18th century. The *bandeirantes* from São Paulo were thus called because they were members of armed

bands called *bandeiras*, who entered the backwoods to enslave Indians and prospect for precious minerals. They moved along the rivers and, as the Karajá Indians have always lived on the banks of the Araguaia River, they ended up having contact with the white and half-bred men trying to occupy their territory. Despite long contact with civilized men, they still preserve their native language and customs such as the making of handicrafts, body painting, family fishing and rituals. They live in 21 villages along the rivers and lakes in the region.

In 1773, when *bandeirante* José Pinto Fonseca was exploring and searching for Indians to enslave in the area, he discovered that he was actually on an island and called it Santa'Anna. Its name was later changed to Bananal Island. The idea of creating a conservation unit in the region was first proposed at the end of the 19th century by André Rebouças, an engineer who supported the international trend of creating national parks. However, the Park only came into being in 1959, when its area enveloped all of the island of Bananal. Because of problems with the Indian communities, the Park had its limits changed and now, in the northern part of the island, it has ¼ of the original area. It includes the Inawebohona Indian land and borders the Araguaia Indian Park, where the Karajá, Javaé and Avá-Canoeiro live. Even today, the conservation unit faces problems as cattle grazing, predatory fishing, gathering of Arrau eggs, hunting, pressure for roads to be built across the Park, fires caused by farmers, and conflict with the Indian population.

HIGHLIGHTS

Amazonian Chelonians Project
Established in the Park since 1985, it aims at protecting the Arrau, or Amazonian Turtle, which lays its eggs in the beaches of the region. The project is developed at the junction of the Javaés and Araguaia Rivers.

Araguaia River
It is possible to sail nearly the whole extension of the main river. From June to September, nice white sandy beaches appear along the river.

Javaés River
This small arm of the Araguaia is another natural border of the Bananal Island, which forms nice beaches during the dry season. Good for a dip.

Mercês River
The main attraction of this river are the clean beaches without vegetation.

SURROUNDINGS

Araguaia Indian Park
It is necessary to get a permit with Funai (Indian Affairs Bureau) to visit the Indian Park, where you will be able to have contact with the Indians and their customs. In the villages, it is possible to buy ceramics handicraft and basketry. Information: Phone (65) 522-1155.

Beaches
During the dry season, from June to September, the long golden sand beaches of the Araguaia and Javaés

Karajá people

According to the Karajá Indians, they are descendants of the Berahatxi Mahadu people, who lived in a cold and small place, at the bottom of the River. One day, a curious young man found a way to the surface, which led him to Bananal Island. He was delighted with the beauty of the beaches and with the vastness of the place. He called the other Karajá Indians, who also came to the surface. There they lived happily for some time, but soon had contact with disease and death and decided to return to the bottom of the river. However, the passage was blocked by a huge snake.

Basket making is typical of the Indians

Thus they spread throughout the Araguaia, discovering its diversity and fish, learning how to grow crops with the Biu Mahadu people. Today, for this reason, they live from fishing and small crops. Apart from these economic activities, they sell handicrafts.

◀   Arrau sideneck (above); beaches with clear sand in the Araguaia

Rivers are good for relaxing and walking. You can also go canoeing, with a permit of the bureau for environmental affairs, Ibama.

Boat Rides

Boat rides allow you to see some of the exuberant local fauna. Don't miss the sunset on the river bank.

Fishing

The Araguaia River is famous for its abounding fish. Canguçu, on the Javaés River, and São Félix do Araguaia, on the Araguaia River, are places with good facilities for fishing. It is necessary to get a permit from Ibama.

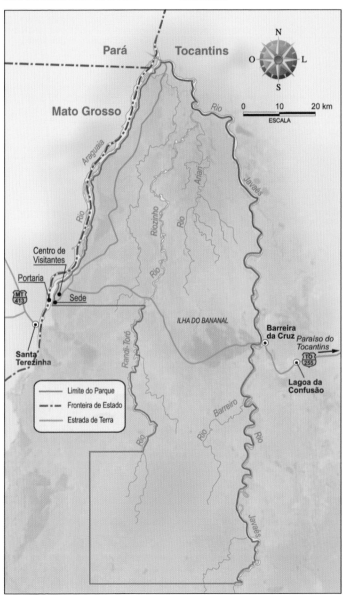

TO VISIT

Access – Not open for visitation.
Address – Aane 20, conj. 03, lote 02, Palmas, TO, 77054-010. Phones: (63) 215-2023 and (65) 558-1138.
How to get there – There is an airstrip in Santa Terezinha, near the Park's headquarters. By car from Palmas: take the TO-447 road towards Paraíso do Tocantins, then BR-153, up to Nova Rosalândia. From this city, take TO-255 to Lagoa da Confusão. It is paved all the way. From Lagoa to Barreira da Cruz, which is on the Javaés River and the Park's limits, it is around 60 km on a dirt road. It is also possible to go via Santa Terezinha, in the state of Mato Grosso.
Infra-structure – Headquarters, dirt roads linking the main points and the Amazonian Chelonians Project.

TIPS

◗ The best time to visit the Park is from May to September, when it rains less and the river beaches appear.
◗ Camping on the beaches around the Park is a good option to get to know the rivers and beaches of the region: take your tent and gear. It is not permitted to camp in the Park.
◗ Boat riders are excellent guides: they know where animals can be spotted and, in case of fishing, they know the best places in the rivers, outside the Park though.
◗ Take care with Stingrays buried in the sand along the rivers. Shuffle in the sand to prevent stepping on them and getting stung by their tail.

To know more
BALDUS, H. **Ensaios de etnologia brasileira.** São Paulo: Nacional/INL, 1979.
VASCONCELOS, J.M. **Kuryala, capitão e Karajá.** São Paulo: Melhoramentos, 1979.

SERVICES . . . .

Lagoa da Confusão
🌐 63
✉ 77493-000

Useful Addresses
City Hall. Rua Firmino Lacerda, 15. Phone: 364-1148.
Bus station. Rua João M. de Alencar, s/n°. Phone: 364-1179.
Post Office. Rua Firmino Lacerda, 15. Phone: 364-1148. At the City Hall.
Hospital. Av. Vicente Barbosa, s/n°.
Ambulatory. Rua Firmino Lacerda, s/n°. Phone: 364-1276.
Bank. Do Brasil.

Support for the Visitor
Tourist Bureau. Rua Filismino de Souza, s/n°. Phone: 364-1271.

Lodging
Lagoa da Ilha. Rua Neusa Ribeiro, s/n°. Phone: 364-1110. 20 rooms, air conditioning, swimming pools, water slides, multi-sport court, bar, parking lot. 💲💲
Pedra. Rua principal, s/n°. Phone: 364-1132. 6 rooms, fans. 💲
Pousada Lady Pleo. Av. Raimundo Filismino de Souza, s/n°. Phone: 364-1118. 15 rooms, air conditioning, tv, frigobar, tel, parking lot. 💲
Real. Av. Vicente Barbosa, 7. Phone/fax: 364-1158. 8 rooms, tv, air conditioning, parking lot. 💲

Dining
Lagoa da Ilha. Rua Lagoa da Ilha. Phone: 364-1110. Varied menu. 💲
Pizzaria da Pedra. Rua Principal, s/n°. Phone: 364-1132. Pizza. 💲
Churrascaria da Lagoa. Na beira da lagoa. Phone: 364-1108. Meat and fish. 💲

River beaches: only from May to September, when it rains less

Cabo Orange

The coastal plain is covered in mangroves, which spread for a stretch about 10 km inland. They are growing upon sedimentary deposits which had their origin in the sea and rivers. The Park has other ecosystems such as the *Cerrado* - a type of open forest formed by stunted, twisted trees - and fields which are seasonally flooded, in a region of difficult access within the Amazon Rain Forest. It has a typical Ecuatorial climate, hot and moist all year round with the hottest months between September and December and rainfall concentrated mainly from March to May. To north is the Oiapoque River; the Uaçá in the northwest; and the Caciporé River cuts the Park in two. The homogeneous vegetation of the mangroves, which has basically three

species of trees, is broken by the presence of colourful Scarlet Ibis which build large collective nests in the region. These birds, as well as Flamingoes, while rare in many parts of the country, are quite common in the Park. Several species of crab, shrimp, fish and a lot of mosquitoes live in the rich ecosystem. Other animals, such as Egrets, Herons, American Storks and Crab-eating Raccoons also enjoy the richness of the region. In the fields where Murici and Cajuzinho predominate, a low vegetation composed mainly of grasses and cyperaceous plants grows. In the areas which are seasonally flooded, there are Pickerelweed, Capim-arroz (an aquatic grass which grows along the banks of rivers) and Panicum. This is where the Buriti Palm stands out. In the water of the rivers it is common to find Piranhas,

Foundation: July 1980
Area: 6.190 km²
Oiapoque: 60 km; Calçoene:
40 km; Macapá: 370 km
○
⊕ (96)
☎ 214-1100

Tucunarés, Surubins, Tamuatás, and Tracajás - a semi-aquatic fresh-water turtle which lays its eggs in the beaches during the dry season. Apart from the fresh-water species, Cabo Orange National Park also has ocean Manatees, which have nearly disappeared from the rest of the Brazilian coast. With such environmental diversity, the fauna is also very rich, with ducks, parrots, Squirrel Monkeys, Night Monkeys, Otters, Jaguars, Capybaras, Tapirs, Great Anteaters, Giant Otters and Pumas among the local species. There are also a small number of sea turtles of the Green and Leatherback species.

HISTORY . . . .

In one of the reports from Vicente Pinzón in 1513 to Spain he mentioned a numerous Indian population, found to the North of the mouth of the Amazon River. After this episode, the land of the Palikur Indians was mentioned more than once in reports and maps of travellers who visited the region. In 1594, Englishmen established trading posts in the Oiapoque and in the 18th century French Jesuits unsuccessfully tried to settle there. In 1900, a dispute with

French Guiana almost caused the two countries to fall into the hands of the French. This area of Amapá, which includes the Cabo Orange National Park, largely borders French Guiana. For the Brazilian authorities, the border was at Oiapoque, while for the French it was much further to the south, at the Araguari River, near the city of Macapá.

Without military power to fight one of the biggest countries at that time, Brazil backed up its claims on the reports from Baron Rio Branco, the famous diplomat who was also a skilled map-maker. Switzerland, which acted as the judge, decided in favour of Brazil, setting the borders of the present day state of

Amapá. After incorporating the land, the Palikur Indians were discriminated for not speaking Portuguese and because they had kept commercial relations with the French for centuries. This led them to move to the other side of the border. Today, they are again settled in Cabo Orange, as well as the Karipunas and the Galibis. Back in 1992, these well organized Indian peoples created the

Fishing is the main activity of the riparian people

Oiapoque Indigenous Peoples' Association. This was one of the institutions responsible for the restitution of the Oiapoque Indian land, including Uaçá, Juminã and Galibi. For years considered the northernmost point of Brazil, Oiapoque has now lost its place to Mount Caburaí, near Mount Roraima. In the surroundings of the Park is located the village of Tapereбá with its nearly 500 inhabitants.

HIGHLIGHTS

Tapereбá Village
The villagers live on small crops which they cultivate for their survival as well as products from the rivers and the sea; they also work on the buffalo ranches in the region. The presence of salty water in the rivers causes difficulties for them, as the only place with fresh-water during the drought is 50 km away at Maruani Lake.

Pororoca
The phenomenon of the pororoca occurs here at the mouth of the Caciporé River. This is when high tide invades the river, thundering and causing big waves to be formed, carrying away whatever lies on the riverbanks.

Manatees inhabit the rivers of the Park

SURROUNDINGS

ⓘ ● São Roque Waterfall
⊖ 17 km from Oiapoque ⊕ One day
On the border of the French Guiana, it is also called La Roque. You get there by road and then take a 15-minute ride on the Oiapoque River by *voadeira*, a small fast motor boat.

Saint-Georges de L'Oyapock
⊖ 10 minutes by boat from Oiapoque ⊕ One day
The city with French style architecture is next to the Park in the French Guiana.

⊙ Indian Villages: Uaçá, Galibi, Açaizal, Encruso, Cumarumã, Cumené, Santa Isabel, Waiábi and Juminã
⊖ From Oiapoque it is 80 km to Uaçá and 50 km to Galibi and Waiábi, on the banks of the Curipi and Uaçá Rivers ⊕ A day for each village
The Indian reservation may be visited with permission of the government bureau for Indian affairs, Funai. Access is via the BR-156 with the villages of Galibi and Waiábi to the right side of the road. To get to the villages Açaizal, Cumarumã, Cumené, Santa Izabel and Juminã, part of the trip is along the river by voadeira.

TO VISIT

Access – Get information at Ibama (government bureau for environmental affairs) about the possibility of visiting the Park.
Mail address – Rua Hamilton Silva, 1570, Macapá, AP, 68902-010.
Phone/fax: (96) 214-1100 and 214-1116.

◀ Scarlet ibis (above); Tapereбá village, on the banks of the Caciporé River

How to get there – From Macapá to Oiapoque it is 540 km via the BR-156; most of it dirt road. From there, you can get to the Park via the Caciporé River. It is also possible to reach the Park by sea, at Vila Taperebá, on the Park's southern border.
Infra-structure – There is none.

To know more
MONTEIRO, S. e KAZ, L. (coords.).

Amazônia fauna e flora. Rio de Janeiro: Alumbramento/Livroarte, 1993-1994.
QUEIXALÓS, F. e RENAULT-LESCURE, O. (orgs.). **As línguas amazônicas hoje.** São Paulo: Instituto Socioambiental, 2000.
RICARDO, C.A. **Povos indígenas no Brasil: Volume 3 - Amapá/Norte do Pará.** São Paulo: CEDI, 1983.
www.socioambiental.org

Jaú

The geologic origin of the Park is recent and its topography is flat, with altitudes around 100 m. The low hills are separated by water bodies or by valleys which are periodically flooded. The climate is typical of the Amazon, hot and moist, with average temperatures around 25°C.

In the Jaú National Park, the Amazonian Rain Forest is represented mainly by dry land forests, which dominate around 70% of the Park's area. These forests are thick, dark and moist with tall trees which are usually taller than 40 m: Kapok Ceibas, *Quarubas*, Cow trees, Brazil nut trees and *Sucupiras*. In order to support such a height, huge tabular roots spread in all directions through the soil. The dry land forests mingle with big rivers, small *igarapés* - waterways in the forest, passable by the natives' canoes - white sand river beaches, open forests and fields that seasonally flood. The *igapó* forests - a kind of forest with palms bordering a dark water river, which is subject to fluctuations in the water level - grow on the plains along the rivers and represent 12% of the conservation unit. The trees spend half of the year under water, a time when the water fauna has a chance of feeding on the plants and enjoying the protection provided. Here, palms like *Açaí* and Caryota Rufflepalm are common. In the zones of sandy soils, between the larger water courses, there are many Buriti and Carnauba palms. The more open formations, such as meadows,

Foundation: September 1980
Area: 22.720 km²
Novo Airão: 3 hours by *voadeira*;
Manaus: 210 km; Barcelos:
190 km; Manacapurú: 80 km
○
⊕ (92)
☎ 613-3277

occur in the drier areas, bringing a change to the green shades of the vegetation. In the water, there is a huge diversity of environments which can change according to fluctuations in the water level. Lakes, *igarapés* and dark water rivers, harbour countless organisms. During the dry season, white sand beaches appear along the rivers.

Jaú's fauna is rich, but difficult to be seen, as the animals hide in the Rain Forest. Several species, such as Manatees, the Black Ouakari - whose regional name is *Bicó* monkey -, Giant Otters and Jaguars are all endangered. Besides these, there are also Capuchin and Howling monkeys, Deer, Agoutis and Tapirs. There is a great diversity of bird species including Tinamous, Trumpeters, Toucans, Curassows, Parrots and Macaws. Big prey birds, such as the Harpy Eagle, are rarer, but a treat for those who see them. Caymans are very common in Jaú and are present in all environments. Among the species found in the Park there are Paraguay Caymans, Black

Caymans and the *Diri-diri* Cayman. Most of the 11 chelonian species which are found in Jaú live in aquatic environments and during the dry season they come onto the beaches to lay their eggs. The eggs are much gathered, as they are considered to be a local delicacy, even in the urban centres. One of the biggest Amazonian fish is among the almost 300 fish species: the *Jaú*, which gives names to the Park.

HISTORY

The river Negro was occupied by Indigenous peoples of several ethnic groups of the Arawak linguistic tree. In the Jaú River basin, archaeologic research has estimated, based on ceramics fragments, that the human occupation began at least 1.000 years ago. Scientists also found in this region several archaeologic sites with rock paintings carved into the rocks, portraying the daily life.

At the end of the 17th century, religious orders founded the first colonial settlement, Santo Elias do Jaú, on the lower river Negro. The settlement, based on the Indian villages, originated the village of Airão where catechizing and Indian slave trading took place and, later on, the exploitation of the "forest drugs". From 1880 until the beginning of the 20th century, with the rubberboom period, the region experienced great economic development, bringing migrants from the northeast region of Brazil.

A decline in latex exploitation during the first decades of the 20th century brought decadence to the region and the inhabitants slowly moved to Tauapessassu. This village, which is closer to Manaus, later became the city of Novo Airão. Today the ruins of Airão are in the process of being declared as National Historic Patrimony by the National Historic Patrimony Institute.

In 1977, after an expedition visited the region, the National Amazon Institute of Research reached the conclusion that the Jaú River basin should be properly protected.

The biggest National Park in the country and the second in Latin America - it is only smaller than the Canaima National Park in Venezuela - lies in an area without Indians and without important mineral reserves. In November of 2000, the Park was acknowledged by Unesco as Patrimony of Human Kind.

HIGHLIGHTS

Some of the local attractions are walking along the trails in the country's biggest Park and sailing the river which winds through the region.

🌀 Igarapé Preto Waterfall

Near the Park's entrance. It only exists from October to January.

🌀 Jaú Waterfall

🕔 Five hours

It is more like 'rapids' than a waterfall; the waterfalls of Jaú can be reached from Ibama's boat-office; it takes half an hour by voadeira (fast motor boat).

🌀 Carabinani Waterfalls

This is a complex of 12 falls on the Carabinani River which appears during the dry season; good for bathing and for taking showers.

🌐 🚣 Boat Tours

The best way to get to know the region is by voadeira, a small fast motor boat, along the Park's water ways. Along the rivers Jaú, Carabinani and Unini, you can watch flocks of Macaws and Parrots flying over the igapó forest. In the parts where the water is still, orchids cast their colours onto the dark waters.

🌐 🐢 Rio Negro Beaches

Between November and January, extensive, clear sandy beaches form along the river Negro, close by the mouth of the Jaú. With a bit of luck, it is possible to watch turtles coming out onto the beach to lay their eggs.

🌐 Paunini River

Some of the families within communities living along its banks accept the lodging of visitors. You can experience something of the natives' lifestyle for some days.

🌐 Unini River

One of the Park's water ways with Riparians living on its banks. You can visit the community who live by hunting and fishing for their own consumption. They also grow small cassava plantations from which an edible flour is made.

◀ Dendrobatideous toad (above); the Negro river is a via to one of the bases in the Park

Seringalzinho

Around 20 families live
in this small community;
they live on fishing and
plant gathering. Handicrafts
made of Titica vine seeds
is one of the attractions
in the community.

SURROUNDINGS

Airão Ruins

⊖ Fifteen minutes by voadeira
from the Park's headquarters
The ruins of this old city
were taken over by the
forest when the place was
abandoned. There are
houses with trees growing
in the middle of the living
room, plants sticking out
of the walls and much
more. The people of Airão
moved to Novo Airão,
the Park's nearest city.

Mariuá Archipelago

⊖ 170 km from the Park
⊕ One day
This is the biggest river
archipelago in the world
and has 1.266 islands spread
over 140.000 km² along the
Negro River. During the dry
season, beaches appear; you can
walk on the white sand and swim
in the river's dark waters.

Anavilhanas

Near Novo Airão, one of the
biggest river archipelagos in the
Amazon is formed by around 400
islands on the Negro River. It envelopes an area of 3.500 km² which
spreads over 90 km along the river.
It harbours hundreds of lakes, bays,
paranás (a stream that leaves and
re-enters the same river), rivers and
igapós. As it is an Ecologic Station,
only researchers with permits are
authorized to enter.

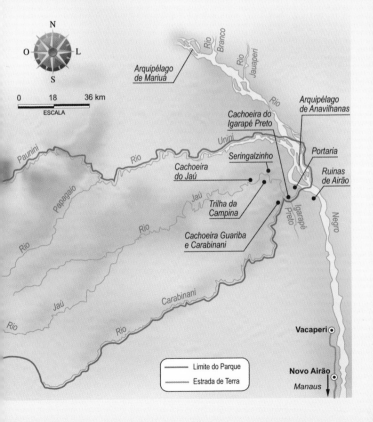

TO VISIT

Acess – The Park is usually closed from November to March, when the water level is too low for navigation. It is necessary to get a permit with Ibama previously. Admission fee: R$ 3,00.

Address – Rua Ministro João Gonçalves de Sousa, s/n°, km 1, BR-319, Manaus, AM, 69075-830. Phone: (92) 613-3277. Fax: 613-3095.

How to get there – from Manaus you get to the Park by boat on a 18-hour trip via the river Negro. Departures are from São Raimundo port to Barcelos. The boat sails past the base of the Park. It is possible to rent a boat in Manaus (R$ 100/1.500,00 per day depending on the boat) for 10 to 12 people. By car: take the Manaus–Manacapuru road up to Novo Airão (80 km paved and 90 km dirt) and then by voadeira to the Park.

Infra-structure – A Visitor's Centre on the Jaú river.

TIPS

❍ The best time to visit the Park is from June to July, when the rivers and *igarapés* are full, and from September to November, when the waterfalls and beaches appear.
❍ Do not forget to take your camera during the hikes: the region has rare plant species, mainly orchids.
❍ Try to drink only mineral water, as there are hepatitis, amoebic dysentery and other tropical diseases in the region.
❍ If you intend to spend the night with the inhabitants of the Park's outskirts, remember to take a hammock and a mosquito net to sleep in.

To know more

Oliveira, A.A. e Daly, D.C. (edits.). **Florestas do Rio Negro.** São Paulo: Companhia das Letras/ UNIP/NYBG, 2001.

FUNDAÇÃO VITÓRIA AMAZÔNICA. **A genêse de um plano de manejo: o caso do Parque Nacional do Jaú.** Manaus: Fundação Vitória Amazônica, 1998.

LEONARDI, VICTOR. **Os Historiadores e os rios – Natureza e ruína na Amazônia Brasileira.** Brasília, Ed. UnB/Paralelo 15, 1999. 270p.

MONTEIRO, S. e KAZ, L. (coords.). **Amazônia fauna e flora.** Rio de Janeiro: Alumbramento/ Livroarte, 1993-1994.

www.fva.org.br

SERVICES

Novo Airão

🌐 92
✉ 69730-000

Useful Addresses

City Hall. Av. Ajuricaba, 979. Phone: 365-1410.
Bus station. Av. Presidente Castelo Branco, s/nº. Phone: 365-5254.
Post Office. Av. Presidente Getúlio Vargas, s/nº. Phone: 365-1179.
Hospital. Av. Tiburcino,s/nº. Phone: 365-1514.
Bank. Da Amazônia.

Lodging

Pousada Ecológica Anavilhanas. AM-010, km 8. Phone: 365-1357. 8 rooms. Trails in the forest. $
Josely. Av. João Paulo II s/nº. Phone: 365-1157. 12 rooms, tv, minibar, air conditioning. Parking lot. $
Rio Negro. Av. Castelo Branco, s/nº. Phone: 365-1102. 14 rooms. Parking lot. $

Dining

Carioca. Av. Ajuricaba, s/nº. Phone: 365-1314. Fish. $
Três Irmãos. Av. Tiradentes, s/nº. Phone: 365-1060. Varied menu. $

It is necessary to get by the Anavilhanas archipelago to go to the Park

Monte Roraima

Mount Roraima is part of the Guianas rock outcrop, which is believed to be two billion years old, the oldest mountainous region on Planet Earth. The sedimentary plateau where the Park is would have appeared around 600 million years ago as the result of earthquakes, when South America and Africa split apart. The mountains and hills were eroded by water until the mountain range arrived at its present day topography. The National Park is only the southern part of a set of sandstone plateaus, which lie on the border with Venezuela and the Guianas. These formations are called tables or tepuis, with altitudes above 1.000 m, flat summits, waterfalls on the rim of the escarpments, cracks and ravines.

The most famous, Mount Roraima with 2.875 m in height, is just like a 'big table' with an irregular shape and steep escarpments at the rim. Only a small area of this plateau lies within Brazilian territory. The weather is tropical, hot and moist with high rainfall, especially on the top, where the temperature falls dramatically. The fascinating landscape, formed by projecting rocks enveloped in forests and permeated by lakes, waterfalls and ravines, is inspiring. The vegetation has stretches of Amazonian Rain Forest and regions of *Cerrado* - a type of open forest composed of stunted, twisted trees. Besides these landscapes on the tablelands, there are high altitude fields among rocky outcrops with many endemic species. It is estimated that endemic species amount to 50% of the vegetation. They have survived and stood out from other

Foundation: June 1989
Area: 1.160 km²
Boa Vista: 334 km;
Pacaraima: 112 km;
Santa Elena de Uairén: 105 km
⊘
🌐 (95)
☎ 592-1085

species due to their isolation and to the extreme weather conditions. Several species of orchids, bromeliads, lichen, Canelas-de-ema, ferns, Cape-las-de-são-joão and insectivorous plants stand out. Growing around the creeks which flow through the area, there are Matchwood, Cordias and several palm species such as *Açaí* and the Caryota Rufflepalm. The forests are tall, with trees like Seringa-brava, Red Ocotea, Tento-amarelo, Timpó-pau, Jungleplum, Matamatá-branco, Tinteiro, Tamaquaré - a tree of the genus Caraipa -, Bebeeru - also called Greenheart Ocotea -, and Matamatá-vermelho.

Due to the diversity of environments, there are many species of native fauna. Big cats such as Jaguars and Ocelots, Tapirs, Peccaries, Armadillos, Anteaters and Sloths stand out. Among the most common monkeys are Capuchins, Howling Monkeys of the genus Alouatta and Spider Monkeys. The diversity of fish in the Park is not so great, due to the geological formation of the Cotingo riverbed, which has many waterfalls and rapids, preventing the fish from going up the river. However, fish is of great importance in the diet of the communities around the Park.

Mount Roraima: local Indians hold that it is the sacred mountain of the god Makunáima

HISTORY

As Mount Roraima is in an area of difficult access, it remained safe from "human conquest" for centuries. Until the beginning of the 20th century, it was only possible to reach the southern part of Roraima by boat. It was almost impossible to travel through the territory's high lands, covered in thick forests and mountains, and only a few adventurers took the risk. One of them was Englishman Walter Raleigh whose expedition travelled past the foot of the Mountain at the end of the 16th century. In the 19th century, many European adventurers and naturalists' expeditions travelled through the Amazonian Rain Forest to try and reach the summit of Mount Roraima. The first man who made it, in 1884, was the English botanist Everard Im Thurn. The expedition of German naturalist Koch-Grünberg resulted in the book Vom Roraima zum Orinoco, one of the sources used by the modernist writer Mario de Andrade to write his classic book Macunaína. In 1927, it was Marshal Rondon's turn to reach "the backwoods of Uraricoera", when he led an expedition to stake out the borders between Brazil, Venezuela and British Guiana. The Park was created in 1989 in order to protect the ecosystems of the Pacaraíma and the Caburaí mountain ranges, besides materializing the "three-way point": the Brazil-Venezuela-Guiana border atop Mount Roraima.

HIGHLIGHTS

Mount Roraima
⊕ Seven days
Its 40 km² are atop a big plateau, with water falling from many spots along its rim, from rivers such as the Cotingo. In order to reach the summit, it is necessary to face the challenges of rivers and rocks at the beginning of the trek, besides a temperature which varies between 35°C and 0°C. If you decide to go via the Venezuelan side, the ascent takes 12 hours and does not require any special climbing technique. But if you choose to go via the Brazilian side, from Uiramutã, then you must be an experienced climber.

Triple Milestone
Border of Brazil, Guiana and Venezuela. The milestone was placed atop Mount Roraima in 1927 by Marshal Rondon.

◀ Altitude vegetation (above); in the sandstone plateaus there are 1.000-m high tables

Crystal Valley

With many crystal outcrops. It is to the northeast of the triple milestone, on the summit of the Mount Roraima.

SURROUNDINGS

⑩ Sete Quedas Waterfall
⊖ 12 km from Uiramutã ⊕ Two hours
You walk on a trail through the forest to reach the Sete Quedas Waterfall.

Mount Caburaí

⊖ 30 km from Uiramutã ⊕ Seven days
The northernmost point in Brazil, on the border with the Guianas, is 1.465 m high. It is the rim of a huge plateau which stretches along the border; the source of the Maú river, which falls off the cliffs forming waterfalls, is here. The Uailã River also has its source here and forms rapids and the Garã-Garã Waterfall, which is 100 m high.

Canaima National Park

⊖ 5 km from Santa Elena de Uairén (Venezuela) ⊕ One to four days
The greatest concentration of tables or tepuis, with ages up to 1,7 million years, lies in the National Park on the Venezuelan side. The attractions are the Indian communities, *Cerrado*, forests, the Carrao River and many waterfalls, including the highest waterfall in the world, the Salto Angel with 1.000 m. The city of Canaima in southeast Venezuela is the base for visits.

Sol Mountain Range

⊖ 40 km from Uiramutã ⊕ Three days
This is a 2.400-m-high plateau in the southeast region of Mount Roraima National Park. To the south, east and northeast, the Park borders the area where Ingaricó, Patamona and Taurepang Indians live.

Uiramutã

⊖ 315 km from Boa Vista ⊕ Four days
The city harbours several Indian communities, with a strong presence of the Makuxi and Ingarikó groups. It lies in the northernmost part of the country and is the only access to reach Mount Roraima via Brazil.

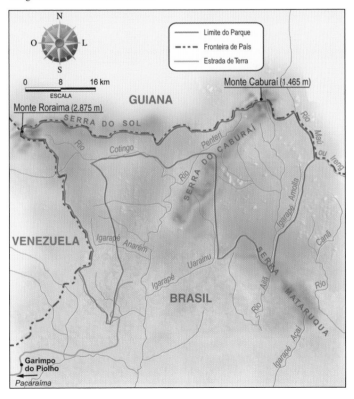

TO VISIT

Access – Via the Brazilian side, it is necessary to be an experienced climber. From the Venezuelan side the base is Paraitepuy, where there are agencies, guides and porters who can accompany your ascent up the mountain. In the village, the Pémon Indians may also be taken on as porters and cooks at an average price of US$ 20,00 per day.

Address – Av. Panamericana, s/nº, Pacaraíma, RR, 69345-000. Phone: (95) 592-1437. Fax: 592-1207.

How to get there – By car from Boa Vista: take BR-174 road for 212 km. There are coaches departing daily between Boa Vista and Pacaraima (bus companies: Eucatur and União Cascavel). You might just as well take a taxi from Pacaraima to Santa Elena do Uairén. From Paraitepuy to the Mount, it is necessary to walk along a trail.

Infra-structure – There is none.

TIPS

❍ The best time to visit the region is between December and March, when the trails are less slippery, there is less moisture and the crossing of rivers is easier. During the rest of the year the adventure is greater and repaid by the spectacle of the waterfalls of the neighbouring tables.

❍ To get to the main mark of the mount, prefer the Venezuelan side, as it is not necessary to be a skilled climber.

❍ In Pacaraima, do not fail to visit the Park's Integration and Control Station, next to Ibama's inspection station. Do visit the City Hall Indian Handicraft Centre, with basketry exhibition and pieces made by the Macuxi, Wapixana and Taurepang Indians.

To know more
ANDRADE, M. **Macunaíma, o herói sem nenhum caráter.** (Edição Crítica em Português). Ed. Fondo de Cultura. Ec. México, 1990.
www.amazoniatourr.com.br/pacaraima.htm

SERVICES

Pacaraíma, RR
⊕ 95
✉ 69345-000

Useful Addresses
City Hall. Rua Monte Roraima, s/nº.
Phone: 592-1286.
Bus station. Rua Brasil on the corner of street Quênio. Phone: 592-1147.
Telephone station. Telemar.
Phone: 592-1101.
Post Office. Rua Monte Roraima, s/nº.
Phone: 592-1269.
Hospital. Rua Caribe, s/nº.
Phone: 592-1160.

Lodging
Pacaraíma. Rua Quênio, s/nº.
Phone: 592-1515. 17 rooms, tv, air conditioning, minibar. $
Pousada do Sossego. Av. Brasil, s/nº. Phone: 592-1187. 12 rooms, tv, air conditioning, minibar, fan. Parking lot. $
Serra Azul. Rua Parima, 101.
Phone: 592-1272. 13 rooms, tv, minibar, fan. Parking lot. $

Dining
El Paradoro. Rua Principal, s/nº.
Phone: 592-1436. Varied menu. $ $
Serra Azul. Rua Parima, 101.
Phone: 592-1272. Meat. $

The topography with altitudes above 1.000 m favours the formation of gigantic waterfalls

Pacaás
Pacaás Novos

With rocks in the upper parts and plains in the the lower parts, covered in more recent sedimentary soils, the table-like topography with steep escarpments stretches for kilometers including the Pacaás Novos and the Uopianes mountain ranges. Its highest peak is the Tracoá at 1.230 m.

The sources of many rivers are in the mountain ranges, off which they fall as waterfalls and form the major basins in Rondônia: Guaporé, Mamoré and Madeira. The climate in the region is hot and humid, with more rains from November to March; the dry season is from May to September, when the *friagem* phenomenon happens. *Friagem* is a sudden, dramatic drop in the temperature. With little or no human interference at all, the landscape includes

the *Cerrado* - a type of forest formed by stunted, twisted trees - in the upper partes and Amazonian Rain Forest in the lower lands. Among the species found in the fields there are Quarubas-do-campo, Shellseeds, Alcornocos, Umiris, Paus-terra, Regal Maximilianas, a species of Rubber tree called Anã - or dwarf -, and several species of grasses. Buriti palm groves and Renealmias appear in the areas near the water courses. In the zone of contact between the two ecosystems, Taboca - a bamboo - is common in the forest. The Amazonian Rain Forest, which has not been thoroughly studied in the Park, has palms such as the Patauá and the Babaçu, besides species like the Tonkabean, Resintrees, Kapok Seibas, Brazil-nut trees,

Foundation: September 1979
Area: 7.648 km²
Ariquemes: 150 km; Porto Velho: 355 km; Montenegro: 100 km
⊘
⊕ (69)
☎ 239-2002

the Amarelão and the Rubber tree. Among the main species of fauna there are endangered Blue Macaws, a species of budgerigar called Tuim, Guans, Toucans, and King Vultures. Among mammals there are Night Apes and Howling Monkeys of the Alouatta genus, Jaguars, Ocelots, Wild Dogs, 9-banded and Giant Armadillos, Agoutis and packs of Peccaries - or Wild Pig.

HISTORY

The region of Pacaás Novos was inhabited by pre-historic people who left their marks in the form of rock paintings and ceramics artifacts. According to the reports of Marshal Rondon - the humanitarian explorer who gave his name to the state of Rondônia -, tribes from the Tupi-Guarani family language have inhabited the area since before the 19th century. Nobody is really sure about the origin of the name, but travellers from the 18th already called it Pacaás Novos. A tribe with the same name and who belong to the same ethnic group still lives in western Rondônia. The Park's area is inhabited by the Uru-eu-wau-wau and Uru-pa-in, whose land was designated back in 1985; the Indians occupy two thirds of the conservation unit area. Besides the Indian groups who are known, there are isolated Indians in the area. Since 1970's, the state of Rondônia has been a rapidly occupied territory due to its position on the country's new agricultural border. This fact has led to the building of the main roads in the region. In order to prevent the region as a whole from being deprived of its character, and because the area has been identified as very rich in terms of natural resources, the National Park was created in 1979.

The Pacaás Novos River has large waterfalls

SURROUNDINGS

Madeira–Mamoré Railroad

In Porto Velho, visit the museum – where there is a locomotive – and go on a short train tour, which operates only on weekends.
In Guajará-Mirim, 360 km from the capital, another museum tells stories about the railroad.

Ji-Paraná

⊖ 370 km from the Park
🕐 Five hours

Ji-Paraná is one of the cities which appeared during the time of the construction of the Madeira–Mamoré railroad. Take a look at the old jail, by the BR-364 road, made out of rails from the railroad.

TO VISIT

Access – The Park is still not open for visitation. This depends on the establishment of the Park's facilities, which, in turn, depends on the updating of the management plan that will have been done by 2003.
Mail Address – Av. Tancredo Neves, s/n. Cep 78967-000. Campo Novo de Rondônia-RO. Phone: (69) 239-2002 Fax: 239-2031.
How to get there – By plane: there are regular flights from the rest of the country to Porto Velho. By car from Porto Velho: take BR-364 up to the city of Ariquemes (205 km of asphalt road); then take BR-421 up to the city of Montenegro (50 km, part asphalt, part dirt), continuing in bad condition to Campo Novo de Rondônia (60 km on dirt road). From this city to the Park it is still 40 km more on a dirt road.
Infra-structure – None.

The village of the Uru-eu-wau-wau Indians

The Madeira–Mamoré Railroad Saga

The first great challenge posed by the Amazon to the white man was due to a great engineering project: to build a railroad that would link the capital of the State of Mato Grosso (Vila Bela) to the Amazon, providing an outlet for the rubber production and an access to the Atlantic for Bolivia.

As the rivers Madeira and Mamoré have many waterfalls, thus impeding them to be used as water ways, the solution found was to build a railroad. A British company was hired and started the works in 1872. They gave up less than one year later. With support and money from Emperor Dom Pedro II, an American company took over the construction of the railroad. In one year,

the Americans also gave up. Meanwhile, workers died from tropical diseases and in battles against the Indians. Even so, the Brazilian and Bolivian governments wanted to finish the railroad and kept building it. At last, another American company managed to face the jungle and, in 1912, finished 360 km of railroad linking the cities of Porto Velho and Guajará-Mirim. In 1972, the railroad was closed because it was worn out. Today there are memories, machines and some rails of the "Devil's Railroad", as it used to be called due to the estimates which figure the number of deaths at around 10.000. Seven kilometers of the rail road still operates from Porto Velho on a historic tour for visitors.

◀ Water lily (above): São Miguel River flows through the southernmost part of the Park

The harpy eagle, the biggest prey bird in the country, can be seen in the Park

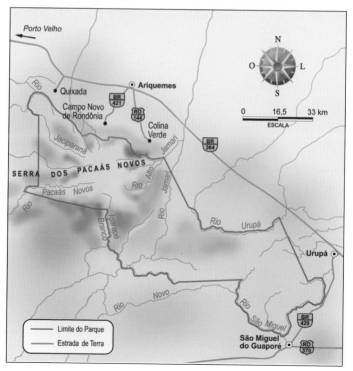

Pico da Neblina

The country's second biggest Park and its neighbour, the Parque Nacional Serrania la Neblina, in Venezuela, envelop one of the largest protected areas of Amazonian Rain Forest. A moist tropical climate is typical of the region, but at high altitudes the wind blows hard and the temperature may drop to nearly 0°C. Its topography includes three distinctive areas: in the lower areas, the Branco and Negro river plains are on pre-cambrian rocks whose altitude ranges from 80 to 160 m; the Amazonas-Orenoco plateau, which lies in the basins of the rivers that name the plateau, includes the Imeri, Padre and Marie-Mirim mountain ranges, with altitudes between 600 and 2.000 m; the Roraima sedimentary plateau, with altitudes above 1.200 m, is where the peaks of Neblina and 31 de Março are located. The 31 de Março (2.992 m), the second highest peak in the country, lies around 700 m from the border of Venezuela. The Amazonian Rain Forest is present in many forms throughout the

Park: in the *campinaranas* - an extensive open sandy soil space in a forest with many shrubs and some trees in a dense formation - trees such as a Copayes, Carnaubas, Tamaquarés - a tree of the genus Caraipa -, and the Brazilian Boxwood are common. Foothill forests grow between 600 and 1.000 m in height, where there are Japurás, Jacanos and *Palmiteiro*. In the forests above 1.000 m in height, trees like Quaruba, Cedars, Ita-ubas, Bacabinha-Quinha, the Jutaí-Pororoca and the Mandioqueira-Azul appear. Above 1.800 m, the rocky outcrops are covered in lichen, insectivorous plants and bromeliads. The peak itself is a small 200-m² plateau, where winds are cruel and mist is everlasting. Among the fauna, a monkey endemic to the region stands out: the Black Ouakari, which are found in groups of 15 to 30 individuals looking for food in the igapós, a kind of temporarily inundated forest which borders a river. All day long, Capuchin and Alouatta Howling monkeys make a lot of noise in the canopies. On the

Foundation: June 1979
Area: 22.000 km²
São Gabriel da Cachoeira: 55 km;
Cucuí: 50 km; Manaus: 960 km

⊕ (92)
☎ 613-3277

ground, Tapirs, Jaguars, Wild Dogs, Armadillos, Anteaters, Peccaries, and Brockets roam about. Among the birds, Tyrant Hawks, Harpy Eagles, the Dusky Trumpeter, the Crested Curassow and the spectacular Cock-of-the-rocks are notable. The male Cocks, with their orange feathers and the helmet-like crest, live in the mountains and stand out from a distance. They feed on fruit, insects and small lizards which they hunt for on the shadowy banks of the creeks.

HISTORY

Before the colonial period, several migratory waves of different Indigenous peoples occupied the region of the Neblina peak. Here there is mountainous terrain on one side and seasonally flooded land on the other, few fish in the rivers and little agricultural land. Carmelite priests arrived here at the end of the 17th century, and in 1759 Portugal had a fort built at São Gabriel da Cachoeira, in order to guard the border with Colombia and Venezuela. The European occupation influenced the distribution of several Indigenous groups in the area: besides the Yanomamis, there are around 20 distinctive groups of the Tukanu, Arwak and Maku linguistic families. In the mid 1970's, the Radam-Brasil Project advised that the region ought to be preserved, as it has great floristic complexity, and in 1979 the Pico da Neblina National

Park was created. The highest point, with 3.014 m, was first valued by a botanic expedition in 1954. For years, it remained as an area between Brazil and Venezuela and only at the beginning of the 1960's it became part of the Brazilian territory, including the country's highest point. Up to that time, the Bandeira Peak, at the Caparaó National Park, was Brazil's highest peak. In the 1970's and 1980's the region of the upper and mid river Negro was considered a priority by the Federal Government because it is a border zone with a high potential of gold reserves. At that time, some bases of the Calha Norte Project were established in the region. In the 1990's, after much pressure, the Indians had their territory declared and

The 3.014-m high Neblina Peak is the highest point in the country

staked out: the Yanomami Indian land envelops the Park and the Negro River Indigenous Land borders it.

HIGHLIGHTS

❶ ✿ Tucano Waterfall and Igarapé

At the foot of the mountain range, it is a place to rest for the adventurers who go climbing the Neblina Peak. It is three days from São Gabriel da Cachoeira. The waterfall provides a refreshing bath which renews the visitor for the hard hikes.

✿ Miuá Igarapé

Igarapés are waterways stretching into the forest, the arm of a river which sometimes goes very deep into the jungle. This one is on the Park border and it is necessary to

Yanomamis: demi-gods and monsters

Yanomami means human beings and these people believe that they are protected by the spirits who dwell on the mountains summits. For centuries, these hunters and farmers have been living in the northern part of the Amazon. Today their population is 26.000. They have only been in touch with white men since the beginning of the 20th century, a fact which helped to keep their customs relatively well preserved. They believe that they are the descendants of the demi-god Omama who married the daughter of Tëpërësiki, a monster who lives at the bottom of the waters. Their offspring was the first shaman. The forest-land, Urihi, is also Yanomami territory. It is the forest which Omama gave them for their sons to live on from generation to generation. This land,

The Indians have many villages in the Park

today staked out by the white man, is around 192.000 km², including parts in Brazil and Venezuela. To the Indians, the forest is a living being, origin of resources, which set into a complex dynamic between Man and the other beings which dwell in it. The Yaropë are supposed to be the offspring of half-man half-animal beings, whose behaviour was unbalanced and they ended up by assuming their animal condition. Urihi is formed by a blow (wixia) and by an image (urihinari), besides remitting to fertility.

◀ Cock-of-the-rocks (above); the Negro River set the southern border of the Park

go by *voadeira*, a fast motor boat, from São Gabriel. It has rapids and is a good place for a dip. An inspection station of the government bureau for environmental affairs, Ibama, will soon be established here.

Neblina Peak
⊕ Ten days

The ascent to the Highest peak in Brazil (3.014 m) is for experienced hikers who don't need to have climbing expertise, but who are used to walking on tough trails. The trail includes passages through narrow cracks in the rocks, vineforests, ascent on irregular terrain and through entangled roots. The higher you go, the more tired and colder you will become. The ascent is 32 km and you can expect rain and much moisture.

Seis Lagos State Biologic Reservation
⊖ Two days by voadeira from São Gabriel da Cachoeira ⊕ Two days

Within the Pico da Neblina National Park, there are six lakes, each of a different colour due to the minerals present. Its area coincides with the Balaio Indigenous land.

Maturacá Village
The nearest village to the peak lies at the foot of the mountain range and is within the Yanomami territory. Access is via the river Cauaburi and the Maturacá canal. There is a Yanomami village, a Salesian mission and an army outpost.

SURROUNDINGS

Cucuí
⊖ 205 km from São Gabriel ⊕ Two days

On the border of Venezuela, the small city offers some boat tours and is the starting point for the Cucuí Rock. Access is via the neighbouring country. Part of the trip is by boat and then a hike in the forest leads to the top of the rock; a nice view of the Amazonian Rain Forest.

São Gabriel da Cachoeira
⊖ 55 km from the Park ⊕ One day

The small town on the banks of the Negro river is interesting for its population, formed mainly of Indigenous peoples, some military personnel and miners. There are beaches formed along the river - the river itself forms waterfalls in the region during the rain season. The name *cachoeira* means waterfall, and it has good places for bathing in the drought season. Take a look at the ruins of the fort, which was built back in 1759.

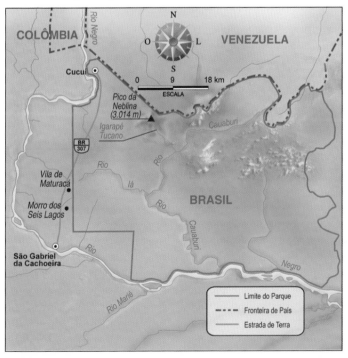

TO VISIT

Access – Visits must be programmed at the Park and visitors must be accompanied with guides. Get information at the Park's headquarters.

Address – Av. Dom José, 52, São Gabriel da Cachoeira, AM, 69750-000. Phone: (92) 613-3277. Fax: 613-3095.

How to get there – It is two hours by plane from Manaus to São Gabriel da Cachoeira. The same trip by boat, on the Negro river, takes four days. From São Gabriel da Cachoeira you get to the Park via the Iá-Mirim igarapé and the rivers Cauaburi and Sá. By car from São Gabriel da Cachoeira: take BR-307. It is 85 km of dirt road; then take the voadeira on the Iá-Mirim igarapé.

Infra-structure – The Park helps people to organize expeditions to the summit; they have boats, cooks, guides and porters for groups who are interested.

TIPS

⟳ The best time to visit the Park is from September to January, when it rains less and the sun shines more often. However, this is also the hottest time and there are more mosquitoes.

⟳ Malaria is endemic to the region. Do use insect repellent and wear long sleeve shirts during the hours when the mosquitoes are more active.

To know more
PERET, J.A. **Amazonas: História, gente, costumes.** Brasília: Senado Federal, 1985.
www.socioambiental.org/website/povind

SERVICES

São Gabriel da Cachoeira, AM

🌐 92
✉ 66060-230

Useful Addresses
City Hall. Av. Sete de Setembro, 84. Phones: 471-1221/1120.
Bus station. Av. Dom P. Massa, s/nº. Phone: 471-1321.
Airport. Estrada do Aeroporto, km 18. Phone: 471-1343.
Port. Barcos Tanaka e Almirante Martins. Phones: 471-1142/1267.
Post Office. Av. Dom P. Massa, s/nº. Phone: 471-1295.
Hospital. Rua Quintino de Sá Cardoso, 1126. Phone: 471-1437/1126.
Banks. BEA, do Brasil.

Support for the Visitor
Tour Agencies. Nature Safáris. Phone 656-6033.

Lodging
King's Island Lodge. Ilha dos Reis, 5 minutes by boat. Phone: 471-1215. Internet: www.naturesafaris.com. 10 rooms, bar, restaurant. Package of three days and two nights. $$$$
Roraima. Av. Castelo Branco, 361. Phone: 471-1576. 18 rooms, tv, air conditioning, minibar. $$
Uaupés. Av. Sete de Setembro, s/nº. Phone: 471-1805. 36 rooms. $

Dining
La Cave du Conde. Rua Brigadeiro Eduardo Gomes, 444. Phone: 471-1435. International. $$
Íris. Av. Sete de Setembro, Bairro Praia, 477. Phone: 471-1288. Fish. $$

Dark water rivers, which carry little sediment, predominate in the Park

Serra da Mocidade

The mountains are the most ancient lands at Mocidade and the low, sedimentary terrain, the most recent one. These sandy plains are prone to flooding and remain covered by water for most of the year. The higher parts form the Mocidade Mountain Range, of low altitudes. The climate is hot and humid with a dry season, more intense between October and April. The scenery in the conservation unit is composed mainly of Amazonian Rain Forest and the *Cerrado* - a type of forest formed by stunted, twisted trees,

Foundation: April 1998
Area: 3.509 km²
Caracaraí: 200 km; Boa Vista: 396 km; Poço Irituba: 314 km

⊘

⊕ (95)

☎ 623-9384

also called *Lavrado* in this part of the country. The little studied fauna and flora are composed of typical species from the two ecosystems. There are water fowl such as Egrets, Herons and King Fishers, besides mammals like the Otter and the Capybara. Migratory species of birds from the northern hemisphere have also been recorded in the Park.

HISTORY

The occupation of Roraima occurred later than the rest of the Amazon, and this has helped to preserve its natural environment. Local residents live basically from exploiting rubber trees, bully trees, Brazil nuts and fishing. With the building of the BR-174 road between the cities of Boa Vista and Caracaraí, back in the 1940's, the region's profile began to change as

The capybara is one of the mammals that inhabit the rivers of the Park

agricultural colonies were established in the old territory. However, more dramatic changes took place in the 1970's, when the military government made big projects for the region. The Yanomami Indians, whose land borders the Park to the west, were much affected by the winds of change. The building of the Perimetral Norte road (BR-210), between 1973 and 1976, subjected them to massive contact with the colonizers, who spread diseases which dramatically diminished the Indians' population. In 1977 the BR-174 road, part which links Manaus to Caracaraí, began to be used resulting in new impact on the Indian population, who, until then, had been living almost completely isolated. In the 1980's, the Indians faced a new threat when miners invaded their land, causing suffering and destruction. The National Park was created on April 29, 1998 and it is also

During the dry season the water level of the rivers lowers several metres

◄   Socó-grande (above); the Cumaru mountains encircle the plain cut by rivers part of a complex of protected areas which include, besides the Viruá National Park, the ecologic stations Caracaraí and Niquiá.

To Visit

Access – The Park is not open for visitation.
Address – Av. Bem Querer, s/n°, Caracaraí, RR, 69350-000.
Phones: (95) 623-9384 and 623-9513.
How to get there – By plane to Boa Vista or Manaus; from these cities the access is via a paved road to Caracaraí (BR-174). From Caracaraí, by boat on the Branco and Água Boa do Univini Rivers, it takes five hours.
Infra-structure – There is none.

The *caçari* is common in the low land

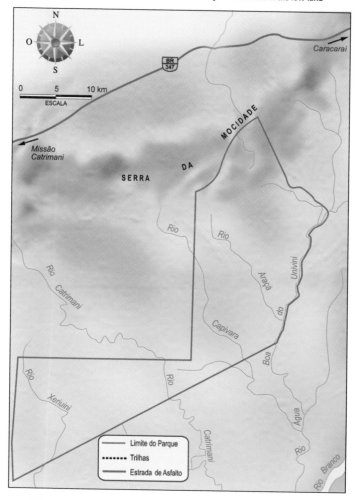

Divisor

Serra do Divisor

The Divisor Mountain Range is formed by lands whose origins are distinct. The most ancient is the Acre basin, around 130 million years old and which was raised by earthquakes. New bends in the crust created faults in the topography, dividing it into three distinct mountain ranges: Moa, Jaquirana and Rio Branco. The influence from the Andes can be seen in the rivers: crystal clear and small, amid mountains with sharper peaks and steep slopes, covered in rain forest; very different from the typical rivers of the Amazon. The Park's mountainous region, which is closer to the Pacific Ocean than to the Atlantic, is covered in Amazonian Rain Forest with the appearance of Andean species; common trees are Uxiranas, Arurás, Red Ant trees, Cariperana, Euphorbiaceous trees, Folha-de-leque, Rosewood, Mahogany, White and Pink Cedar. In the low lands, there are many Guariúbas, Matchwood, Macucus, Andirobaranas and Sapotes.

In the more open parts, palms like Ubim and tangled vines predominate. Where bamboos take over, there are species like the Abiorana-seca, the Axixá, the Enrira-preta, the Ingá-xixica and the Matamata. Among the palm species, there are *Açaí*, *Buriti*, Patauá, and species of the Ruffle

Foundation: June 1989
Area: 8.430 km²
Cruzeiro do Sul: 90 km; Rio Branco: 700 km; Pucallpa (Peru): 150 km
○
🌐 (68)
☎ 322-3380

palm. Along the watercourses, there are forests which are seasonally flooded. Typical trees of this type of forest are the Guiana Crabwood, the Axixá, the Monkeycomb, the Rubber tree, Muiratinga, Piquiá, Peroba, the Brazil Beautyleaf, species of Sweetwood and the Brazilian Andira. The Divisor Mountain Range is considered to be one of the areas with the highest rate of biologic diversity in the Amazon. There are many endemic species, mainly in the mountainous region. So far, scientists have identified 102 species of mammals, 485 fowl, 40 reptiles and 683 amphibians. This number doesn't take into account the fossils of pre-historic animals like mastodons, cliptodons and taxodons found in the region.

Several mammals draw the visitor's attention: monkeys such as Howling, Capuchin, Big-bellied Wooly and Red Ouarakari Monkeys, Jaguars, Mountain Lions and Ocelots. There are also Deer, Tapirs, Agouti Pacas, Squirrels, Armadillos, and several bat species. Among birds, there are Macaws, Toucans, Curassows, Agamis, and Guans. Due to difficulty in reaching the mountains, the region has always been a natural refuge for the fauna. With occupation of the valleys of the high and mid Juruá River, many animals which used to abound are now rare. *Tracajás*, for instance have nearly disappeared from the area, as their eggs and meat are much enjoyed by the natives.

Formosa waterfall: fall from the Moa River

HISTORY

Before European colonization, the state of Acre was a mosaic of various Indigenous ethnic groups who spread throughout the valleys of the rivers Acre, Jordão, Envira, Iaco and Juruá. Among the main groups are the Kaxinawás, the Ashaninkas, the Kulinas, the Jaminauás, the Katunikas, the Manchineris, the Yawanauás and the Nukinis.

With the economic rubber boom, in the 19th century, a massive migratory wave from the northeastern region of the country hit the Amazon. Abused by the owners of the rubber plantation, the seringueiros, as they got to be called, worked almost only for their food. When cheaper rubber from southeastern Asia led to a decline in the Brazilian production, these people found themselves in the middle of the jungle, where they stayed on and lived. At the end of the 1970's, with the expansion policy of the military government, farmers and wood cutters took over large areas in the state of Acre, cutting the trees and destroying the resources of the local population. In the 1980's, more people were becoming organized in order to fight for the defense of the forest and for the rights of seringueiros and Indians. As a result, the land

of the indigenous people was staked out, sustainable use was planned and environmental reservations were created. The Serra do Divisor National Park was created in 1989, based on the study done by the Radambrasil Project, which identified the area as one of the eight Amazonian areas recommended for conservation units due to its high rate of biologic diversity.

HIGHLIGHTS

The Park is divided into two parts: in the North are the Moa River, many waterfalls and a mountainous landscape; in the South the landscape is cut through by the Juruá River. This is where the local population is concentrated.

❿ Ar Condicionado Waterfall
⊕ Four hours
The peculiar name - air conditioning - is due to the cold watersprays from the waterfall, which cool down the area and give a sensation of a lower temperature. It is necessary to walk a twenty minute trail in the forest.

❿ Buraco da Central Waterfall
This 'artificial' waterfall appeared after the oil company Petrobrás drilled this site while prospecting for oil, back in the 1930's. Nobody found oil, but they left a well which gives off sulphureous steam and whose water is warm; a good option for a bath.

❿ Formosa Waterfall
⊕ Two days
The waterfall, around 12 m in height, is in the Park's northern region. It is necessary to walk around four and a half hours in the forest to get to the waterfall.

❿ Véu-da-Noiva Waterfall
⊕ Two hours
It is 30 minutes from the river bank, with an excellent pool for a dip.

● Moa River
⊕ Three hours
The major part of the river is navigable and allows bathing in several places. The Moa River trail is reached in 10 minutes by voadeira, a fast motor boat. It is then 40 minutes more to walk to the top of the foothills of the mountain range, where there is a bromeliad forest and the Jaquirana lookout. The trail is very steep.

◄ Curassow (above); forest has the biggest biologic diversity in the Amazon

SURROUNDINGS

Meeting of the waters

Fifteen minutes by boat from Cruzeiro do Sul ☺ One hour
The place where the muddy waters of the Juruá River meet the dark waters of the Moa.

TO VISIT

Access – It is necessary to get a permit to visit the Park at the local Ibama.
Address – Rua Jaminaua, s/nº, Cruzeiro do Sul, AC, 69980-000.
Phone/fax: (68) 322-3380.
How to get there – There are flights from Rio Branco to Cruzeiro do Sul. From the city to the Park, access is via the Moa or Juruá Rivers by boat. By car, only a part of the BR-364 road which links the city of Mâncio Lima to the Park is passable during the dry season.
Infra-structure – It still does not exist.

To know more
LEÃO, M. da S. e CAVALCANTE, M.E. (orgs.). **Mapinguari comedor de carne e outras histórias do seringal.** Rio Branco: Poronga, 1996.
SOUSA, M. **O Empate contra Chico Mendes.** São Paulo: Marco Zero, 1990. www.amazonia.org.br

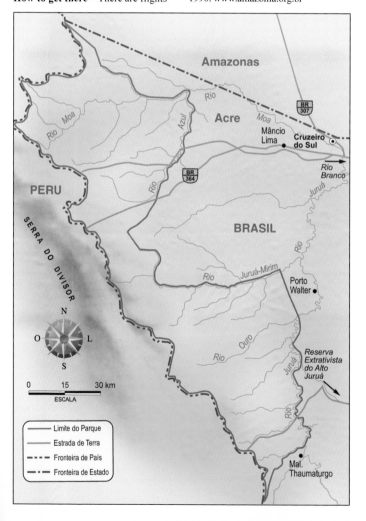

Viruá

The park is located on a sedimentary plain with some low altitude hills. In places, the sandy soils are hydrophobic and do not allow the rain water to drain; because of this many lagoons form amid flood-prone land. To the west, the Park's border is the Branco River and to the south it is the Anauá River; the conservation unit is cut from northeast to southwest by the Viruá *Igarapé* - a waterway which flows into the forest. Only during the dry season the rivers flow independently; during the rest of the year, the water takes over the whole landscape. The climate is hot and humid all year round, but drier from October to April. The landscape is formed of grassy fields to fields with some trees: a large mosaic of meadows and *campinaranas* - an extensive open space in a forest but with many shrubs and some trees in a dense formation. In the Northern region of the Park, there are also dry land forests, vine forests with palms and *igapó* forest. In the transition zone between meadow and forest, flooded land form the countless lagoons in the Park. Buriti palm groves, common on land with water, stand out in the landscape. The fields include a number of grasses and, in the forest, a multitude of orchids hanging from trees attract the visitor's attention. Among the animals, the Little Anteater, the Peccary, the Tapir, the Jaguar, the Capybara and several species of monkeys stand out.

Due to the existence of flooded lands, water fowl and birds which depend on water are common; there are Jabiru Storks, Fisher Eagles, Egrets, Tiger Herons and Jacanas. It is estimated that there are more than four hundred bird species in the Park, many of which have little record of

Foundation: April 1998
Area: 2.270 km²
Caracaraí: 66 km; Poço Irituba: 114 km; Boa Vista: 196 km; Manaus: 545 km

⊘
⊕ (95)
☎ 532-1462

occurrence in Brazil. In the water there are fish like *Tucunarés, Pirapitingas* and *Matrinchãs.* There are also several chelonians, such as the *Tracajá* and the Arrau Sideneck.

HISTORY

The first inhabitants of the region which today is the state of Roraima were Indians of Arawak language. The Karib Indians, escaping from the Spanish invasion from the north of South America, entered their territory and battles between the two groups occurred. When the *bandeirantes* - a colonial character from the 17th and 18th centuries who explored the backwoods in search of precious minerals and Indians to enslave - arrived in the region, the Indians were separated, enslaved and almost annihilated. The area from the middle of the Negro, Venezuela and Guiana Rivers, which once belonged to the state of Amazonas, was transformed into federal territory in 1943. In the beginning, the territory was called Rio Branco, but after two decades the name was changed to Roraima. With the building of the highway BR-174, which links Manaus to Venezuela and the Caribbean, the occupation of the region increased rapidly. There was to have been established a rural colony on the banks of the Branco River, but because of poor soils and flooding the plans were changed. For this reason, human presence in the region is almost non-existent and part of the environment, which is well preserved, became the Viruá National Park in 1998. It is part of a large complex of protected areas which includes the Serra da Mocidade National Park and the Caracaraí and Niquiá Ecologic Stations, created back in the 1980's.

Flooded campina near a wine palm grove

HIGHLIGHTS

Viruá Igarapé

It is only possible to reach the igarapé during the flood season, when voadeiras - a fast motor boat - are able to make it. There is a 15-km trail, which can be travelled from the Park's inspection station.

Lakes

Formed nearly over all Viruá's extension, the lakes offer good opportunities to observe the fauna, mainly long-legged water fowl which go to the lakes in order to feed.

Anauá River

The Park's southern region is a good place for a dip, mainly in the dry season when beaches appear.

SURROUNDINGS

Jaru Ecotourist Complex

13 km from Caracaraí Four hours
The complex, which was recently established, has beaches, rapids and a stretch of forest. You can also go fishing for Pirapitinga and Matrinchã. There are facilities as chalets, camping ground, restaurant and trails.

Bem Querer Rapids

16 km from Caracaraí Five hours
Access Branco River and BR-174 road
The rapids on the Branco River are the main attraction in the region, despite impairing local navigation. Try the tasty cooking which is based on Amazonian fish, specially the Pirapitinga. Facilities include restaurants, chalets and boats for fishing.

Dry land area: common in the north of the Park

Amazonian Chelonians

In the dry season, when beaches appear along the rivers, turtles come out onto the sand in order to lay their eggs. They lay more than a hundred eggs in each nest and these are incubated by the sun's heat. When the eggs hatch, the offspring run to the water, the environment which offers some protection. On their way to the river, they are menaced by a number of species in the natural course of the Amazonian food chain. However, with the increase in the region's occupation and the resulting consumption of the animals and their eggs - chelonians are reputed as a local delicacy - the population of these reptiles have dramatically decreased. One of the goals of the Amphibians and Reptiles Management and Conservation Centre is to assure that several chelonian species, such as turtles, semi-aquatic turtles and the fruit-eating Brazilian land turtle, actually mate. The Chelonians Project work includes the protection of mating grounds, research on the species, the development of an environmental education program with the river communities and the establishment of experimental centres for breeding the species. The focus is on the economic potential of these species. So far, the project has returned 20 million baby-turtles to the region's rivers. It is working in nine states in the north and central-west regions of Brazil, protecting around 115 mating grounds on beaches.

TO VISIT

Access- The Park is still not open for visitation. You can get up-to-date information at the local government bureau for environmental affairs, Ibama, **Address** – Av. Bem Querer, s/n° Caracaraí, RR, 69350-000. Phone: (95) 532-1462.

Fax: (95) 623-9161 (Ibama Boa Vista). **How to get there** – Access is via BR-174 from Boa Vista to Caracaraí and then by boat on the Branco and Anauá Rivers (5 hours), or continuing on BR-174 up to the village of Petrolina and then to the Park's inspection station. **Infra-structure** – An inspection station.

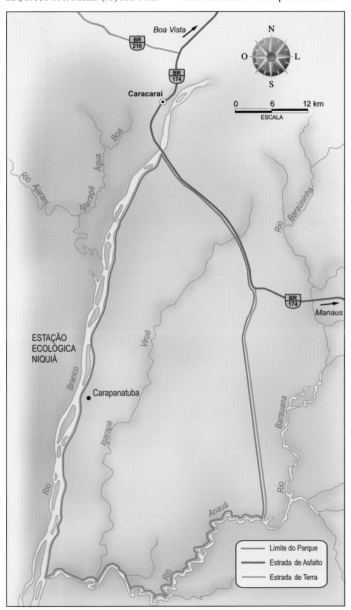

CREDITS

A: top - C: centre - Cd: centre-right
Ce: centre-left - E: bottom - Pd:
double page - Pi: whole page

Cover

Macaw: Zig Koch / Chapada: Araquém
Alcântara / Foz do Iguaçu: Daniel Gonzalez
Counter-cover: Jaguar: Zig Koch /
Fernando de Noronha landscape: Ivan
Carneiro / Rupestrian paintings: André
Pessoa/ Waterfall: Márcio Cabral/ Boat:
Christian Knepper

Legends of the chapter's opening photos

South: P. N. da Serra Geral
Northeast: P. N da Chapada Diamantina
Centre-West: P. N. do Pantanal
Mato-grossense
North: P. N. do Araguaia
Southeast: P. N. da Serra dos Órgãos

Presentation

5 Pi Zig Koch / 9 Pi Zig Koch / 10 E Victor
Andrade / 11 Pi Zig Koch / 12/13 Pd Araquém
Alcântara / 16 A Zig Koch / E Victor Andrade
/ 17 Pi Zig Koch / 18/19 Pd André Pessoa /
20/21 Pd Victor Andrade / A Zig Koch

South Region

22/23 Pd Zig Koch / 24 E Zig Koch/ 26/27 A
Zig Koch / Pd Peter Milko / 28 A Peter
Milko/ E Zig Koch/ 30 E Zig Koch/E Peter
Milko/ 31 A Zig Koch/ 32 A/E Zig Koch/
C Peter Milko / 34/35 Pd Christian Knepper/
A Zig Koch/ 36 A/E Zig Koch/ 37 A Leonardo
Papini/E Christian Knepper/ 40 E Christian
Knepper/41 A Zig Koch/ 42 A Leonardo
Papini/C Christian Knepper/ E Denise Greco /
44/45 Pd Renato Grimm/A Zig Koch/ 46 E
Zig Koch/ 47 A Renato Grimm/ 48 A/C/E
Renato Grimm/ 49 E Adriano Gambarini /
50/51 Pd /A Zig Koch/ 52 A/E Zig Koch/ 54
A Zig Koch/ 55 Pi Zig Koch/ 56 A/C/E Zig
Koch/ 57 A Zig Koch / 58/59 Pd/A Zig Koch/
60 A Zig Koch/E Leonardo Papini/
62 A Zig Koch/ E Peter Milko/ 63 C Zig
Koch/ 64 A Peter Milko/ C/E Zig Koch /

66/67 Pd Peter Milko/ A Zig Koch/68 A Zig
Koch/ E Peter Milko/ 70 Pi Victor Andrade/
71 A Zig Koch/ E Peter Milko/ 72 A/E Peter
Milko/ C Zig Koch / 74/75 Pd/A Zig Koch/
76 A/E Zig Koch/78/79 A/E Zig Koch/
80 A/C/E Zig Koch/ 81 E Zig Koch

Southeast Region

82/83 Pd Paulo Miranda/ 84 A Victor
Andrade / 86/87 Pd Araquém Alcântara /
A Zig Koch / 88 E Victor Andrade /
90 A Zig Koch/91 Pi Victor Andrade /
92 A Peter Milko / C Leonardo Papini/ E
Victor Andrade/93 A Leonardo Papini / 94/95
Pd Peter Milko / A Mario Friedlander/
96 A José Ayrton Labegalini / E Peter Milko/
97 José Ayrton Labegalini / 98/99 Pd Marcelo
Andrê/ A Zig Koch/ 100 E Zig Koch/ 101 A
João Correia / 102 A/C/E Marcelo Andrê/ 103
E Marcelo Andrê/ 104/105 Pd/A Zig Koch/
106 A Paulo Miranda/E Zig Koch/ 107 A
Paulo Miranda/E Zig Koch/110 E Zig Koch/
111 A Mauri Santos/ 112 A Peter Milko/ C / E
Mauri Santos / 114/115 Pd Rômulo Campos/ A
Enrico Marone/ 116 A/E Rômulo Campos/117
C Rômulo Campos / 118/119 Pd Marcelo
Venturini/ A Zig Koch/ 120 E Victor Andrade/
121 Pi Peter Milko/ 124 A/C Marcelo
Venturini/E Peter Milko /126/127 Pd Victor
Andrade/ A Zig Koch/ 128 A Victor Andrade/
E Adriano Gambarini/ 129 E Adriano
Gambarini/ 131 A Ivan Carneiro/132 A/C/E
Victor Andrade / 134/135 Pd Victor Andrade/
A Zig Koch/ 136 Pi Victor Andrade/ 137 C
Cristiano Burmester/ E Zig Koch/140 A
Cristiano Burmester/ C Zig Koch E Gabriela
Michelotti/ 141 A Zig Koch /142/143 Pd
Victor Andrade/ A Zig Koch/ 144 E Peter
Milko/145 A Victor Andrade/ 148/149 Pd Zig
Koch/ 150 A Peter Milko/ C Paulo Miranda/ E
Paulo Miranda / 152/153 Pd / A Zig Koch/
154 A Paulo Miranda/ E Peter Milko/155 A
Victor Andrade/E Paulo Miranda/ 158 Imagem
Satélite divulgação / 159 E Peter Milko/ 160
A Zig Koch/ C Paulo Miranda E Zig Koch

Centre West Region

162/163 Pd Denise Greco/164 E Denise
Greco /165 A Peter Milko / 166/167 Pd/
Marcio Cabral / A Zig Koch/ 168 E
Marcio Cabral/ 170 E Zig Koch/

172 A/C Marcio Cabral/E Claudia Vieitas / 174/175 Pd/ Peter Milko/A Zig Koch/ 176 A Mario Friedlander/ 177 A/E Mario Friedlander/ 180 Pi Peter Milko/ 181 A Zig Koch/ 182 A Peter Milko/C Mario Friedlander/ E Zig Koch / 184/185 Pd Lizimar Dahlke/A Marcio Cabral/186 A Marcio Cabral/ 187 A Peter Milko/E Marcio Cabral/ 188 A Victor Andrade/E Mario Friedlander/190 Pd 191A Victor Andrade/ 192 A Lizimar Dahlke/C Victor Andrade/ E Lizimar Dahlke / 194/195 Pd Adriano Gambarini/ 195 A Claudia Vieitas/ 196 A Peter Milko/ C Zig Koch/197 A Zig Koch/ E Claudia Vieitas/200 A Victor Andrade/C/E Adriano Gambarini / 202/203 Pd/A Adriano Gambarini/204 Pi Peter Milko/ 205 A Denise Greco/ 206/207 Pd/ A Paulo Robson de Souza/ 208 A Victor Andrade / E Adriano Gambarini/ 209 Divulgação Prefeitura de Bodoquena

Northeast Region

210/211 Victor Andrade / 212 E Araquém Alcântara / 214/215 A André Pessoa/Pd Victor Andrade/ 216 A Adriano Gambarini/ 217 A Lizimar Dahlke/E Carolina da Riva/ 220 A Adriano Gambarini/221 C Adriano Gambarini / 222 A Adriano Gambarini C/E Vitor Andrade 224/225 Pd Gabriela Michelotti/ A Enrico Marone/226 A/E Enrico Marone/ 227 A Enrico Marone / 228/229 Pd/ Christian Knepper/ A Zig Koch/230 E Zig Koch/ 231 A Christian Knepper/233 A Zig Koch/ 234 A Zig Koch/ C Denise Greco/ E Christian Knepper/235 E Victor Andrade / 236/237 Pd/ Zig Koch/A Cristiano Burmester/ 238 E Denise Greco/239 A Ivan Carneiro/242 A Ivan Carneiro/C Zig Koch/E Peter Milko / 244/245 Pd Cristiano Burmester/ A Zig Kock/ 246 A Ivan Carneiro E Denise Greco/ 247 A/E Zig Koch/ 248 A Carolina da Riva/ 250 A Carolina da Riva/ C Cristiano Burmester/ E Denise Greco / 252/253 Pd Victor Andrade/ A Zig Koch/ 256 Pi Gabriela Michelotti/ 257 A Enrico Marone / E Peter Milko/ 258 A Leonardo Papini / C/E Enrico Marone / 260/261 Pd Gabriela Michelotti/A Zig Koch/ 262 A Gabriela Michelotti/263 A Zig Koch /

264/265 Pd Victor Andrade/A Lizimar Dahlke/ 268 A André Pessoa/E Victor Andrade/ 269 A André Pessoa/E Divulgação / 270/271 Pd Adriano Gambarini/ 272 A/C/E André Pessoa 273 A André Pessoa / 274/275 A Adriano Gambarini/Pd Jurandir Lima/ 276 A/E André Pessoa/ 278 A/C/E André Pessoa/279 A André Pessoa / 280/ 281 Pd Victor Andrade/ A André Pessoa/ 282 E André Pessoa/283 A Victor Andrade/E Zig Koch/ 284 E Zig Koch/ 286 A Adriano Gambarini/C Victor Andrade/E André Pessoa/ 287 E André Pessoa / 288/289 Pd Adriano Gambarini/ A Zig Koch/ 290 A Adriano Gambarini/ E Divulgação/ 291 E Adriano Gambarini/ 292 E Peter Milko/ 294 A Victor Andrade/C Adriano Gambarini/E Victor Andrade/295 E Peter Milko

North Region

296/297 Adriano Gambarini / 299 A Zig Koch/ 300/301 Pd/A Araquém Alcântara/ 302 A Araquém Alcântara/ 303 A Araquém Alcântara/ 304 A Araquém Alcântara/C Mario Friedlander/ E Zig Koch/ 305 E Zig Koch /306/307 Pd/A Araquém Alcântara/ 308 E Peter Milko/ 310 A Jurandir Lima/ C Victor Andrade/ E Araquém Alcântara/311 E Adriano Gambarini / 312/313 Pd/A Zig Koch/314 A Zig Koch/ E Peter Milko / 316/317 Pd/A Araquém Alcântara/320 A/E Peter Milko/ C Araquém Alcântara/ 321 E Araquém Alcântara / 322/323 Pd/ A Araquém Alcântara/ 324 E Zig Koch/ 325 A Araquém Alcântara/ 326 A/E Araquém Alcântara/ C Zig Koch/ 327 E Araquém Alcântara / 328/329 Pd/ A Araquém Alcântara/330 A/C Araquém Alcântara/331 A Araquém Alcântara / 332/333 Pd/A Zig Koch/ 334 A/E Leonide Príncipe/336 A/C/E Zig Koch/ 337 E Zig Koch / 338/339 Pd Taylor Nunes /A Zig Koch / 340 A Zig Koch/ E Taylor Nunes/ 341 A Taylor Nunes / 342/343 Pd Araquém Alcântara Divulgação SOS Mata Atlântica/ A Araquém Alcântara/ 344 A Araquém Alcântara / 346/347 Pd/A Taylor Nunes/ 348 A/Cd Taylor Nunes

ACKNOWLEDGEMENTS

Adão Moreira Rodrigues
Adiraci Oliveira de Almeida
Alair Garcia
André Pessoa
Andrea Curi Zarattini
Antônio Fernandes dos Santos
Apolônio Rodrigues
Célio Albuquerque
Cherezino Cherer
Claudia Camurça
Cláudio Bellini
César Vitor
David Clearly
Denise Arantes
Douglas Simões
Ecoparaná
Edair Corteletti
Enrico Marcovaldi
Eugênia Vitória e Silva de Medeiros
Fabiana Prado
Fundação Ecoa
Fundação Ecotrópica
Fundação Vitória Amazônica
Geraldo Machado Pereira
Gigi Pati Pataxó
Heitor Reali Fragoso
Hélio de Antiqueira Bulhões
Ireno Alberto da Costa
José Carlos Corteletti
José Maria Canavieira
Jota Marincek
Juarez José Vasto
Lana Guimarães
Laurenz Pinder
Leila Zanardini Hoffmann
Luiz Marcio Haddad Pereira Santos
Luis Meneses
Luís Renato Ulhoa C. Lopes
Márcia Brambilla
Márcia Engel
Márcio Cabral
Marco Aurélio da Silva
Maria Inês Miranda
Maria Luiza Monteiro da Costa
Marieta Borges Lins e Silva
Mario Barroso Ramos Neto
Paulo César Boggiani
Paulo Robson
Paulo Sérgio
Rosa Trakalo

Rosamaria Muller
Sandra Serra de Miranda
Suely Ortega
Tito de Paula Couto
Ulisses Souza Scoufield

Directors of the National Parks
Adílio Augusto Valadão de Miranda
Albino Batista Gomes
Antônio Galdino de Souza
Antônio Emanuel Barreto Alves de Sousa
Carlos Lamartine Torres Mello
Carlos Rangel da Silva
Dion Ferreira Barros de Almeida
Eduardo Gomes da Costa
Elmo Monteiro da Silva Junior
Emerck Lima Cipriano
Estevão José Marchesini Fonseca
Fernando Atayde Nóbrega
Francisco Celso de Medeiros
Gabriel Botelho Marchioro
Gabriel Cardoso Borges
Gaspar Saturnino Rocha
Gilson Costa Homobono
Guadalupe Vivekananda
Henrique Horn Ilha
Inara Auxiliadora Rocha Santos
Isaac Simão Neto
Ivone Lima Fecury
José Augusto Ferraz de Lima
José Carneiro Bruzaca
José Gaudêncio Filho
José Ponciano Dias Filho
José Sales de Sousa
José Wilmington Paes Landim Ribeiro
Jovelino Muniz de A. Filho
Julio César Gonchorosky
Leo Nascimento
Luisa Juliana Silveira Lopes
Luiz Alberto Fernandes
Mario Augusto Bernardes Rondon
Maude Nancy Joslin Motta
Milene Maia
Paulo Antônio Damasceno da Rosa
Paulo Cezar Reys Bastos
Ricardo Magalhães Barbalho
Rosa Lia Gondin de Castro
Rosemeri Lodi
Rosilene Aparecida Ferreira
Sérgio Pedreira Pereira de Sá
Sônia Peixoto

Dados Internacionais de Catalogação na Publicação (CIP)
(Câmara Brasileira do Livro, SP, Brasil)

Philips guides : Amazônia : Brasil : Amazonas,
    Acre, Rondônia, Pará, Amapá, Roraima e Mato
    Grosso / general coordinator Beatriz Santomauro ;
    translation to English Cláudio Blanc ; associate
    contributors Bárbara Schmal ... [et al .]. --
    São Paulo : Horizonte Geográfico, 2001. --
    (Series Philips guides of Brazilian ecological tourism)

    Patrocínio: Projeto Philips Brasilis.
    ISBN 85-88031-09-4

    1. Amazônia - Descrição e viagens 2. Amazônia -
História I . Santomauro, Beatriz. II. Série.

02-0553   CDD-918.1

Índices para catálogo sistemático:
1. Parques nacionais brasileiros : Descrição
918.1

T

VENEZUELA

GUIAN

RORAIMA

BOA VISTA

COLÔMBIA

Rio Negro

Rio Solimões

Rio

MANAUS

AMAZONAS

Madeira

Rio

PORTO VELHO

ACRE

RIO BRANCO

RONDÔNIA

PERU

BOLÍVIA

PARAGUA

Oceano Pacífico

CHILE

ARGENTINA

1	Amazônia
2	Araguaia
3	Cabo Orange
4	Jaú
5	Monte Roraima
6	Pacaás Novos
7	Pico da Neblina
8	Serra da Cutia *
9	Serra da Mocidade
10	Serra do Divisor
11	Viruá
12	Abrolhos
13	Chapada Diamantina
14	Descobrimento
15	Fernando de Noronha
16	Jericoacoara *
17	Lençóis Maranhenses
18	Monte Pascoal
19	Pau-Brasil
20	Serra da Capivara
21	Serra das Confusões
22	Sete Cidades
23	Ubajara
24	Brasília
25	Chapada dos Guimarães
26	Chapada dos Veadeiros
27	Emas
28	Pantanal Mato-grossense
29	Serra da Bodoquena
30	Caparaó
31	Cavernas do Peruaçu
32	Grande Sertão Veredas
33	Itatiaia
34	Restinga de Jurubatiba
35	Serra da Bocaina
36	Serra da Canastra
37	Serra do Cipó
38	Serra dos Órgãos
39	Tijuca
40	Aparados da Serra
41	Iguaçu
42	Ilha Grande
43	Lagoa do Peixe
44	Saint-Hilaire/Lange*
45	São Joaquim
46	Serra Geral
47	Superagüi

* Parks founded recently. Do not appear in the itineraries of the Guide.